LIBRARY IN A BOOK

IMMIGRATION

John Powell

Facts On File

An imprint of Infobase Publishing

Immigration

Facts On File, Inc.
An imprint of Infobase Publishing
132 West 31st Street
New York NY 10001

Library of Congress Cataloging-in-Publication Data
Powell, John.
    Immigration/John Powell.
        p. cm.—(Library in a book)
    Includes bibliographical references and index.
    ISBN 0-8160-6234-X (alk. paper)
    1. Emigration and immigration—Juvenile literature. 2. United States—Emigration
and Immigration—Juvenile literature. 3. Immigrants—United States—Juvenile literature. I. Title. II. Series.
    JV6201. P68 2006
    304.8—dc22   2006006898

Facts On File books are available at special discounts when purchased in bulk
quantities for businesses, associations, institutions, or sales promotions. Please call
our Special Sales Department in New York at (212) 967-8800 or (800) 322-8755.

You can find Facts On File on the World Wide Web at http://www.factsonfile.com

Text design by Ron Monteleone
Maps and graph by Sholto Ainslie

Printed in the United States of America

MP Hermitage 10 9 8 7 6 5 4 3 2 1

This book is printed on acid-free paper.

CONTENTS

ACKNOWLEDGMENTS

My thanks to the editorial team at Facts On File who do excellent work and are such a pleasure to work with. I am also grateful to friends and colleagues at Oklahoma Baptist University who have been most understanding regarding my occasional absences. I would like to specially thank my editorial assistant, Heather Johnson, who was superb throughout. Finally, for that trip into the mystic, my lifelong companions have earned the best I have to give—thanks to Janice, Grady, Tessa, and Ellen.

For Tai Tai

PART I

OVERVIEW OF THE TOPIC

CHAPTER 1

INTRODUCTION TO IMMIGRATION

America, it has frequently been observed, is a land of immigrants. The first immigrants to North America came across a land bridge and by sea from northern Asia more than 10,000 years ago. When Christopher Columbus arrived, there were thriving, advanced civilizations in what are now Mexico and Peru and many less complex tribal societies throughout the Americas. When England established its first permanent settlement at Jamestown in 1607 with 104 immigrants, there were probably more than 4 million Indian inhabitants in what is now the United States, with the largest numbers concentrated east of the Mississippi River. In less than 400 years, however, American Indians composed less than 1 percent of the country's population. The story of this dramatic population reversal began in the early 16th century, when the first Spanish explorers ventured northward from their central bases in Cuba and Mexico.

IMMIGRATION IN THE COLONIAL PERIOD (TO 1775)

Spanish conquistadores found limited riches in America, despite their determined explorations. Expeditions led by Juan Ponce de León (1513), Pánfilo de Narváez (1528), Álvar Núñez Cabeza de Vaca (1528–36), Hernando de Soto (1539–41), Juan Rodríguez Cabrilho (Portuguese explorer in service of Spain) (1542), and Francisco Coronado (1540–42) led to no lasting settlements. The Spanish fort at St. Augustine, Florida, founded in 1565, became the first permanent European settlement in the present-day United States, though it remained largely a military and administrative center. Spain was more successful in colonizing what would become New Mexico, when in 1598 Don Juan de Oñate led 500 men north from Mexico. In 1609 these settlers established Santa Fe. By 1680, when the Pueblo Indians revolted,

3

there were 2,000 Spanish settlers there, and by 1750 the number had increased to 4,000. A pattern of population reversal had been established, for while the Spanish population was doubling, the Pueblo population was declining by nearly 60 percent as a result of war, disease, and migration. Although Spain continued to claim control and exert some influence in the American Southwest, there was no significant settlement until the 1760s, in the wake of the Seven Years' War.

As other European states recovered from wars of religion and developed a stronger sense of nationalism during the late 16th century, they, too, began to covet the trade and possible riches offered up by the New World. Under the leadership of Queen Elizabeth I (r. 1558–1603), England allied itself to the Netherlands, under Spanish control, and from the 1570s began to raid Spanish settlements in the New World and around the globe. Simultaneously, English entrepreneurs established joint-stock companies and sought charters from the queen for the purpose of finding wealth in the Americas; any successful settlement would be a diplomatic bonus. England's earliest attempts to settle—in Newfoundland in 1583 and Roanoke (in present-day North Carolina) in 1585—were part business venture, part challenge to Spanish dominance in the Western Hemisphere, and equally unsuccessful. The 1606 charter authorizing the London Company (soon renamed the Virginia Company) to establish settlements in the region of Chesapeake Bay, however, would finally pay dividends. In December the *Susan Constant*, the *Godspeed*, and the *Discovery* landed 104 men and boys whose first concern was to locate a position that could be secured from attack. Although early reports observed "faire meaddowes and goodly tall trees," Jamestown had many weaknesses as a site. Located in a marshy peninsula more than 30 miles from the mouth of the James River, it was disease-ridden, deficient in pure water, and located in territory controlled by the powerful Powhatan confederacy. Furthermore, the group consisted of many immigrants of noble birth who were searching for easy wealth. In the first year, disease, laziness, and ignorance nearly destroyed the colony, with only about 40 men surviving into the new year. The colony was saved only by an influx of immigrants and the discipline imposed by Captain John Smith, who gained control of the governing council in 1609.

A new royal charter in 1609 gave more power to the Virginia Company, which again sought colonists and investors, but military rule prevailed and conditions remained desperate until John Rolfe successfully developed a mild tobacco that appealed to Europeans. Between 1617 and 1622, settlers abandoned all other work in order to profit from the new cash crop. Sir Edwin Sandys led stockholders in a series of reforms designed to make the colony more attractive to speculators, including establishment of America's first representative assembly, the House of Burgesses (1618), and institution of the "headright" colonizing system for distributing land, which provided

50-acre plots for those paying their own way to the New World and additional headrights if they also paid for the passage of servants. Between 1619 and 1622, more than 3,000 people immigrated to Virginia. Most were young indentured servants, though there were significant numbers of Scots-Irish and Irish and a few Germans who had been recruited by the Virginia Company. After a brief period of success on the back of high tobacco prices, Jamestown declined, leading King James I to transform Virginia into a royal colony in 1624. By 1635 the population had grown to 5,000, and four years later, the House of Burgesses was officially recognized by King Charles I, establishing an important precedent of self-government in the English colonies.

At the same time, 600 miles northward along the Atlantic seaboard, two groups of dissident English Christians were establishing a new home in Massachusetts. Pilgrims and Puritans were the spiritual children of the 16th-century Protestant Reformation, believers in the holiness of God, the sinfulness of humankind, and the ultimate authority of the Bible in matters of faith. When King Henry VIII rejected the authority of the pope and the Roman Catholic Church in 1535, the Anglican Church became the new establishment, with an official hierarchy and many ceremonial elements derived from the Roman Church. English Christians who sought to "purify" the Anglican Church by removing the old elements of Romanism by the 1560s were derisively called Puritans. Because it was a crime to worship outside the Church of England, "separatist" congregations either had to worship secretly or leave the country. In 1608 a small congregation of Separatists moved to the Netherlands, where they were granted complete freedom of worship. Fearing loss of their English identity, however, and recognizing the limited economic opportunities in a foreign land, they migrated again. In 1620, 102 settlers—mostly separatist Pilgrims—as they called themselves headed to northern Virginia on the *Mayflower*. Blown off course from their original destination, they established Plymouth at their landing spot in present-day southern Massachusetts. Because they were technically outside of English jurisdiction, family heads joined to produce the Mayflower Compact, the first written framework for a government in what is today the United States. Poor soil and limited economic opportunities kept immigration to Plymouth small. After 20 years, the population was still only about 2,500.

More prosperous was Salem, a Puritan settlement some 40 miles to the north and the center of the Massachusetts Bay Colony. In 1629 John Winthrop and a group of wealthy Puritans who had become convinced that reform of the Church of England was impossible, secured a charter from King Charles I (r. 1625–49). Curiously omitting the standard requirement stipulating where meetings of the joint-stock company were to be held, the charter enabled the 12 associates to move to America, where they could settle with little royal interference. The *Arbella* carrying Winthrop and other Puritan leaders was one of 17 ships carrying more than 1,000 settlers in March 1630. With the rise of religious oppression in Britain and the outbreak of civil war, by the early 1640s, the "Great Migration" had brought about 20,000 settlers to Massachusetts. Though this was less than one-third the total number of Britons coming to the New World, it was enough to make it the largest colony on the northern Atlantic seaboard. Although immigrants came for many reasons, religion played a larger role in New England than in other colonial regions. The Puritans experimented with a kind of civil government that would create a "city on a hill," to show the benefits of godly living. Town life predominated, with men and women voluntarily covenanting to follow local ordinances. A small amount of land was provided free to each immigrant family, though all were expected to pay local and colony taxes and to contribute in support of the minister. Whereas the Pilgrims of Plymouth had removed themselves from the Church of England, the Puritans sought to purify it from within. Eventually, they developed a church structure known as Congregationalism, in which each village church was independent, with members agreed in "the presence of God to walk together in all his ways."

In between these two largely English outposts in Virginia and New England, King Charles I granted a proprietary charter to the openly Catholic Cecilius Calvert, second Lord Baltimore. Charles favored the establishment of a refuge for Catholics who were no longer free to worship in England. Realizing the importance of Protestant immigration to the economic success of the settlement, however, Catholics were ordered to "be silent upon all occasions of discourse concerning matters of Religion." On March 25, 1634, the *Ark* and the *Dove* landed about 150 settlers, the majority of whom were Protestants. Maryland was unique in that its charter made Baltimore a "palatine lord," with outright ownership of almost 6 million acres. He hoped to fund his venture by re-creating an anachronistic feudal system, with purchasers of 6,000 acres enjoying the title lord of the manor and having the right to establish local courts of law. Landowners bristled at the attempts of the Calverts to restrict traditional English legislative liberties, plunging Maryland into a long period of political instability that almost destroyed the colony. English religious divisions were mirrored in Maryland, with Catholics in the upper house and Protestants in the lower house vying for control of the government, a conflict that sometimes erupted into open warfare. With the Puritan victory in the English Civil War (1642–49), Baltimore feared he might lose Maryland. Thus, he drafted his "Act concerning Religion," extending freedom of worship to all who accepted the divinity of Christ, though the act of toleration was repealed when Puritans gained control of the government (1654).

Maryland remained predominantly English throughout the colonial period, developing a culture similar to that of neighboring Virginia, though with somewhat greater social mobility. The cultivation of tobacco defined its economic and social structure. Farms and plantations, almost always owned by English settlers, were widely dispersed along the Chesapeake Bay, and a steady stream of indentured servants, predominantly English, Scots, and Scots-Irish, were hired and sent over from their home lands to work the fields. By 1700 Maryland's population of about 34,000 made it the third most populous colony, behind only Virginia and Massachusetts.

The Spanish presence in Florida and English settlements in Virginia, Maryland, and New England left hundreds of miles of coastline and virtually the whole of the interior of the continent open to development. Sweden settled the area of modern Delaware as a commercial venture in 1638, eventually settling several hundred Swedes and Finns in the area. Disease, lack of support, and conflict with the Dutch kept overall numbers small, and by 1655 New Sweden was incorporated into the Dutch colony of New Amsterdam—modern New York. The coastal region of New York was probably first explored by Europeans when Giovanni da Verrazano, an Italian serving the French government, mapped the area. The Dutch visited the region as early as 1609 and eventually established Fort Orange (modern Albany) in 1624 and New Amsterdam at the mouth of the Hudson River in the following year. From these settlements, they created a trading network that extended into the Hudson, Connecticut, and Delaware River valleys. Under the patroon system, members of the Dutch West India Company were granted larger tracts of land in return for bringing settlers. Although the maximum number of Dutch settlers in the mid-Atlantic region was only about 10,000, they generally enjoyed good relations with the Indians and developed a thriving commercial community. From its establishment, the area was a polyglot mixture of Dutch, Belgians, French Huguenots, Finns, Swedes, Portuguese Jews, and English.

French explorer Jacques Cartier had claimed Acadia and the St. Lawrence Seaway in the 1530s, though the bitter winters had restricted French interest to fishing along coastal waters. Explorer Samuel de Champlain established the first permanent French settlement in North America at Quebec (1608), where only eight of the original 24 Frenchmen survived the first winter. In 1627 he became head of the Compagnie de Nouvelle France, which was granted title to all French lands and a monopoly on all economic activity except fishing, in return for settling 4,000 French Catholics in Canada. Although the fur trade flourished, the French were little interested in farming settlements. French America—known as New France—was composed of three distinct areas of settlement: Acadia, the mainland and island areas along the Atlantic coast; Louisiana, the lands drained by the Mississippi, Missouri, and Ohio River valleys; and Canada, the lands on either side of the St. Lawrence Seaway and just north of the Great Lakes. Among these only Canada, with the important settlements of

Quebec and Montreal, developed a significant population. A harsh climate, and continual threats from the British and the Iroquois, made it difficult for private companies to attract settlers to French territories. In 1663 Louis XIV (r. 1648–1713) made New France a royal colony, but it was only moderately successful at enticing colonists.

Though Spain, the Netherlands, France, and Sweden all established footholds in America, Britain was the only country to send substantial and increasing numbers of settlers into the region. In addition to thriving settlements in Virginia, Maryland, and New England, in 1663 King Charles II (r. 1660–85) granted eight courtiers proprietorship of the Carolinas, where favorable land policies and religious tolerance led to a diverse population that by the mid-18th century included large numbers of Scots (15 percent of the European population), Irish and Scots-Irish (11 percent), Germans (5 percent), and French Huguenots (3 percent). In 1664 Britain wrested control of New Amsterdam—renamed New York—from the Dutch, finally gaining permanent control in 1673, when it was agreed that Dutch commercial and religious rights would be respected. After the conquest, the region was granted to James, duke of York, brother of the English king Charles II, and included present-day Maine, much of the Massachusetts coast, Long Island, and New Jersey. Originally part of the newly conquered territory of the New Netherlands, in 1664 New Jersey was granted by the duke of York as a proprietary colony to John, Lord Berkeley, and Sir George Cateret, two courtiers who had supported the Crown during the English Civil War and interregnum (1642–60). Promising freedom of worship and government, they attracted a sizable population—about 14,000 by 1700—but the absence of a deepwater port kept it mainly an agricultural colony, developing in the shadow of neighboring New York. Shortly after Colonel Richard Nicolls was made governor, he learned that the duke of York had given New Jersey to Berkeley and Cateret. Confusion was rampant, as settlers authorized by Nicolls prior to the transfer clashed with those recruited by Berkeley and Cateret. Although Dutch settlers were allowed to keep their lands, they were sometimes drawn into the disorder. Out of the turmoil, a group of Quaker investors, including William Penn, bought Berkeley's stake in 1674, leading to division of the territory into East Jersey and West Jersey. West Jersey became the first Quaker colony in America. Both halves struggled and were reunited in 1702 as a royal colony.

Penn was more successful in his new venture beyond the Delaware River. As early as 1677, he began to sell land there to German Rhinelanders and in 1681 was granted a charter by Charles II, perhaps in payment of a debt owed to Penn's father. His new colony of Pennsylvania was founded on principles of liberty of conscience and due process of law, and in the first instance as a refuge for Quakers. During the 1660s, Penn himself had embraced Quakerism, the most democratic and anarchic of the Protestant sects. Unlike the

Introduction to Immigration

Puritans who emphasized original sin, predestination, and strict principles of governance, Quakers recognized an "inner light" that could guide people to salvation. Adding to their unpopularity, they were pacifists and therefore regarded as unpatriotic. Many Quakers then responded with alacrity to Penn's new project. The new proprietor also advertised tirelessly in England, Ireland, and Germany, lauding the rich soil and high degree of personal freedom. As a result, in 1685 alone, 8,000 immigrants arrived. Within a few years, Penn boasted that the people of Pennsylvania were "a collection of diverse nations in Europe," including "French, Dutch, Germans, Swedes, Danes, Finns, Scotch, Irish, and English."

The revocation of the Edict of Nantes in 1685, which had provided French citizens freedom of worship, drove 15,000 Protestant French Huguenots, many of whom were wealthy or skilled artisans, to British colonies. Most settled in New York, though important settlements were also founded in Pennsylvania, Virginia, and South Carolina. By the 1680s, Britain had gained political control of the eastern seaboard from New England to the Carolinas and was beginning to press inward toward the Appalachian Mountains.

One of the secrets to the extension of British influence was the very diversity of their settlements. In terms of ethnicity, while the New England colonies and old Virginia and Maryland remained largely English, the middle colonies of New York, New Jersey, and Pennsylvania were ethnically heterogenous, and the southern backcountry was becoming increasingly so. In terms of religion, there was a place for everyone. Puritans found a home in New England, Quakers and other dissenting groups in Pennsylvania and Rhode Island, Catholics in Maryland, and Anglicans in New York, Virginia, and the Carolinas. The backcountry, largely free of hierarchical influences, was open to all. By the 18th century, however, religion played less a role in settlement choices, and all the colonies became more religiously diverse. In terms of economy, there was considerable variety, from the great tobacco, rice, and indigo plantations of Virginia and the Carolinas, to the small wheat and produce farms, small-scale industry, and developing commercial activity of the central and northern colonies. Ports from Charleston to Boston became important centers of trade and depots for newly arriving immigrants.

INDENTURED SERVITUDE AND SLAVERY

Out of this rich mix of ethnicities, religions, and economic activity there developed two general patterns of settlement in the English colonies. In the southern colonies, including Virginia and the Carolinas, wealthy proprietors closely associated with the English Crown and the Anglican Church, controlled most of the land and dominated social life. Economies were generally agricultural, and the work was often done by indentured servants and, after 1660, by slaves brought from Africa. The second general pattern of settlement occurred in New England, where small landowners predominated, commercial interests were more influential, and democratic tendencies more prevalent. Indentured servitude was common, but slavery was seldom practiced. In both instances, however, immigrant laborers had a profound effect on the development of the colonies.

Indentured servants agreed to work exclusively for one employer for a fixed number of years, in return for training and other financial considerations. The normal contract of indenture in colonial North America provided the servant with cost of passage from Europe; food, shelter, and clothing during the period of indenture; and land or other provisions when the contract was completed. Indentures in the middle and southern colonies were usually fixed at five to seven years, with seven being most common. In New England, a period of three or four years was more common. The indenture system was most common in the middle and southern colonies, where it accounted for more than half of all colonial immigrants, but it was utilized widely throughout the British and French colonies. Servants came from all classes and races and from many European countries, though English paupers and convicts made up the majority. A few rose in society according to their early expectations, with some becoming landowners and legislators. Most, however, remained servants or were provided with marginal lands when their contracts were fulfilled. Often pushed into the most dangerous and least profitable areas of settlement, these poor whites became discontented and hard to govern. They also helped to settle the more remote and mountainous areas beyond the seaboard. After the 1660s, indentured servants were almost always European, and the majority survived their indenture. As late as the 1770s, more than 40 percent of immigrants to America were indentured servants.

The indenture system worked because it met the needs of North American entrepreneurs and agriculturalists, who were short of labor; European paupers, who were short of money; and European governments that had too many paupers and criminals with which to deal. Private companies such as the Virginia Company, the Plymouth Company, or the Company of New France realized that the lure of land for potential investments would not suffice were there not also a laboring class to do most of the menial work. Companies advertised some combination of free passage to the Americas, land, tools, and clothing for a servant who completed the period of servitude. Some servants were prepurchased by colonial merchants or landowners. During the first half of the 17th century, prepurchasing posed a considerable risk for the buyer, however, for the servant was more likely to die than to complete his or her term of service. To address the risk, the Virginia Company developed a headright system that rewarded the purchaser with 50 acres of land for every servant brought to the colony at their own expense. In other cases, prospective settlers would indenture themselves to the company, which would then sell the contracts upon arrival in American ports. Most indentured servants were from the agricultural classes, though craftsmen and artisans were always in demand. By the 18th century, skilled workers were sometimes able to negotiate especially favorable terms of indenture.

Many servants, like settlers generally, did not survive the voyage to the New World. If they did successfully complete their indenture, there were often legal challenges to obtaining what they had been promised. Life was harsh, and laws were passed prohibiting servants from marrying, trading, or having children. Corporal punishment was common, and infractions of the law often included extension of the term of service. Men and women indentured as a couple were sometimes divided, and if one spouse died, the other was required to serve both terms. Children were indentured until the age of 21. As news of these hardships filtered back to Britain, fewer paupers willingly undertook to indenture themselves. In the second half of the 17th century, people were frequently forced into servitude through deceit, brutality, or as an alternate punishment for crime. In some years, thousands of criminals were deported to America as indentured servants.

More dramatic than the impact of indentured servants was the importation of African laborers. Although the use of indentured servants was common in the southern colonies, planters realized that a seven-year term of service created an unsteady supply of labor. As a result, landowners increasingly turned to slavery for their labor needs. Most slaves were taken in Africa by African middlemen, who sold them to European merchants at the coast. Captives were held in European forts or slaving depots until their sale could be arranged with merchants bringing a variety of manufactured items from Europe or America, including textiles, metal wares, alcohol, firearms and gunpowder, and tobacco. Africa thus became part of the infamous triangular trade, in which New England merchants would exchange simple manufactured goods on the western coast of Africa for slaves, who would in turn be shipped to the West Indies, where they were traded for rum and molasses. Once a merchant had secured a full cargo, African slaves were inhumanely packed into European ships for the Middle Passage—a voyage of anywhere from five to 12 weeks from West Africa to the Americas. Some slavers were loose packers, which reduced disease, while others were tight packers who expected a certain percentage of deaths and tried to maximize profits by shipping as many slaves as space would allow. It is estimated that 15 to 20 percent of African slaves died en route during the 16th and 17th centuries, and 5 to 10 percent died during the 18th and 19th centuries. Men, who were most highly valued, were usually separated from women and children during the passage. The holds of the ships rarely allowed Africans to stand, and they were often uncleaned throughout the voyage. Upon arrival in the Americas, slavers would advertise the auction of their cargo, often describing particular skills and allowing Africans to be inspected before sale. It was common for slaves to be sold more than once, and many came to North America after initial sales in the West Indies.

The number of slaves remained relatively small throughout the 17th century, and slavery was not officially sanctioned until the 1660s, when slave codes began to be enacted. This enabled a small number of African Americans to maintain their freedom and even to become landholders, though it was not common. By the early 18th century, the prevalence of slavery increased dramatically, especially when Britain acquired the right to trade slaves in the Spanish American empire in 1713. In 1700 slaves comprised about 11 percent of the colonial population and twice that in Virginia and Maryland. By 1750 Africans comprised 40 percent of the populations of Virginia and the lower South. Slaves were never widely used in northern colonies, though keeping them as domestic servants was not uncommon, and pockets of rural agricultural areas sometimes had slave populations of up to 10 percent.

The massive forced migration of Africans to North America created a unique African-American culture based on a common African heritage, the experience of slavery, and the teachings of Christianity. As a result of the patterns of the slave trade, it was impossible for most slaves to identify the exact tribe or ethnic group from which they came. Most early slaves were taken from the coastal regions of Senegambia, Sierra Leone, the Gold Coast, the Bight of Benin, the Bight of Biafra, Angola, and Mozambique, but by the later 17th century, most were being brought from interior regions, further diversifying the ethnic background of Africans brought to the Americas. Yet skin color gave all slaves an assurance of a common homeland. African music and folktales continued to be told and adapted to changing circumstances. Although African rituals of magic and voodoo were occasionally maintained, most often the belief in spirits was combined with Christian teaching and the slave experience to produce a faith emphasizing Old Testament themes of salvation from bondage and God's protection of a chosen people. The majority of slaves labored on plantations in a community of 20 or more slaves. They were subject to beatings, rape, and even death; did not have the protection of the law; and were usually denied access to education. Despite the fact that slaves could not legally marry, the family was the principal bulwark against life's harshness, and marriage and family bonds usually remained strong. Strong ties of kinship extended across several generations and even to the plantation community at large.

NON-BRITISH IMMIGRANTS

The 18th century was a period of unprecedented growth in the American colonies. Noting such trends as early marriage, large families, and high wages, Benjamin Franklin observed in a celebrated essay of 1751 that "our people must at least be doubled every twenty years." He was very nearly right. Not only did the population grow from fewer than 300,000 in 1700 to more than 1 million in 1750; by 1775 it stood at more than 2 million. A significant part of the increase was due to high birth rates and low mortality rates—15–20 percent lower than in Europe. Equally important, however, was the significant immigration that occurred between 1700 and 1775. Almost a quarter-million Africans were forced to migrate; more than 100,000 Scots-Irish; a similar number of Germans; more than 150,000 English, Welsh, and Scots; and smaller numbers of Swiss, Swedes, and Jews.

As in the 17th century, the largest number of immigrants came from Great Britain, but non-British nationals continued to pour in, sometimes in large numbers. With the devastation of the European War of the Spanish Succession (1702–14), significant numbers of German and Scots-Irish immigrants added to the ethnic mix that already predominated in the middle colonies. Germans began to immigrate to North America in large numbers around 1709, when war, bad crops, and heavy taxes drove several thousand of them to western New York and Pennsylvania. Most of the 100,000 or more Germans who emigrated between 1700 and 1775 came from Dutch ports on the North Sea, easily accessed by citizens of states near the Rhine River: Palatinate, Baden, Württemberg, Hesse, Nassau, Cologne, Osnabrück, Muenster, and Mainz. Most entered through Philadelphia, settling in the nearby countryside, where they became known as the Pennsylvania Dutch—from a corruption of the German word for Germans, the *Deutsch*. They came in such numbers that Franklin wondered why "the Palatine Boors [Germans] be suffered to swarm into our Settlements, and by herding together establish their Language and Manners to the Exclusion of ours? Why should Pennsylvania, founded by the English, become a Colony of Aliens, who will shortly be so numerous as to Germanize us instead of our Anglifying them, and will never adopt our Language or Customs." But Franklin was wrong on this count. With the Seven Years' War (1756–63) and the American Revolution (1775–83), German immigration came to a virtual standstill for 50 years, leading to the gradual assimilation of the first wave of German Americans.

Although Scots had been among the earliest immigrants to the Americas, the first widespread Scottish immigration to the New World came between 1717 and 1775, when more than 100,000 Presbyterian Scots-Irish settled in America, mainly because of high rents or famine, and with most coming from families having been in Ireland for several generations. In the colonial period, they were in fact usually referred to simply as Irish, making it difficult to determine exact figures. Additionally, large numbers of rebellious Scots were exiled to America by the British government. But there was also a significant voluntary migration of Scots directly from Scotland, especially after 1730, with some 40,000 coming between 1763 and 1775 alone. While

Immigration

Scots and Scots-Irish became prominent throughout the colonies, they frequently settled along the Appalachian frontier and largely influenced the religion and culture of the frontier regions as they developed. Altogether this represented the largest movement of any group from the British Isles to British North America in the 18th century.

Although war usually restricted immigration, during the Seven Years' War 6,000 French speakers in present-day Nova Scotia, New Brunswick, and Prince Edward Island were exiled to Britain's southern colonies and to Louisiana, then still in the hands of France. There they became the largest French-speaking enclave in the United States—the Cajuns. Canada's remaining French population of some 70,000 was brought under control of the British Crown, which organized the most populous areas as the colony of Quebec.

SETTLEMENT OF GEORGIA

The settling of Britain's last Atlantic seaboard colony suggests many of the patterns already implicit in immigration elsewhere during the 18th century. The Georgia colony was unique among the American colonies, as it was founded in 1732 as a penal colony for the "worthy" poor in the disputed territory between the Carolinas and Spanish Florida. Fearing the possible northward expansion of Spain, the British Crown granted General James Oglethorpe and a board of trustees a charter for settling the land between the Savannah and the Altamaha rivers. Oglethorpe believed that while giving London paupers a fresh start in the New World, he could also thwart any Spanish aggression. Colonists were encouraged to immigrate, but the terms were not generous. A head of household could claim a grant of 50 acres of land and an additional 50 acres for each servant. On the other hand, he could not amass more than 500 acres of land and could only pass it down to the eldest son; otherwise the land reverted to the trustees. Slavery was prohibited.

Because the trustees in London retained total control of the government of Georgia, the colonists complained from the beginning. They harried Oglethorpe and the trustees into making fundamental reforms. In 1738 land and inheritance laws were made more liberal, and in 1750 settlers were allowed to import slaves. In 1751 Georgia was returned to the Crown, which authorized an assembly. With the purchase of large tracts of lands from local Indian tribes in 1763, 1766, and 1773, the government was able to attract a wide variety of settlers seeking lands of "the most fertile quality," most notably several thousand Scots-Irish who arrived by way of Charleston, as well as small numbers of Austrian Lutherans and Moravians, and a Jewish community in Savannah. The coastal region remained predominantly English,

14

while the backcountry filled with what Bernard Bailyn calls "a remarkably poly-ethnic and poly-linguistic community."

Paradoxically, while the English colonial settlement as a whole was diverse, including large numbers of German, Dutch, Scandinavian, French, and African inhabitants, British immigrants far outnumbered all others combined, and it was from their political, cultural, and religious sensibilities that the dominant patterns of American culture emerged. From the time of the first permanent British presence in the New World at Jamestown, Virginia, in 1607 until 1900, British immigrants outnumbered all others in the United States and Canada. In the colonial period between 1607 and 1776, more than 300,000 British immigrants came to America for a variety of reasons. There was no typical British immigrant to North America. They were English, Welsh, Scots, Scots-Irish, and Irish. Some came as proprietors or representatives of the government, some as soldiers, some as seekers of religious freedom, some as indentured servants, and some as paupers. Most of them came to better their economic circumstances in some way, driven by overcrowding and poor economic conditions in Britain.

THE PERIOD OF OPEN IMMIGRATION

EARLY PHASE (1775–1830)

Britain's loss of the American colonies led to a dramatic demographic shift in her remaining North American colonies. Before the end of the 1780s, 40,000–50,000 Loyalists left the new republic for Nova Scotia, New Brunswick, and Quebec. In addition several thousand additional Americans seeking better farmlands moved into western Quebec. As a result of this great influx of largely English-speaking settlers, in 1791 Quebec was divided into Upper Canada (Ontario) and Lower Canada (Quebec), roughly along British and French lines of culture. Despite these losses, the United States continued to grow at a phenomenal rate. The French Revolution and Napoleonic Wars (1789–1815) significantly hindered immigration, but the Scots-Irish continued to come, perhaps 100,000 during this period. Some 10,000 French émigrés also made their way to the United States.

By the time the young Americans had won their independence from Great Britain in 1783, they were one of the most rapidly growing—and diverse—countries in the world. When the first U.S. census was taken in 1790, the population stood at just over 3.9 million. Less than half were English or Welsh (49 percent); Africans, mostly slaves, comprised 19 percent of the population, followed by Germans (7 percent), Scots (7 percent), Scots-Irish (5 percent), Irish (3 percent), and Dutch (3 percent). There was considerable regional variation, with New England remaining most thoroughly English (more than 75 percent); Pennsylvania almost 40 percent German;

Immigration

coastal regions of the south almost 50 percent African; and the entire back-country from New York to Georgia heavily Scots-Irish.

There were no specific provisions regarding immigration in the new Constitution ratified in 1788. As a result of varying policies among the states for naturalizing citizens during the 1780s, however, the U.S. government passed "an act to establish an uniform rule of naturalization" on March 26, 1790. Under provisions of Article 1, section 8, of the Constitution, the measure granted citizenship to "all free white persons" after two years' residence and provided that the children of citizens born outside the borders of the United States would be "considered as natural born citizens." A new Naturalization Act was passed on January 29, 1795, repealing the old act, raising the residency requirement to five years, and requiring three years' notice of intent to seek naturalization. This greater stringency regarding the naturalization of immigrants was continued in the Alien and Sedition Acts (1798). With Thomas Jefferson becoming president, there was a relaxation of the hostility toward immigrants that had prevailed during the administration of John Adams (1797–1801). The Alien and Sedition Acts were repealed or allowed to expire, and Jefferson campaigned for a more lenient naturalization law, observing that, under the "ordinary chances of human life, a denial of citizenship, under a residence of fourteen years, is a denial to a great proportion of those who ask it." On April 14, 1802, a new naturalization measure was enacted, reducing the period of residence required for naturalization from 14 to five years. In addition the new law required that prospective citizens give three years' notice of intent to renounce previous citizenship; that they swear or affirm support of the Constitution; that they renounce all titles of nobility; and that they demonstrate themselves to be of "good moral character." The Naturalization Act was supplemented on March 26, 1804, by exempting aliens who had entered the United States between 1798 and 1802 from the declaration of intention. The three-year notice was reduced to two years on May 26, 1824.

In response to the ideals of natural rights and political liberty that were espoused during the Age of Enlightenment, as well as the evangelical concern for humanitarianism and Christian justice, between 1777 and 1804, the northern states gradually abolished slavery. The slave trade was prohibited throughout the United States by statute in 1808, though more than 500,000 Africans had been forced into the country by that time, and their natural rate of increase made them a self-sustaining population. By 1860 another considerable demographic shift had taken place, as more than 500,000 slaves were sold from farms and plantations in Virginia, Maryland, Kentucky, and other states to the cotton plantations of the Deep South.

Concern with the dramatic increase in immigration in 1818 led to passage of the Manifest of Immigrants Act (March 2, 1819), the first piece of American legislation regulating the transportation of migrants to and

16

from America, and the first measure requiring that immigration statistics be kept. (The United States maintained uninterrupted data on individuals coming into the country from the time this act was passed.) The act limited the number of passengers on each ship, required adequate water and food provisions, and required ship captains or masters to report a list of all passengers taken on board abroad, including name, sex, age, and occupation.

The economic recession in England and Ireland led to a steady immigration from the 1820s. Of the 152,000 immigrants that arrived between 1820 and 1830, 82,000 came from Great Britain and Ireland, about 9,000 from France, and almost 8,000 from the German states.

THE FIRST GREAT WAVE (1830–65)

Although the United States had always been a land of immigrants, the period between 1830 and the outbreak of Civil War in 1860 saw a rapid acceleration of the rate of immigration. Of the 4.9 million immigrants who arrived between 1831 and 1860, 1.9 million were from Ireland, and more than 1.5 million from the German states; together they represented almost 70 percent of all immigrants during the period. Also notable during the period was the advent of Chinese immigration, from fewer than 200 between 1831–50, to more than 41,000 between 1851 and 1860.

Poor Irish laborers had been prominent among the 17th- and 18th-century indentured servants brought to America. During the 18th century, Ireland grew more rapidly than any European country, with the population of the island increasing from 3 million in the 1720s to more than 8 million by the early 1840s. With no system of primogeniture, Irish farms were quickly divided among large families, with plots soon becoming too small to support a family. During the late 18th century, most Irish immigrants arrived in ports along the eastern seaboard of North America, often making their way to the Appalachian backcountry of Pennsylvania, South Carolina, and Georgia. A series of potato famines made conditions still worse, leading to a steady stream of mostly Scots-Irish Presbyterian immigrants during the 1820s and 1830s. Most immigrants landed first in Canada, as transportation rates to Montreal, Quebec, and Halifax, were considerably less than to the United States. The vast majority nevertheless eventually made their way to the United States. Between 1820 and 1840, more than a quarter-million Irish settled in the United States, the largest immigrant group by far.

The Great Famine of 1845–49 dramatically accelerated the process of immigration. Although famines caused by potato blight were common in the 18th and early 19th centuries, impoverished Irish citizens had never been so dependent on the potato. The outbreak of 1845 did not seem unusual. In the following year, however, virtually the entire crop was destroyed. A million or more Irish may have died as a result of famine and disease; another million chose to emigrate. With friends or family already in the United States and British North America, the decision to leave their ravaged land became easier. Between 1845 and 1860, about 1.7 million Irish settled in the United States, and another 360,000 in Canada. Although the rate of immigration declined as the century progressed, the aggregate numbers remained large. Whereas 18th-century Scots-Irish had often headed for the frontier, Irish immigrants after the Great Famine almost always settled in eastern cities, before moving on to jobs in canal and railway construction, and thus filtering westward along with the progress of the country.

The Irish were widely discriminated against during the 19th century, mainly because they were Catholic. Throughout American history, there had been periodic peaks of antiforeign sentiment. From the earliest colonial days, there had been a fear that immigrant lifestyles would erode the distinctive features of the majority culture. An early nativist movement had developed in the 1790s, when Federalists hoped to exclude the corroding influence of radical immigrants by passing the Alien and Sedition Acts. With the majority of settlers in British territories being Protestant Anglicans and Puritans, Quakers and Roman Catholics were seen as potential threats to the traditional English order. While these attitudes persisted in the early republic, they remained largely out of the public discourse until the 1830s. As most Americans were members of Protestant denominations that fostered the ethic of American individualism, it was easy to convince people in hard times that papal schemes were afoot. The influx of more than a quarter of a million, mostly Catholic, Irish between 1820 and 1840 led to the second great wave of nativism in the United States. Samuel F. B. Morse's *Foreign Conspiracy against the Liberties of the United States* (1834) and Rev. Lyman Beecher's *A Plea for the West* (1835) suggested to Americans that clandestine plots to impose Catholic culture were being masterminded in Rome. Sensational exposés of Catholic practices became common in the press. Maria Monk's *Awful Disclosures of the Hotel Dieu Nunnery of Montreal* (1836), purporting to tell the firsthand account of the author's imprisonment in a Catholic monastery, was a best seller and remained so long after she was discredited. In addition to vague fears of conspiracy, many Americans feared the potential power of the Roman Catholic Church to overturn the Protestant foundation of the emerging public system of education. This sometimes led to violence, as in the Philadelphia riots of 1844, when a number of Irish Catholics were killed and several churches burned.

The second major migration of the 1830s and 1840s came from the German states of central Europe. The southwestern German states, which had been particularly hard hit by the effects of rapid population growth, crop failures, high taxes, and an antiquated cottage industry, continued to supply most of the emigrants via the Rhine River and the port cities of Amsterdam, Rotterdam, and Antwerp. The situation was worsened by declining potato crops in 1842 and the complete failure of the crop in 1846. German rulers sometimes sponsored organizations such as the Central Society for German Emigrants (Berlin, 1844) and the National Emigration Society (Darmstadt, 1847) in order to alleviate domestic problems. With the reduction of interstate German tolls by the Zollverein (tariff union) in 1834, travel to the more desirable German ports of Bremen and Hamburg became easier, encouraging emigration from Westphalia, Oldenburg, Saxony, Prussia, and Mecklenburg. The typical German immigrant after 1830 was more likely to be skilled and with some education, choosing America or Canada as a place to maintain family status, rather than to establish it. German immigration to the United States peaked proportionally in the 1850s, with nearly a million German speakers emigrating to escape the effects of the abortive democratic Revolutions of 1848, to flee social or religious persecution, or simply to take advantage of the burgeoning American economy. The economic downturn of the late 1850s and the American Civil War (1861–65) discouraged immigration for a decade, but a strong support base for future German immigrants had already been established.

Finally, immigration during the late 1840s and 1850s was spurred by the discovery of gold at Sutter's Mill in the Sacramento Valley of California in January 1848. Between 1848 and the granting of statehood in 1850, more than 90,000 people migrated to California, most from the United States, but large numbers also from Mexico, Chile, Australia, and others from many regions of Europe. Almost all arrived through the port of San Francisco, turning a sleepy village into a city of 25,000 in less than two years. By 1852 the Californian population had risen to more than 250,000.

Among the immigrants were large numbers of Chinese workers from the impoverished and flood-ravaged province of Guangdong, who were especially responsive to the attractions of Gam Saan ("Gold mountain"), as California was called in China. Between 1850 and 1852, more than 20,000 Chinese, almost all men, entered California. In the early years, 70 percent of Chinese immigrants were miners, though they moved into railroad construction and a variety of service industries as the ore deposits—most easily mined with simple and inexpensive equipment—played out.

With the rapid influx of Irish, German, and Chinese immigrants after 1845, a series of steamship disasters, and the prevalence of cholera, typhus, and smallpox among arriving immigrants, in late 1853 Senator Hamilton Fish (R-N.Y.) called for a select committee to "consider the causes and the extent of the sickness and mortality prevailing on board of emigrant ships," and to determine what further legislation might be necessary. With the support of President Franklin Pierce, Congress repealed the Manifest of Passengers Act (1819) and subsequent measures relating to transportation of immigrants, replacing those laws, on March 3, 1855, with "an act to extend the provisions of all laws now in force relating to the carriage of passengers in merchant-vessels, and the regulation thereof." The measure not only limited the number of passengers per vessel but also required 14–18 square feet of deck space per passenger, an increased provision of food, and the maintenance of sanitary conditions on board.

Also as a result of the ever-increasing numbers of immigrants, the New York State Board of Commissioners of Immigration opened Castle Garden at the southern tip of Manhattan Island as America's first formal immigrant depot. Built as a fort prior to the War of 1812, it had become an entertainment center, before being converted into a model processing station for immigrants arriving in New York City. This central point of debarkation enabled commissioners to count immigrants and glean information about religion, occupation, age, and value of property brought into the country. Immigrants were required to bathe with soap and water and were then provided numerous services to help them avoid the predatory practices that had been common, as unscrupulous "providers" took advantage of new arrivals. Basic food supplies could be purchased, and kitchen facilities were available. Immigrants could also change their money there and purchase railroad and canal tickets.

Not all Americans welcomed the nearly 5 million immigrants who arrived during this first great wave of immigration. Whether in rural or urban centers, German clannishness and Irish Catholicism had by mid-century already led to the rise of a strong nativist movement that continued to play a major role in the development of immigation policy prior to World War I. During the 1850s anti-Catholic nativism led to the rise of the Secret Order of the Star-Spangled Banner, more commonly known as the Know-Nothing or American Party. The Know-Nothings were particularly strong in the Northeast and border regions. In the wake of their strong showing in 1854 and 1855, in which they gained control of several state governments and sent more than 100 Congressmen to Washington, they attempted to restrict immigration, delay naturalization, and investigate perceived Catholic abuses. Finding little evidence to support Catholic crimes or conspiracies, and with the country embroiled in pre–Civil War states' rights and slavery issues, Know Nothing political influence and anti-Catholic nativism waned.

POSTWAR PHASE (1865–82)

Few emigrated to America during the Civil War (1861–65), but two pieces of legislation suggested their continued desirability. Though the Homestead Act of 1862 originated in the opposition of workers' groups, western settlers, and agriculturalists to the government's policy of using western lands to raise revenue, it was a powerful magnet for attracting immigrant farmers. The measure provided 160 acres of free land to any head of household who would develop the land and live on it continuously for five years. It not only made it possible for immigrant agriculturalists to establish themselves on the frontier with relatively low capital investments, but it also enabled them to maintain a strong sense of Old World identity, as their lands were often taken up in remote regions. Many land reformers were dissatisfied, as the act was not accompanied by legislation to explicitly halt land speculation, and much land was reserved for railway grants and American Indian reservations. Prospective farmers nevertheless flocked to the lands thus opened. By 1890, 957,902 homestead claims had been filed. German and Scandinavian immigrants were particularly attracted, as they often had modest amounts of capital to establish themselves. Wisconsin, Minnesota, the Dakotas, Kansas, and Nebraska were substantially developed by immigrant farmers.

The 1864 Immigration Act was designed to increase the flow of laborers to the United States following the disruptions of the Civil War. In his message to Congress in December 1863, President Abraham Lincoln urged "the expediency of a system for the encouragement of immigration," noting "the great deficiency of laborers in every field of industry, especially in agriculture and our mines." After much debate, Congress enacted legislation on July 4, 1864, providing for appointment by the president of a Commissioner of Immigration, operating under the authority of the secretary of state, and immigrant labor contracts, up to a maximum of one year, pledging wages against the cost of transportation to America. Though the measure itself did not greatly alter patterns of immigration, it suggested a clear recognition of the importance of immigrants as the country expanded and developed economically.

With the war's end, traditional prewar patterns of immigration resumed. More than 700,000 Germans immigrated by 1870, and another 1.5 million in the 1880s. The revival of the American economy in 1866–73, endemic low wages in Germany, and the unsettling effects of Prussian president Otto von Bismarck's wars of German unification (1863–71) led many Germans to believe that prosperity would never return to their homeland. Most of the 5 million Germans who immigrated to America in the 19th century were attracted to the Midwest—Ohio, Illinois, Michigan, Wisconsin, Minnesota, and Missouri.

After the Civil War, some whose families had migrated to Russia in the late 18th century began to immigrate to America. Like their cultural brethren from Germany, they were divided, based upon location (Black Sea area, Caucasus area, Volga area, Volhynia area) and religious affiliation (Lutheran, Mennonite, Hutterite Brethren). The freeing of Russian serfs (1862), the introduction of compulsory military service (1871), and attempts to force Russian education upon their communities drove a substantial minority of the 1.5 million German-speaking Russians to the United States, where they tended to settle in the Plains states. No matter the country of origin, however, German immigrants usually resisted assimilation. German-language parochial schools were common. In rural areas, the immigrants clustered around their particular churches—Lutheran, Reform, Catholic, or one of the Pietist denominations. In cities such as Milwaukee, St. Louis, Louisville, and Cincinnati, where Germans sometimes numbered more than a quarter of the population, they played a large role in shaping urban culture, establishing newspapers, educational clubs, beer gardens, and mutual-benefit societies.

British citizens also continued their migration to the United States, with more than a million English, Welsh, Scots, and Irish coming in the immediate aftermath of the Civil War. British immigrants (including the Irish) constituted the largest national immigrant group by decade until 1900, peaking from 1863 to 1873, and from 1879 to 1890. Many were escaping famine in Ireland and economic hardship elsewhere, but the rapidly industrializing United States also lured large numbers of skilled workers, machinists, and miners to help drive industrial development. In 1860 more than half of America's foreign-born population was British. By the 1890s, however, British immigration to the United States was declining, with an increasing percentage of British immigrants choosing Canada, Australia, or New Zealand. Inexpensive land in the United States had become difficult to find, and the specialized skills of British workers were less needed as industry became more developed.

Canada played an important role in postwar immigration both as a direct source of immigrants and as a stopover for European-born immigrants who eventually found their way across the southern border. The first major migration of French Canadians had come during the Seven Years' War (1756–63). Until the 1850s, however, immigration remained small, as Canada itself could still offer desirable farmlands in relatively accessible regions. By 1860 Canadians were taking advantage of the demand for labor, moving across the international border much as if they were moving internally. French Canadians in Quebec, dissatisfied with the working of the old seigneurial land system, left en masse, usually for the textile mills of New England. Farmers dissatisfied with weather and isolation in the prairie provinces frequently sought better conditions to the south. In the 1870s alone, some 380,000 Canadians immigrated to the United States, and a like number did so in the following decade. As in the case of British immigration, however, the 1890s saw a rapid decrease, as Canadian emigrants looked elsewhere for their opportunities.

Three of the most significant new immigrant groups of the period between the Civil War and the 1880s were from the Scandinavian region of northern Europe. Though the effects of industrialization in Scandinavia had lagged behind the countries of western Europe, by the 1860s land enclosure and more efficient farming techniques promised to create a large class of landless farmers. Given an ongoing opposition to state Lutheranism, the lack of future prospects among agriculturalists drove Norwegians, Swedes, and Danes to the United States, where, with a relatively modest investment, they could rebuild their ways of life. Norwegians had begun emigrating in significant numbers during the 1850s and continued to be the largest of the Scandinavian groups into the 1920s. Despite the relatively small number of Scandinavian immigrants—about 1.4 million between 1861 and 1900—they played a disproportionate role in establishing culture patterns in the upper Midwest and Plains states, most notably in Wisconsin, Minnesota, and the eastern Dakotas.

NEW IMMIGRATION AND THE CLOSING DOOR (1882–1943)

During the 1880s, immigration rapidly increased—between 1871 and 1880, it had averaged about 280,000 per year; in the following decade, some 525,000 per year. The source countries were also shifting, away from western Europe and Scandinavia ("old immigration") toward eastern and southern Europe, especially Italy, Austria-Hungary, and Russia ("new immigration"). Germans still came—almost 1 million between 1890 and 1914—but they were increasingly drawn to new German factories, and their numbers paled in comparison to their neighbors to the east and south. Between 1881 and 1900, almost a million Italians immigrated to the United States; between 1901 and 1920, another 3.2 million. As a result of the unification of Italy during the 1860s, the more industrialized and advanced north of Italy benefited, while the economy of the agricultural, feudal south was decimated. As population soared—increasing from 25 million in 1861 to 35 million in 1901—desperate sharecroppers and laborers left the worn-out soil for new opportunities in the United States. Between 1876 and 1924, when the restrictive Johnson-Reed Act was passed, more than 4.5 million Italians immigrated to the United States, about three-quarters of them from the impoverished south. Italian immigration reached its peak in the first decade of the 20th century, when more than 2 million Italians settled in the United States. Italians— generally poor, uneducated, and Roman Catholic—suffered severely from American nativist attitudes. As a result, they created social enclaves—Little Italies—in most of America's major eastern cities, fostering a love of the old country and traditional ways of life.

Immigration figures were comparable for Austria-Hungary (946,426 between 1881 and 1900; slightly more than 3 million between 1901 and 1920). Only a handful of Austrians had immigrated to North America prior to the mid-19th century. When Leopold Anton von Firmian the Catholic bishop-prince of Salzburg (r. 1727–44) exiled 30,000 Protestants from his lands in 1728, several hundred settled in the state of Georgia. A few radical reformers fleeing the failed revolutions of 1848 settled in the United States as

Immigration

political refugees. Most were middle class and reasonably well educated and tended to cluster in New York and St. Louis, where there were already large German-speaking settlements. Although the official estimate that fewer than 1,000 Austrians were in America in 1850 is almost certainly wrong, it does suggest the limited migration that had taken place by that time.

By the 1870s, however, several factors led to a rapid increase in immigration. The emancipation of the peasantry beginning in 1848 led to the creation of a market economy and the potential for wage earnings and individual choices about migration. Overpopulation also contributed to the rapid increase in immigration. With a rapidly growing population, laws and inheritance patterns reduced the majority of farms to tiny plots that could barely support a family. As more agricultural workers were uprooted from the land, it became more common for them to try their hand in North America when prospects in Austrian cities failed. Finally, a heightened sense of nationalism encouraged Austrian minorities to escape the discriminatory policies of the Austrians and Hungarians. From 1870 to 1910, immigration increased dramatically each decade despite restrictions on immigration propaganda. Many ethnic groups, including Poles, had high rates of return migration, suggesting immigration as a temporary economic expedient. On the other hand, German Austrians, Jews, and Czechs tended to immigrate as families and to establish permanent residence. With the United States and Austria-Hungary on opposite sides during World War I, immigration virtually ceased. At the end of the war, the anachronistic, multiethnic Austro-Hungarian Empire was dismembered and replaced by the successor states of Austria, Hungary, Poland, Czechoslovakia, Romania, and Yugoslavia.

Russian immigration figures (almost 820,000 between 1881 and 1900; more than 2.5 million between 1901 and 1920) were almost as high as those for Italy and Austria-Hungary, drawn largely from non-Russian ethnic groups. Russia had acquired much of Poland in the late 18th century, and throughout the 19th century, it continued to expand, especially into the Caucasus Mountain region and central Asia, occupying areas that would later become the modern countries of Armenia, Azerbaijan, Georgia, Kazakhstan, Kyrgyzstan, Turkmenistan, Tajikistan, and Uzbekistan, as well as into Finland in the north. As a result, during the great age of immigration after 1882, more than a dozen major ethnic groups were often classified by immigration agents as "Russian," though they were in fact members of these older nations.

This "new immigration" was troubling to many Americans. Most of the "old immigrants" had been Protestants (the Irish being the notable exception), and few had been destitute. A much higher percentage of "new immigrants" came with little education and few resources. Few of them knew anything of representative institutions or the democratic process. Virtually all Italians were Roman Catholics, and more than 2 million Russians and

Introduction to Immigration

Austrians were Jews. The greatest phase of Jewish immigration to the United States came between 1880 and 1924, a period that saw the Jewish population rise from about 250,000 to 4.5 million and saw the center of Jewish life shift from Europe to the United States. With Jewish persecution on the rise during an intensely nationalistic period in European history, some 2 million Jews—known as Ashkenazic Jews—fled Poland, Russia, Romania, Galicia (in the Austro-Hungarian Empire), and other regions of eastern Europe. Also during this period, about 35,000 Sephardic Jews arrived, mainly from Turkey and Syria. These mainly Orthodox Jews from eastern Europe and the Middle East were often an embarrassment to well-established Reform Jews who were well on their way toward assimilation, creating some tension within the American Jewish community. After 1890 the vast majority of Jews settled in New York City and other parts of the northern seaboard. Although half of America's Jews lived in New York City by 1914, there were many thriving, independent Jewish communities spread throughout the country.

The massive wave of immigrants during the 1880s—including more than 2 million between 1881 and 1883—rendered obsolete the old Castle Garden immigration station of lower Manhattan that had opened in 1855. Although reluctant to spend federal monies on immigrants, the government found a ready source of income to defray the costs of processing. Immigrant head taxes, begun at 50¢ in 1882, were gradually raised to $8 in 1917, providing a regular source of funding for the immigrant process, including the construction of more suitable facilities. Officials chose the site of the former naval arsenal as the location for a new processing center on Ellis Island. With its completion in 1892, officials could process up to 5,000 immigrants per day. After being ferried from the ships on which they had arrived, most immigrants were given a cursory medical examination, had their papers checked against shipping manifests, and were briefly interviewed. Those admitted typically purchased tickets by rail or coastal steamer to their final destinations and were then ferried to either Manhattan or the Jersey shore. The small number who were refused entry were detained pending an appeal or deportation. Ellis Island became the first stop for more than 12 million immigrants to the United States, including three-quarters of all those entering the country between 1892 and 1924.

As most of the new immigrant groups clustered together in enclaves in major industrial cities, many nonimmigrants questioned the ability of the country to assimilate these newcomers. Between 1890 and 1910, the foreign-born population averaged more than 14 percent of the American population. More significant, by 1920 immigrants and their children comprised more than 70 percent of the populations in Boston, Chicago, Milwaukee, and New York. In time all the major immigrant groups of the period worked their way up the socioeconomic ladder, but not before nativism, World War

Immigration

I, and the Bolshevik Revolution in Russia led to a series of restrictive immigration measures that completely transformed what had been a largely open immigration process prior to 1882.

ASIAN EXCLUSION ACT

The first overtly racist restrictions on immigration were aimed at the Chinese and Japanese, just as the "new immigrants" were beginning to make their presence felt in the east. West coast immigration was much smaller and was mainly limited to Chinese and Japanese migrants processing through San Francisco. For almost two decades after the Civil War, there were virtually no limitations on immigration on either coast. The Burlingame Treaty between the United States and China (1868) granted "free migration and immigration" to the Chinese. Although it did not permit naturalization, it did grant Chinese immigrants most-favored-nation status regarding rights and exemptions of noncitizens.

Although emigration from China was officially forbidden, within four years of the discovery of gold in California (1848–52), 25,000 Chinese had immigrated to California in the hope of striking it rich on "Gold Mountain." The bloody Taiping Rebellion (1850–64) against the Qing dynasty led thousands more to seek asylum abroad. The Chinese were generally well received. With the United States embarking on a period of rapid development of mines, railroads, and a host of associated industries in the west, Secretary of State William H. Seward sought a treaty with China that would provide as much cheap labor as possible. Negotiating for China was a highly respected former U.S. ambassador to China, Anson Burlingame, whose principal goal was to moderate Western aggression in China. The Burlingame Treaty, signed on July 28, 1868, recognized "the inherent and inalienable right of man to change his home and allegiance" and provided nearly unlimited immigration of male Chinese laborers.

The end of the initial railway boom and the depression that began in the early 1870s, however, led to America's first major piece of restrictive immigration legislation, the Chinese Exclusion Act of 1882. When the Chinese first came to California in large numbers in the 1850s in the wake of the gold rush, they generally had been well received and by the 1870s constituted almost 10 percent of the population of California. With the advent of depression from 1873, many people living in the western states blamed the 100,000 Chinese immigrants for taking jobs and depressing wages. Increasing agitation was for a time deflected by merchants, industrialists, steamship companies, missionaries, and eastern intellectuals who argued in favor of the Chinese presence in America. By the late 1870s, however, politicians in the midwest and east took an interest in placating an increasingly violent white labor force, and thus were inclined to agree to limitations on Chinese immigration. In addition to organized opposition from labor groups such as the Workingmen's Party, racism played a large role in anti-Chinese attitudes. A growing opposition led to passage of the Page Act (1875), which prohibited forced contract laborers from China and appointed a Senate committee to investigate the question of Chinese immigration (January 1876). In 1879 Henry George published *Progress and Poverty*, one of the most influential economic tracts of the 19th century, in which he concluded that the Chinese were economically backward and "unassimilable." After much debate and many abortive bills, the United States and China signed the Angell Treaty (1881), which gave the United States authority to regulate the immigration of Chinese laborers. A bill was quickly brought forward to exclude Chinese laborers for 20 years, but it was vetoed by President Chester A. Arthur, who argued that such a long period of exclusion would contravene the articles of the Angell Treaty. Arthur reluctantly signed a revised measure on May 6, 1882, excluding all Chinese laborers for 10 years and denying naturalization to Chinese aliens already in the United States.

The Chinese Exclusion Act was the first measure to specifically exclude an ethnic group from immigrating to the United States. Chinese officials and their domestic servants were exempted from the prohibition. In 1888 the Scott Act imposed new restrictions on Chinese immigration. The exclusions were extended in 1892 and again, for an indefinite period of time, in 1902. As a result of the 90-day deferment period, almost 40,000 additional Chinese laborers entered the United States, raising the Chinese population to about 150,000.

Significant Japanese migration to the West only began after passage of the Chinese Exclusion Act (1882). Prohibited from hiring Chinese laborers, Hawaiian plantation owners turned to laborers displaced by the modernizing Meiji regime in Japan. Between 1885 and 1904, more than 100,000 Japanese were brought to work in Hawaii, making them the largest ethnic group in the islands. At the same time, many Japanese students and other travelers were venturing to the mainland. By 1900 they had been joined by laborers, making a Japanese population of almost 30,000 in California. As thousands of Japanese migrated to North America annually in the wake of U.S. annexation of Hawaii in 1898, Americans in California protested strongly, leading to diplomatic agreements by which the Japanese government agreed to stop issuing passports to laborers. Japan's emergence as an important East Asian power following the Russo-Japanese War (1904–05) heightened tensions between the United States and Japan. In the wake of the war, Japanese immigration to the United States exploded, reaching up to 1,000 a month by 1906. Japan also posed a potential threat to the Philippines, an American colony since 1898. Tensions were to some extent alleviated with the signing of the Taft-Katsura Agreement (1905), by which Japan agreed not to invade the Philippines in return for U.S. recognition of

Immigration

Japanese supremacy in Korea. In the same year, however, both houses of the California legislature urged their Washington delegation to propose formal limitations on Japanese immigration. The crime and uncertainty following the San Francisco earthquake in April 1906 led to increased hostility toward Japanese immigrants. The city's mayor and the Asiatic Exclusion League, with almost 80,000 members, pressured the San Francisco school board to pass a measure on October 11 segregating Japanese students. The resolution deeply offended the Japanese nation and led to talk of war between the two countries.

Not wishing local affairs to undermine the international policy, President Theodore Roosevelt sought a diplomatic solution. In his annual address on December 4, he repudiated the school board's decision and praised Japan. Between December 1906 and January 1908, three separate but related agreements were reached that addressed both Japanese concerns over the welfare of the immigrants and Californian concerns over the growing numbers of Japanese laborers. In February 1907, immigration legislation was amended to halt the flow of Japanese laborers from Hawaii, Canada, or Mexico, which in turn led the San Francisco school board to rescind on March 13 their segregation resolution. In discussions of December 1907, the Japanese government agreed to restrict passports for travel to the continental United States to non-laborers, former residents, or the family members of Japanese immigrants. At the same time, the U.S. government allowed migration of laborers to Hawaii and access to the United States by travelers, merchants, students, and "picture brides" whose marriages were arranged in Japan on behalf of women in the United States.

With the dramatic decline in the numbers of Japanese laborers, Filipinos were increasingly recruited to take their place. To demonstrate that America's East Asian policy was not made from a position of weakness, Roosevelt followed this "Gentlemen's Agreement" with a world tour of 16 American battleships, including a symbolic stop in Japan. With provisions of the Chinese Exclusion Act (1882) and the Gentlemen's Agreement (1907) largely excluding Chinese, Japanese, and Korean laborers, the high demand for cheap agricultural labor in Hawaii and California led to a rapid influx of Filipino workers.

THE NEW IMMIGRATION

While anti-Asian sentiments were centered in the West, suspicion of Italians, Germans, Austrians, Hungarians, Poles, Russians, Jews, Greeks, Ukrainians, and a host of other central and eastern European groups was growing in the East. Much of this was rooted in hostility toward non-Protestant religious practices; more generally in customs strange to peoples whose ancestors had come from northern and western Europe. In part,

28

too, many Americans were fearful of links between the "new immigrant" groups and the rise of socialism, particularly as represented by the threat of organized labor.

Ironically, until the early 20th century, most immigrants preferred to work at home, where they could care for their children and protect their cultural values. They were generally suspicious of labor organizers, preferring to work through their own intermediaries, while labor organizers almost universally decried America's open immigration policy. In the minds of most Americans, however, it was always a radical European immigrant behind labor disorder. As a result, most labor unions did all they could to present themselves as "American" first and foremost. The first national labor organization, the National Labor Union (NLU), was formed in 1866. Widespread unemployment in the wake of the Civil War heightened concern over jobs, and the NLU almost immediately lobbied against the Immigration Act of 1864, which provided for entry of contract laborers. The NLU disappeared during the 1870s, with the Knights of Labor emerging as the premier labor organization in the United States during the 1870s and 1880s. The Knights opposed immigration, especially that of Chinese peasant workers, and worked vigorously for the repeal of the Burlingame Treaty. In decrying the Chinese "evil," labor leaders emphasized the fraudulent means of migrant entry, often coming across the Canadian border or under false names. Knights pressure contributed to the Chinese Exclusion Act, but they were equally concerned with general labor recruitment in Europe, which was undertaken, they argued, in order to create a labor surplus. The Knights did manage to secure amendments that put some teeth into the ineffective Alien Contract Law (1885), but the decline of union membership after 1886 rendered the organization less important in immigrant reform than in the previous decade.

More influential than either the NLU or the Knights of Labor was the American Federation of Labor (AFL), founded in 1881. The AFL encouraged organization of workers into craft unions, which would then cooperate in labor bargaining. Under the energetic leadership of Samuel Gompers, an English immigrant from a Jewish family, the AFL gained strength as it won the support of skilled workers, both native and foreign-born. Ethnic concerns soon became entwined with the general depression of wages caused by the massive immigration of the 1880s and 1890s. Chinese immigration was condemned from the first, and the flood of unskilled workers from southern and eastern Europe after 1880 generally was not eligible for membership in craft unions.

As nativism began to rise in the 1880s, Americans were more fearful of racial and political, rather than religious, incursions. The Haymarket bombing in Chicago in 1886, for which several German anarchists were convicted and hanged, confirmed for many the inferred link between aliens

29

and radical politics. Although the Immigration Restriction League, founded in 1894, was at first unsuccessful, it gradually chipped away at the open door for immigration, leading to rising immigrant head taxes, greater restrictions on Asian immigration, and, finally, the advent of a literacy test. In 1896 the AFL established a committee on immigration and in the following year passed a resolution calling on the government to require a literacy test as the best means of keeping out unskilled laborers. They also continued to oppose Chinese and Japanese immigration.

Despite the exclusion of most Asians, during the first decade of the 20th century an average of almost 900,000 immigrants came to the United States each year, almost 70 percent of them from eastern and southern Europe. Alarmed at the influx of immigrants, Congress passed an Immigration Act in 1907, codifying and extending previous restrictive legislation and establishing a commission to evaluate American immigration policy. The commission included members from the Senate—Chairman William Paul Dillingham (R-Vt.), Henry Cabot Lodge (R-Miss.), and Asbury Latimer (D-S.C.); members from the House of Representatives—Benjamin F. Howell (R-N.J.), William S. Bennet (R-N.Y.), and John L. Burnett (D-Ala.); and presidential appointees—William R. Wheeler, Jeremiah W. Jenks, and Charles P. Neill. On December 5, 1910, a two-volume summary of the commission's findings was presented to Congress, and early the following year, the massive 42-volume report was released. The commission's study concluded that during the 1880s a fundamental change occurred in immigration to the United States. Most who had come under the "old immigration" "mingled freely with . . . native Americans" and thus were assimilated. The "new immigration" that began around 1883 was marked by an increase in transient, unskilled laborers who flocked to urban enclaves where they resisted assimilation. The committee made several recommendations to limit the "new immigration," including a five-year period of deportability for immigrants accused of serious crimes and a three-year period of deportability for those who became public charges; continued restrictions on Chinese, Japanese, and Korean immigration; restrictions on unskilled immigrants; and, most controversially, a literacy test as the best means of restricting immigration. Although there was much of value in the information and statistics gathered by the commission, its conclusions reflect the restrictionist bias of the committee members, who established an artificial dichotomy between "old" and "new" immigrants that obscured many variations from one ethnic group to another. The commission also failed to consider the effect of the recency of immigration, which clearly affected education, achievement, and rate of assimilation.

Racism and international politics combined during World War I to produce an especially strong sense of xenophobia. The Chinese Exclusion Act of 1882 had been seen by most policy-makers as a reaction to an excep-

Introduction to Immigration

tional case, but attitudes gradually shifted with the influx of poorly educated southern and eastern Europeans who arrived in the hundreds of thousands in the 1880s. Pseudoscientific anti-immigrant literature became prevalent from the 1890s and found one of its most eloquent exponents in Madison Grant, who argued in *The Passing of the Great Race* (1916) that interracial unions led to reversions to a "more ancient, generalized and lower" race. Though it was widely accepted that racial distinctions should be recognized, the real debate revolved around how best to ensure that the bulk of immigrants were of the best kind. The idea of imposing a literacy test to restrict the tide of "undesirable" Europeans was first widely proposed by progressive economist Edward W. Bemis in 1887. It found relatively little political support until the cause was taken up by the Immigration Restriction League, founded and supported by members of a number of prominent Boston families. Measures incorporating a literacy test came near success in 1895, 1903, 1912, and 1915, only to be vetoed by presidents Grover Cleveland, William Taft, and Woodrow Wilson.

With the United States moving ever closer to joining the Great War in Europe, hostility increased toward Germany, Ireland, and Austria-Hungary, leading to increasing support for policies supporting "one hundred percent Americanism." Rep. John L. Burnett (D-Ala.) revived his bill first introduced in 1913 and vetoed by Wilson in 1915. In this atmosphere, Americans watched in horror as the Bolshevik Revolution in Russia led to the establishment of the world's first communist state in 1917. Blaming the Central powers (Germany, Austria-Hungary, Bulgaria, Ottoman Empire) for World War I and Russians and Jews for the Bolshevik Revolution, Americans widely accepted the qualitative distinction between "old," pre-1880 immigration from western and northern Europe and "new," post-1880 immigration from southern and eastern Europe. Wilson's veto was overridden by both the House (287 to 106) and the Senate (62 to 19), and the Immigration Act was formally passed on February 5, 1917. Popularly known as the Literacy Act, it marked a turning point in American immigration legislation. Prohibiting entry to aliens over 16 years of age who could not read 30–40 words in their own language, it was the first legislation aimed at restricting, rather than regulating, European immigration. It further extended the tendency toward a "white" immigration policy by creating an "Asiatic barred zone" that prohibited entry of most Asians.

When the Immigrant Act of 1917 failed to halt a continuing flood of hundreds of thousands of Europeans after the war, support for an ethnic quota grew. Support for immigration restriction included, for the first time, many within the business community, who found that immigrants from Canada, Mexico, and the West Indies were generally less radicalized than European laborers. In order to ensure that Bolsheviks, anarchists, Jews, and other "undesirables" were kept to a minimum, the Emergency Quota Act

Immigration

of 1921 set the number of immigrants from each national origin group at 3 percent of the foreign-born population of that country in 1910, a date chosen because immigration from England, Ireland, Scotland, and Scandinavia had been particularly high in 1909 and 1910. The measure limited immigration to 357,800 annually from the Eastern Hemisphere, with more than half the number reserved for immigrants from northern and western Europe. About 1 percent of the quota was allotted to non-Europeans.

As the politics of eastern Europe remained turbulent, the Soviet experiment of communism became more publicized, and the racialist message of eugenics became more widely accepted, American politicians determined that a permanent measure to dramatically reduce immigration was needed. The Johnson-Reed Act of 1924 ensured that the vast majority of future immigrants would, in the words of Tennessee congressman William Vaile, "become assimilated to our language, customs, and institutions" and "blend thoroughly into our body politic." The measure established an overall annual quota of 153,700 immigrants, allotted according to a formula based on 2 percent of the population of each nation of origin according to the census of 1890. Under this formula, Great Britain, Germany, and Ireland were favored, while quotas for Italy, Russia, Austria-Hungary, and Greece were cut dramatically. As in the Emergency Quota Act, immigrants from the Western Hemisphere were excluded from the quota. The Johnson-Reed Act of 1924 also prohibited entry of aliens not eligible for citizenship, formally excluding entry of Japanese, Chinese, and other Asian immigrants. The 2 percent formula was designed to be temporary and was replaced with an equally restrictive formula in 1927 that provided the same national origin ratio in relation to 150,000 as existed in the entire U.S. population according to the census of 1920.

Even in special cases, restrictionists carried the day. Widespread opposition to Filipino agricultural laborers led to passage of the Tydings-McDuffie Act in 1934, which granted the Philippines commonwealth status and promised independence within 10 years. As a result, Filipinos were reclassified as aliens, with an immigrant quota of only 50 per year. As nonwhites, the 50,000 Filipinos in the country were also ineligible for naturalization and thus prohibited from participating in President Franklin Roosevelt's depression era New Deal work programs. The measure was only slightly ameliorated by exemptions that allowed Hawaiian employers to import Filipino farm labor and enabled the U.S. government to recruit Filipinos into the military.

Although nativism declined somewhat in the late 1920s, American immigration policy remained consistently restrictionist until World War II. Father Charles Coughlin, head of the Christian Front against communism, spoke out against the "problem" of the American Jew to an estimated 30 million listeners during the mid-1930s. Most of the 150,000 Jews who immigrated to the United States in the years leading up to World War II were professionals and other members of the middle classes, about 3,000 of whom were admitted under special visas aimed at rescuing prominent artists and scientists. By and large, however, few special provisions were made for Jewish immigrants. Nativism undoubtedly contributed to Franklin Roosevelt's unwillingness to support the Wagner-Rogers Bill (1939), which would have allowed annual admission beyond quotas, for two years, of 20,000 German refugees under the age of 14. As late as 1941, a bill that would have allowed entry to 20,000 German Jewish children was defeated in Congress. Also during the 1930s, more than 500,000 Mexican Americans were repatriated to Mexico. With the outbreak of war in Europe in 1939, restrictions on immigration were increased. Fear of undercover agents led to a drastic reduction of admissions from Nazi-occupied countries. In addition the Immigration and Naturalization Service (INS) was moved from the Department of Labor to the Department of Justice and a network of law-enforcement agencies was authorized to compile a list of aliens for possible internment should the United States enter the war. Finally, with the outbreak of war in Europe in 1939, the U.S. Congress passed the Alien Registration Act (1940), requiring all non-naturalized aliens 14 and older to register with the government and tightening naturalization requirements.

WORLD WAR II, COLD WAR, AND IMMIGRATION (1943–91)

The threat of war had been looming since the Japanese invasion of the Chinese territory of Manchuria in 1931. In 1935 Benito Mussolini's fascist Italy invaded Ethiopia, and the following year, Adolf Hitler's Nazi Germany remilitarized the Rhineland on the border with France reinforcing a growing militarism in both Europe and Asia. With the Japanese invasion of China proper in 1937 and the German invasion of Poland in 1939, the next world war was underway. The American public, highly isolationist, remained out of the fray until December 7, 1941, when Japanese aircraft attacked Pearl Harbor, in Hawaii, damaging or sinking much of the U.S. military's Pacific fleet. During the next almost four years, the United States directed all its energies toward the defeat of the fascist and militarist governments of Japan, Germany, and Italy.

The cataclysm of World War II (1937–45) had a profound effect on immigration to North America. With restrictive immigration policies in place by the 1920s and the Great Depression ravaging the economy during the 1930s, interwar immigration to the United States had been dramatically curtailed from the peak years just before World War I. In 1907 the United States admitted almost 1.3 million immigrants; 30 years later, when Japan invaded China, the United States admitted 50,000; by 1943 fewer than 24,000 were admitted. Gradually, however, the war changed people's attitudes toward immigrants and those who might become immigrants and presented enormous challenges to current policies. First raised were security questions regarding potential enemies: What should be done with the millions of Japanese, Germans, and Italians living in the United States? Also, with millions of men and women serving abroad, labor needs had to be met at home, and provisions had to be made for foreign families acquired while overseas. Finally, there were humanitarian questions regarding the protection of children threatened by war and the eventual resettlement of refugees and other persons displaced by the war. As a result of these challenges, a number of important exceptions were made to the various immigrations restrictions then in effect. Anti-Catholicism and anti-Semitism declined, and there was a generally less hostile attitude toward non-founding ethnic groups. Though major new immigration legislation was not passed, changing attitudes as a result of the war did pave the way for more far-reaching legislative changes in the future.

With the declaration of war against Germany, Italy, and Japan following the attack on Pearl Harbor, more than 1 million foreign-born immigrants from those countries became "enemy aliens." Italians and Germans were so deeply assimilated into American culture, however, that they were largely left alone. More visibly distinct, and ethnically related to the attackers, Japanese immigrants and Americans of Japanese descent were quickly targeted in the early war hysteria. The territory of Hawaii was put under military rule, and the 37 percent of its population that was of Japanese ancestry was carefully watched, though they were not interned or evacuated. On the mainland, many politicians and members of the press, along with agricultural and patriotic pressure groups, urged action against the Japanese, leading to Executive Order 9066, empowering the secretary of war to remove people from any area of military significance.

Japanese Americans were forced to quickly dispose of their property, usually at considerable loss. They were often allowed to take only two suitcases with them. Camp life was physically rugged and emotionally challenging. Most nisei—second-generation Japanese—thought of themselves as thoroughly American and felt betrayed by the justice system. They nevertheless remained loyal to the country, and eventually, more than 33,000 served in the armed forces during World War II. Among these were some 18,000 members of the 442nd Regimental Combat Team, which became one of the most highly decorated of the war.

Throughout the war, about 120,000 Japanese Americans were interned under the War Relocation Authority in one of 10 hastily constructed camps in the desert or rural areas of Utah, Arizona, Colorado, Arkansas, Idaho, California, and Wyoming. In three related cases that came before the

Introduction to Immigration

Supreme Court—*Yasui v. United States* (1942), *Hirabayashi v. United States* (1943), and *Korematsu v. United States* (1944)—the government's authority was upheld, though a dissenting judge noted that such collective guilt had been assumed "based upon the accident of race." The camps were finally ordered closed in December 1944. The Evacuation Claims Act of 1948 provided $31 million in compensation, though this was later determined to be less than one-10th the value of property and wages lost by Japanese Americans during their internment.

POSTWAR IMMIGRATION

Militarism, nationalism, and racism had been common features of political life under the totalitarian governments of Italy, Germany, and Japan during the 1930s. Almost 16 million American soldiers saw firsthand the result of such attitudes, and after fighting side by side with Chinese and Filipino soldiers against imperial Japan, many came to have a new respect for them and potential immigrants. By 1943 the ban on Chinese immigration and naturalization was lifted, and naturalization was granted to Filipinos in 1945 and to Asian Indians in 1946. By the end of the war in 1945, more than 15 million combatants had been killed and more than 30 million displaced from their homes. In addition the full extent of the Holocaust was quickly revealed—6 million Jews dead at the hands of Adolf Hitler.

With the ending of the war, two problems immediately affecting immigration came to the fore. One involved thousands of war brides and their hero husbands seeking legal means to bring home their wives. Congress passed the War Brides Act in December 1945, authorizing admission to the United States of alien spouses and minor children outside the ordinary quota system. Amendments in 1946 and 1947 authorized admission of fiancées for three months as nonimmigrant temporary visitors, provided they were otherwise eligible and had a bona fide intent to marry. Eventually, some 115,000 British, 7,000 Chinese, 5,000 Filipina, and 800 Japanese spouses were brought to the United States, as well as 25,000 children and almost 20,000 fiancées.

The larger problem involved the disposition of some 20 million people who had been displaced in Europe, including more than 2 million living in refugee camps, mostly in Germany and Austria. Among the displaced were some 9 million Germans returning to their homeland, more than 4 million war fugitives, several million people who had been forced into labor camps throughout the German Reich, millions of Russian prisoners of war and Russians and Ukrainians who had served in the German army, and half-a-million Lithuanians, Latvians, and Estonians fleeing occupation by Soviet troops. Only 60,000 Jews remained to be liberated from Hitler's death camps, while another 200,000 had survived in hiding. New humanitarian measures were imperative to cope with the crisis. As a result, President Harry Truman issued a directive on December 22, 1945, instructing U.S. consulates to give first preference in immigration to displaced persons. No particular ethnic group was singled out, but Truman insisted that "visas should be distributed fairly among persons of all faiths, creeds, and nationalities." Of the 40,000 visas issued under the program, about 28,000 went to Jews. Truman realized that such a measure could only be temporary.

In the debate over a more substantial solution, it became clear that anti-Semitism remained strong in some quarters of the country. As a result, the Displaced Persons Act of 1948 superseded Truman's 1945 directive. Although the new measure provided for 220,000 visas to be issued for two years without regard to quota, it required that they be charged to the appropriate quotas in future years. It also provided up to 3,000 non-quota visas for displaced orphans and granted the attorney general, with the approval of Congress, the right to adjust the status of up to 15,000 displaced persons who entered the country prior to April 1, 1948. The act was amended in 1950 to add another 121,000 visas, for a total of 341,000, through June 1951, chargeable against future quotas at a maximum rate of one-fourth of quotas for three fiscal years (1951–54), and at one-half of quotas thereafter as needed. The number of visas for orphans was raised to 5,000 and taken as a part of the total authorization of 341,000. The provision for adjusting the status of previously admitted displaced persons was extended to those who had entered the United States prior to April 30, 1949. An additional section was added to the Displaced Persons Act, providing 5,000 additional non-quota visas for orphans under the age of 10 who were coming for adoption, to an agency, or to reside with close relatives. Most important, the new measure gave preference to persons from areas occupied by Soviet troops—particularly the Baltic republics and eastern Poland—and to agriculturalists.

COLD-WAR IMMIGRATION

Immigration priorities quickly shifted from the war against fascism to the war against communism. The expansion of Soviet political power during the late forties and the victory of the communist army in China in 1949 led many Americans to fear Karl Marx's promised international communist revolution. The intense ideological struggle thus set up between democratic countries led by the United States and communist countries headed by the Soviet Union is often referred to as the cold war (1945–91). As the Soviet Union sought to surround itself with friendly communist states in the wake of the enormous devastation of World War II, the United States aided anticommunist, right-wing governments in all parts of the world. Ideological differences thus permeated the processes of modernization and decolonization of European empires. Millions of people were displaced in the struggle between communism and democracy and sought permanent haven in North America.

In the United States, many feared that the immigration policy was too lax, and thus might allow undesirable communists or communist sympathizers into the country. This led to passage of the McCarran Internal Security Act (September 1950), authorizing the president in time of national emergency to detain or deport anyone suspected of threatening U.S. security. Senator Patrick McCarran (D-N.Y.) went on to argue against a more liberal immigration policy, fearing an augmentation of the "hard-core, indigestible blocs" of immigrants who had "not become integrated into the American way of life." Together with Representative Francis Walter (D-Pa.), they drafted the McCarran-Walter Act (Immigration and Nationality Act, 1952), which preserved the national origins quotas then in place as the best means of preserving the "cultural balance" in the nation's population. Both measures were passed over President Truman's veto.

The main provisions of the McCarran-Walter Act provided for a new set of preferences for determining admittees under the national quotas, based principally on the need for skilled workers and family reunification; eliminated racial restrictions on naturalization; and provided 2,000 visas for countries within the Asia-Pacific triangle, with quotas applied to ancestry categories rather than countries of birth. The attorney general was also granted the power to temporarily "parole" refugees into the country in times of emergency. Allotment of visas under the McCarran-Walter Act still heavily favored northern and eastern European countries, which received 85 percent of the quota allotment. Although eliminating race as a barrier to naturalization, the measure retained the national origins formula of 1924 and strengthened the government's ability to denaturalize and deport immigrants associated with subversive groups.

In the spirit of cold-war rejection of all things communist, in 1953 Congress passed the Refugee Relief Act. By the measure's provisions, 205,000 visas were authorized to individuals in three classes, along with their immediate families: refugees (those unable to return to their homes in a communist country "because of persecution, fear of persecution, natural calamity, or military operations"); escapees (refugees who had left a communist country fearing persecution "on account of race, religion, or political opinion"); and German expellees (ethnic Germans living in West Germany, West Berlin, or Austria who had been forced to flee from territories dominated by communists). The measure also authorized 2,000 visas for Chinese immigrants fleeing in the wake of communist victory in the Chinese Civil War (1945–49). No provision was made for refugees from right-wing regimes, a critical distinction that would later be highlighted with respect to immigration from Latin America.

Immigration

With the discrediting of Joseph McCarthy's extreme anticommunism campaign in 1953, and the ongoing processes of decolonization around the world and the civil rights movement in the United States, support grew for a liberalization of immigration policy. Senator John F. Kennedy's *A Nation of Immigrants* (1958) espoused the ideological value of a racially neutral immigration policy, and one that might at the same time attract Third World allies in the cold-war contest with the Soviet Union.

Both fear of communism and a more liberal immigration policy were combined in the case of Cuba. In 1952 former president Fulgencio Batista took control of the government and established himself dictator, with tacit support of the American government. Beginning in 1956, Fidel Castro led an open rebellion against the increasingly harsh and corrupt government. Batista fled in 1959, and Castro assumed dictatorship. Mass emigration, principally to the United States, followed, with some 700,000 Cubans leaving the island by the early 1960s. Within his first year in power, Castro nationalized the majority of the country's industries and began to accept aid from the USSR and other communist nations. In 1961 then-President Kennedy supported the invasion of Cuba by Cuban émigrés at the Bay of Pigs, an unmitigated disaster that heightened tensions between the two countries. The United States followed with an export embargo in 1962. Later that year, the United States discovered that Cuba was harboring Soviet nuclear missiles. Kennedy warned Cuba of impending military consequences and imposed a military blockade to prohibit Soviet warheads from reaching the island—moves that led to the eventual withdrawal of the missiles. Cuba's ongoing involvement in support of marxist movements in Central America and Africa, including sending military troops to aid a civil war faction in Angola from 1975 to 1978, further strained relations with the United States. Between 1959 and 1980, almost 1 million Cubans emigrated from their Caribbean island home to the United States, where they enjoyed preferential treatment by the American government as victims of Castro's communist regime.

In order to ease the transition of Cubans into the United States and establish a clear commitment to resisting communism, the Dwight Eisenhower administration established the Cuban Refugee Emergency Center (1960), and President Kennedy established the Cuban Refugee Program (February 3, 1961), which provided a wide range of social services, for Cuban immigrants, including health care and subsidized educational loans. The United States also suspended parts of its immigration policy, waiving numerical restrictions on the number of visas that could be issued to Cubans. During 1961 and 1962, 99 percent of all waivers were granted in order to provide for "refugees from communism."

Kennedy believed that immigrants were valuable to the country, and members of his administration argued that both the cold war and the civil

Introduction to Immigration

rights movement dictated a more open policy toward nonwhite immigrants. As a result, he recommended that the quota system be phased out over a five-year period, that family reunification remain a priority, and that the Asiatic Barred Zone, prohibiting immigration from most of Asia, be eliminated. After Kennedy's assassination in November 1963, the Lyndon Johnson administration took up the cause in earnest, and on October 3, 1965, the president signed the Immigration and Nationality Act (INA) into law. Though it was technically an amendment of the McCarran-Walter Act of 1952, the measure profoundly altered the course of U.S. immigration policy, ending national quotas and making special provisions for the reunification of families. National origins quotas were replaced with hemispheric caps of 170,000 from the Eastern Hemisphere and 120,000 from the Western Hemisphere. The measure also established a new scale of preferences, including first, unmarried adult children of U.S. citizens (20 percent); second, spouses and unmarried adult children of permanent resident aliens (20 percent); third, professionals, scientists, and artists of exceptional talent (10 percent); fourth, married children of U.S. citizens (10 percent); fifth, siblings of U.S. citizens who were over 21 years of age (24 percent); sixth, skilled and unskilled workers in areas where labor was needed (10 percent); and seventh, those who "because of persecution or fear of persecution ... have fled from any Communist or Communist-dominated country or area, or from any country within the general area of the Middle East" (6 percent). Unlike the provisions of previous special legislation, the 10,200 visas were allotted annually, to deal with refugee situations without further legislation. The number of refugees admitted was always higher, however, as all presidents employed parole authority to exempt hundreds of thousands of refugees, principally those fleeing communist regimes.

Although the new legislation was designed to diversify immigration, it did so in unexpected ways. Many of the Old World slots expected to go to Europeans were filled by Asians, who tended to fill higher preference categories. Having become permanent residents, and then citizens, a wide range of family members then became eligible for immigration in high-preference categories. The INA was successful in bringing highly skilled professional and medical people to the United States. Within 10 years, for instance, immigrants comprised 20 percent of the nation's total number of physicians. At the same time, it was not effective in limiting the overall number of immigrants. Exemptions and high numbers of refugees led the government to exceed quotas permitted under the act.

Cold-war concerns quickly led to new waves of migration from Cuba and Vietnam that could not be accommodated by INA quotas. In the autumn of 1965, Castro opened the port of Camarioca to anyone seeking to bring relatives out of Cuba and promised not to prosecute those who gathered for the purpose of immigration. President Johnson responded by declaring that "those who seek refuge here in America will find it," immediately undermining the limitations established by the newly passed immigration measure. After heated debate, Congress passed the Cuban Adjustment of Status Act (1966), exempting refugees who had been admitted as parolees without a visa from the requirement of traveling to a third country to formalize their status. This measure established a legal distinction between Cuban and all other immigrants from the Western Hemisphere, based upon America's cold-war ideology. As a result of these policies, almost 300,000 Cubans entered the United States between 1965 and 1973, most on chartered "freedom flights." This wave of migration was more diverse racially than the first and included a much higher percentage of women, as Castro had forbidden skilled workers to emigrate. It also included up to half of Cuba's doctors, lawyers, professors, and other professional groups.

Cuba's special treatment was highlighted during the 1970s as Haitians began leaving their country in large numbers. The first and most important factor in driving Haitians to the United States was poverty. Haiti was the poorest country in the Western Hemisphere, and as much as half the population was unemployed. A second factor leading many Haitians to seek personal freedom was the repressive violence of dictator Jean-Claude Duvalier's secret police. It is estimated that more than 60,000 Haitians arrived in south Florida in small sailboats between 1971 and 1981, with thousands of others dying in the attempt. With the Duvaliers as cold-war allies, the United States refused to grant Haitians refugee status and routinely deported them. Though the administration of President Jimmy Carter granted these "boat people" special Cuban-Haitian Entrant Status in 1980, American policy throughout the 1980s opposed a broad expansion of Haitian immigration.

Another cold-war conflict led to a massive influx of a new immigrant group and a further reason for reconsidering American refugee policy. There had been almost no Vietnamese in the United States prior to the war in Vietnam (1963–75). As the United States withdrew its troops from Vietnam in 1975, the government assisted some 125,000 Vietnamese in relocating to the United States, including most high government and military officials and their families. Between 1975 and the early 1980s, an additional quarter-million refugees arrived—most of them "boat people" who risked everything to escape from Vietnam, had little education or money, and came to the United States after first landing in Thailand, Indonesia, or Malaysia. About 100,000 of the "boat people" were ethnic Chinese. The Orderly Departure Program (ODP), established in 1979 with the help of the United Nations, sought to regularize and legalize the process of refugee flight and eventually assisted 50,000 Vietnamese refugees in entering the country by 1987 when the program ended. Once again, however, numerical quotas had been exceeded, laying the foundation for massive new immigration on the basis of the family reunification provisions of the INA. By the mid-1980s, there were more than 650,000 Vietnamese in the United States.

With more than 2 million refugees being paroled into the United States between 1948 and 1980, it became clear that migration pressures brought on by the cold war could not adequately be met by the provisions of the Immigration Act of 1965. The need was addressed in the Refugee Act of 1980, which increased the normal refugee flow to 50,000 annually and accepted the 1968 United Nations definition of a refugee as one unwilling to return to his or her native land "because of persecution, or a well-founded fear of persecution." The measure also established a new category—asylee—which allowed 5,000 refugees already in the country illegally or as students to apply for formal entry. Whereas America's ideological commitment to deter communism overrode all other considerations in the 1960s, the governmental consensus in favor of granting Cubans special immigration status began to break down in the following decade. The resulting Refugee Act of 1980 required Cubans to meet the same "strict standards for asylum" as other potential refugees from the Western Hemisphere, placing them in the same category as Haitians who had been arriving illegally in large numbers throughout the 1970s.

Almost immediately the new policy was tested by the Mariel Boatlift. After seven years of hostility toward emigration (1973–80), a worsening economy encouraged Castro to reverse his policy, leading to the migration of 125,000 Cubans to Florida in 1980 and 1981. Though virtually all the Cubans were allowed to remain in the United States, negotiations by the Carter and Ronald Reagan administrations led to agreements in the mid-1980s that came close to normalizing immigrant relations between the two countries. In the meantime, however, Cubans and Nicaraguans fleeing communist regimes had fared better than Haitians, Guatemalans, and Salvadorans fleeing right-wing authoritarian governments. Between 1946 and 1994, more than 90 percent of 3 million refugees admitted to the United States were fleeing communist regimes, principally those in Poland, the Soviet Union, Romania, China, Nicaragua, Vietnam, Laos, Cambodia, Ethiopia, and Afghanistan.

MEXICAN IMMIGRATION

As the cold war began to wind down after 1985, it appeared that future immigration policy would be driven principally by economic, rather than ideological, factors, with Mexican immigration of growing concern. Between 1881 and 1910, more than 90 percent of all immigrants to the United States were Europeans or Canadians. Mexican immigration increased as a result of the temporary worker programs between 1917 and 1922, with some 700,000 arriving between 1911 and 1940. But this was seen by most as a temporary migration, a view supported by the meager number of slightly more than 20,000 Mexicans who immigrated in the 1930s. By comparison in the same period almost 1.8 million Canadians and more than 7.1 million Europeans had migrated. Although there were no official limits on immigration from countries in the Western Hemisphere, only Canada and Mexico provided significant numbers of immigrants. From the late 1940s, however, the demands of the U.S. labor market and the cold-war conflict led to a dramatic shift in the nature of immigration, with Latin America rapidly developing into the principal source area for immigrants. During the 1950s, legal immigration from Mexico, the Caribbean, Central America, and South America rose to 56,000 per year, while tens of thousands of illegal immigrants waded across the Rio Grande, seeking economic opportunity in the United States.

The urgent demand for labor during World War II led to creation of the Bracero Program in August 1942, which provided the United States with a large, dependent Mexican agricultural labor force, working for 30–50 cents per day under the most spartan conditions. Between 1942 and the ending of the Bracero Program in 1964, almost 5 million Mexican laborers legally entered the country, with several million more entering illegally to work for even lower wages. Mexican immigration rose significantly in each decade following World War II, with almost 300,000 immigrants arriving in the 1950s and some 454,000 during the 1960s. With the end of the Bracero Program, neither the demand for Mexican labor nor the desirability of American employment abated. Mexican immigration rose from about 30,000 per year in the 1950s to 165,000 per year in the 1980s, with perhaps an equal number of illegal immigrants entering the country each year. Once naturalized, Mexican immigrants were then able to seek reunification with their families under provisions of the Immigration and Nationality Act of 1965.

The massive influx of Mexicans, especially illegal aliens, fueled a new round of nativism in the United States during the 1980s. In 1983 the Official English movement was launched in response to the growth of bilingualism that had become common in the 1970s to accommodate the increasing number of Spanish-speaking children in the public schools. By the late 1980s, it became clear that Official English was closely linked to various restrictionist movements, including the controversial Pioneer Fund, which supported eugenics research. Restrictionists redoubled their efforts when the Immigration Reform and Control Act (IRCA) of 1986 legalized the status of nearly 3 million undocumented aliens.

In the wake of massive refugee crises in Southeast Asia and Cuba, in 1981 a Select Commission on Immigration and Refugee Policy recommended to the U.S. Congress that undocumented aliens be granted amnesty and that sanctions be imposed on employers who hired them. After years of heated debate involving ethnic and religious groups, labor and agricultural organizations, business interests, and the government, a compromise measure was reached. IRCA provided amnesty to undocumented aliens who had continuously resided in the United States, except for "brief, casual, and innocent" absences, from the beginning of 1982; provided amnesty for seasonal agricultural workers employed at least 90 days during the year preceding May 1986; required all applicants to take courses in English and U.S. government to qualify for permanent residence; imposed sanctions on employers who knowingly hired illegal aliens, including civil fines and criminal penalties up to $3,000 and six months in jail; prohibited employers from discrimination on the basis of national origins; increased the Border Patrol by 50 percent in 1987 and 1988; and, in a matter unrelated to illegal aliens, introduced a lottery program for 5,000 visas to countries "adversely affected" by provisions of the INA.

Because the measure was meant as a onetime resolution of a long-standing problem, a strict deadline for application was established, all applications for legalization being required within one year of May 5, 1987. At the insistence of state governments, newly legalized aliens were prohibited from receiving most types of federal public welfare, though Cubans and Haitians were exempted. By the end of the filing period, about 1.7 million people had applied for general legalization and about 1.4 million as special agricultural workers. Of the successful applicants, almost 70 percent were from Mexico and more than 90 percent from the Western Hemisphere. The measure was not highly effective in curbing employment of illegal aliens, as Border Patrol officers were prohibited from "interfering" with workers in the field without a search warrant. This further angered and stimulated restrictionists, who believed that no effective government policy in fact existed.

IMMIGRATION AFTER THE COLD WAR (1991–2006)

The same questions that had dogged immigration policy since the Immigration and Nationality Act (INA) of 1965 continued into the 1990s along three lines—what standard policy should be regarding legal immigration, what exceptions should be made, and what were the best means of stemming the tide of illegal immigration. The Immigration Act of 1990 addressed the first of these concerns. In the first major revision of U.S. immigration policy since the INA, immigration preference classes were divided into two broad categories—family sponsorship and employment-related—with an annual review of the number limits in each category. Those who wished to restrict immigration favored the measure because it established an annual cap on family based immigration. Those opposed to restriction supported the measure for its minimum base of preference visas and for the raising of per country visas annually from 20,000 to 25,600, which promised some relief for the backlog of applications from Mexico and the Dominican Republic, among other countries. The measure also provided for an 18-month "temporary protected status" for Salvadorans who had fled political violence in their country during the 1980s. In fact the measure's caps were easily "pierced," because refugees, asylees, Immigration Reform and Control Act legalizations, and Amerasians fell outside its provisions. The measure also provided visas for 55,000 annual "diversity immigrants" (40,000 during the first three years), applying from underrepresented countries. Between 1992 and 1998, the average immigration under the act per year was just over 825,000.

In the 1990s, the issue of the special status of Cubans had not yet been fully resolved. With the ending of Soviet subsidies following the breakup of the Soviet Union in 1991, the Cuban economy neared collapse, driving increasing numbers of *balseros* (ferry people) onto rafts that attempted to reach American shores. Between 1985 and 1990, only a few hundred *balseros* arrived each year. In 1991 the number increased to more than 2,000 and two years later to 3,656. In 1994 Castro ended his policy of pursuing Cubans who sought to flee to the United States, leading to the departure of 37,000 Cubans during August and September. Faced with a potential repeat of the Mariel influx, the Bill Clinton administration ordered rafters to be intercepted and sent to refugee camps at Guantanamo Naval Base or in Panama. On May 2, 1995, the U.S. government ended its policy of automatically admitting Cuban refugees, stipulating that future Cuban immigrants would be required to apply under normal procedures. By an agreement signed on September 9, 1995, the United States agreed to a minimum annual level of 20,000 Cuban immigrants, excluding relatives of American citizens. In return the Cuban government reinstated border controls in order to prevent illegal departures.

Finally, and most contentious, was the question of the unabated illegal immigration, especially from Mexico. Though illegal immigration had been growing steadily throughout the 1980s, two events in 1994 had significant implications for Mexican immigration, especially to the United States. On January 1, the North America Free Trade Agreement (NAFTA) went into effect, gradually reducing tariffs on trade between the United States, Canada, and Mexico and guaranteeing investors equal business rights in all three countries. Although thousands of jobs moved from the United States to Mexico, it did little to stem the tide of illegal immigration. In December 1994, a financial crisis in Mexico led to the devaluation of the peso in early 1995 and a potential defaulting on international obligations. International loans of more than $50 billion staved off bankruptcy, but the accompanying austerity plan in Mexico led to higher interest rates and dramatically higher consumer prices. Growing concern over the cost of providing assistance to illegal immigrants, and fear of an increased flow from Mexico as a result of the economic crisis, led Californians to approve (59 percent to 41 percent) Proposition 187, which denied education, welfare benefits, and nonemergency health care to illegal immigrants. Anticipating legal challenges, proponents of Proposition 187 included language to safeguard all provisions not specifically deemed invalid by the courts. Decisions by federal judges in both 1995 and 1998, however, upheld previous decisions regarding the unconstitutionality of some of the proposition's provisions, based upon Fourteenth Amendment protections against discriminating against one class of people (in this case, immigrants). At the same time, the U.S. government passed a measure that embodied many of the aspects of Proposition 187 that did pass constitutional muster. The Welfare Reform Act of 1996 included clauses specifically related to immigrants, denying cash welfare, food stamps, Medicaid, and supplemental security income. Some food stamp and other benefits were subsequently restored.

An Immigration and Naturalization Service (INS) report of February 1997 showed that there were an estimated 5 million illegal immigrants in the United States as of October 1996; four years later, the number had risen to 7 million (8.7 million according to the Census Bureau). Almost 70 percent of unauthorized residents in 2000 were from Mexico, and another 14 percent were from El Salvador, Guatemala, Colombia, Honduras, Ecuador, and the Dominican Republic. About 40 percent entered with tourist or worker visas but failed to return to their home countries when the visas expired. After years of debate, the U.S. Congress passed the Illegal Immigration Reform and Immigrant Responsibility Act (IIRIRA) in 1996 to curb illegal immigration. The measure authorized a doubling of the number of Border Patrol agents between 1996 and 2001 (5,000 to 10,000) and the building of additional fences along the U.S.-Mexican border south of San Diego. It also provided tougher penalties for those engaged in document fraud and alien smuggling and greater controls on public welfare provided to illegal aliens. The most controversial aspects of the measure involved the streamlining of detention and deportation hearings. This enabled illegal aliens to be deported without appeal to the courts, unless they could demonstrate a realistic fear of persecution in their home country. A review of decisions was required within seven days but could be conducted by telephone or teleconference. As restrictionist fervor diminished somewhat in the late 1990s, several adjustments amended some of the harsher provisions of IIRIRA.

POST-9/11 IMMIGRATION

The terrorist attacks on New York City and Washington, D.C., on September 11, 2001, intensified the decadelong debate about America's moral commitment to immigrants and demonstrated just how far the United States had moved from their cold-war priorities only 10 years earlier. President George W. Bush proposed a series of sweeping measures designed to combat terrorism, including strengthened border controls. The Uniting and Strengthening America by Providing Appropriate Tools Required to Intercept and Obstruct Terrorism (USA PATRIOT) Act was quickly passed and signed into law by Bush on October 26, 2001. The PATRIOT Act, as it became commonly known, provided for greater surveillance of aliens and increased the power of the attorney general to identify, arrest, and deport aliens. It also designated "domestic terrorism" to include "acts dangerous to human life that are a violation of the criminal laws of the United States or of any State that appear to be intended to intimidate or coerce a civilian population; to influence the policy of a government by intimidation or coercion; or to affect the conduct of a government by mass destruction, assassination, or kidnapping." Also, monitoring of some aliens entering on nonimmigrant visas was instituted, passport photographs were digitalized, more extensive background checks of all applications and petitions to the INS were authorized, a Student and Exchange Visitor Information System (SEVIS) database was created to track the location of aliens in the country on student visas, and the U.S. attorney general was given the right to expel immediately anyone suspected of terrorist links. Also, the State Department introduced a 20-day waiting period for visa applications from men 16 to 45 years of age from the predominantly Muslim countries of Afghanistan, Algeria, Bahrain, Djibouti, Egypt, Eritrea, Indonesia, Iran, Iraq, Jordan, Kuwait, Lebanon, Libya, Malaysia, Morocco, Oman, Pakistan, Qatar, Saudi Arabia, Somalia, Sudan, Syria, Tunisia, United Arab Emirates, and Yemen. Any application considered to be suspicious was forwarded to the Federal Bureau of Investigation (FBI), creating a further delay.

Though initially widely supported by the American public, the PATRIOT Act remained a focal point of the evolving debate about the nature of terrorism, the means necessary to combat it, and the wisdom of sacrificing civil liberties for security. Although the act specifically affirmed the "vital role" in American life played by "Arab Americans, Muslim Americans, and Americans from South Asia" and condemned any stereotyping and all acts of violence against them, some groups believed that the PATRIOT Act enabled the federal government to target their activities and to suppress a variety of activist groups that disagreed with the government on a wide array of issues. Civil libertarians continued to warn about the potential for abuse and spoke in favor of allowing a number of the more controversial provisions to lapse at the end of 2005. After several extensions, however, and extensive debate in Congress and throughout the country, all provisions of the measure were reinstated in March 2006. In a concession to those concerned with the permanent extension of government powers, it was agreed that two of the most controversial sections—206 authorizing "roving surveillance" and 215 authorizing access to library and business records—would expire at the end of four years.

In another direct outgrowth of the terrorist attacks, Congress enacted the Homeland Security Act in November 2002. The measure established a new Department of Homeland Security (DHS) to coordinate most anti-terror elements within the U.S. government at the cabinet level and completely reorganized the administration of immigration policy. Already under fire by restrictionists for its ineffectiveness in combating illegal immigration, INS inefficiencies were publicly displayed when it was learned in March 2002 that the agency had approved visas for two of the September 11 hijackers. The DHS, which became fully operational on March 1, 2003, was divided into five directorates, including Border and Transportation Security (BTS), responsible for securing the nation's borders and protecting its transportation systems. Other agencies working under the umbrella of the DHS included the Bureau of Citizenship and Immigration Services, incorporating the U.S. Citizenship and Immigration Services, which administers immigration policy and provides services to all immigrants. The relative importance and particular responsibilities of the various directorates and agencies are likely to change as the DHS develops.

The reorganization did little to stem the immigration debate. In September 2003, the California legislature passed legislation allowing illegal immigrants to receive a California driver's license. With the October recall of Governor Gray Davis, new governor Arnold Schwarzenneger rescinded the measure in December, adding fuel to the debate over U.S. obligations to Mexicans in the country illegally. In January 2004, President Bush, who while governor of Texas had developed a good working relationship with Mexican president Vicente Fox, proposed "fair and secure immigration reform" that would recognize the role of Mexican labor in the U.S. economy while channeling that labor through a temporary worker program that would allow legal residency for up to six years. According to Bush's plan, illegal workers would be granted "temporary" worker status, then be required to return to Mexico; Mexicans seeking visas through legal channels would gain preferential positions; and programs would be established to match willing workers and employers when American citizens could not be found to undertake specific jobs. Little was done regarding its implementation until a fuller proposal was floated to the public in November 28, 2005. According to Bush, "comprehensive immigration reform begins with securing the border," including returning all illegal entrants; deploying increased manpower and technology; constructing physical barriers; and enforcing worksite violations involving illegal immigrants.

By early 2006, there was no consensus regarding immigration policy in the United States. Americans were deeply divided over almost every area

Immigration

affecting immigration, including the appropriate rate of legal immigration; how to deal with more than 11 million illegal immigrants already in the country; the relationship between immigrants and the American economy; the heavy financial burden falling upon a handful of states; and the relationship between immigration and national security. On December 16, 2005, the House of Representatives passed a harsh measure that included the building of extensive border fences and provisions for forcing employers to verify the legality of their workers but without any of Bush's guest-worker provisions. The bill passed with 36 Democrats joining 203 Republicans in favor, while 17 Republicans joined 164 Democrats and 1 Independent in opposing the measure.

By the time the Senate opened debate on March 31, it appeared that a compromise measure was within reach, potentially legalizing millions of illegal immigrants who had been in the United States for more than two years and including a guest-worker program. However, disagreements over increased border security led to the bill's failure in early April, leading to some 140 pro-immigration rallies around the country, drawing an estimated 500,000 supporters in Washington, D.C.; 200,000 in Phoenix; and 30,000 in Atlanta, where the Hispanic community had grown rapidly in recent years. In the wake of the failed compromise, Republican leaders distanced themselves from an earlier proposal to make illegal residence in the country a felony but continued to press for more stringent border control. Government arrests of a handful of employers hiring illegal workers was seen as a superficial attempt to demonstrate a commitment to immigration law, though Bush himself argued on April 23, 2006 that "massive deportation of the people here is not going to work." Those supporting legalization for undocumented workers carried out a new round of coordinated demonstrations on May 1, known as "A Day Without Immigrants," seeking to demonstrate the vital economic role that Latino immigrants—both legal and illegal—play in the country.

Although the economic impact of the demonstrations was relatively small, perhaps a million or more people showed their support for some kind of compromise policy. This was the mood of most Americans, who nevertheless felt that there should be some recognition of illegal activity. According to an Opinion Research Corporation/CNN poll from late April, 77 percent of Americans favored citizenship for illegal immigrants who had worked in the country for five or more years, had a job, and were willing to pay a fine and back taxes. As lawmakers sought a new basis for compromise, tensions increased as Mexican support for a boycott of all U.S. goods, and the involvement of a number of leftist Latino organizations, suggested outside meddling. Given the strong partisan divisions in the American electorate, it is still not clear whether Democrats and Republicans in the U.S. Congress can find enough common ground to pass comprehensive immigration reform.

CURRENT IMMIGRATION ISSUES

Immigration policy is unique among the most contentious issues in the United States. Unlike supporters of particular positions on questions involving abortion, drugs, or war, proponents of immigration policies are seldom able to advance compelling moral grounds in determining who should be admitted to the country and in what numbers. Unlike Social Security or health-care issues, which affect the government's relationship to its citizens, immigration policy deals with noncitizens—people without direct claims on the U.S. government. And unlike any other policy debate, decisions regarding immigration will eventually reconstitute the very nation that made those decisions. In every other issue facing the country today—from terrorism, to global warming, to the United States' role in the world community—U.S. citizens shape their own policies. In the immigration debate, decisions now will determine how many tens of millions of current noncitizens will be influencing every policy question, including immigration, in one's own lifetime. As a result of the Immigration and Nationality Act of 1965, the Immigration Reform and Control Act of 1986, the Immigration Act of 1990, the North American Free Trade Agreement of 1994, and a host of enforcement decisions, there were 35.2 million immigrants living in the United States in 2005, up more than 11 million in only 10 years. Almost 1.5 million new immigrants were arriving every year, and the rate of immigration is likely to grow. New immigrants and recently naturalized citizens will play an increasing role in shaping the values and nature of American culture. Finally, the immigration issue is unique in its ability to baffle and blindside politicians from both major parties. Almost every important policy decision of the past 20 years has had unexpected consequences; none has stabilized the number of immigrants coming into the United States or established a coherent and enforceable policy for regulating the size and nature of the immigrant community.

If there is no clear moral imperative that can be wielded by any camp, upon what basis can immigration policy decisions be made? A traditional answer—"national interest"—is ever more difficult to define as the global economy expands and international conflict evolves to include multinational and terrorist groups, in addition to traditional states. Economics alone will seldom lead to a clear policy, for whatever choices are made will be costly, in both provision to immigrants and enforcement of exclusions. While the costs associated with hosting mostly poorer immigrants is substantial and easy to see, the economic benefits to the United States are mostly potential and difficult to define. It is clear that immigrants make economic progress the longer they live in the United States, but even those who have lived there for more than a decade have, according to the Center for Immigration Studies, "dramatically higher rates of poverty, lack of health insurance, and

49

welfare use than natives."[1] Even the most immediate benefit of extensive immigration—cheap labor—threatens to displace native jobs and to culturally transform many neighborhoods and cities.

Most Americans recognize some humanitarian obligation as citizens of the richest country on Earth, living in the midst of endemic disease, poverty, and death. Even groups largely hostile toward immigration (Americans for Immigration Control, Federation for American Immigration Reform) argue only for reduction to manageable levels and enforcement of immigration laws. But in immigration policy debates, the question is always asked, either directly or implicitly, "to what degree is the United States responsible for providing homes for those in distress?" In some cases, as with the AIDS crisis in southern Africa, the United States had little to do with creating the problem; in some cases, as in Vietnam and Cambodia, U.S. foreign policy was directly responsible; in most parts of the world, a general American economic influence played some part in creating existing economic and political conditions. Even when one accepts some level of U.S. responsibility, however, or wishes to extend a humanitarian hand on other grounds, important questions remain to divide those who otherwise agree. What are manageable levels of immigration? Are there more effective means than open borders for helping those in need? Should some immigrants be considered more valuable to the United States than others, and upon what basis should they be evaluated for admittance? Should the limited allotment of visas be linked to foreign policy considerations? Should the citizens of every country be treated equally? Almost everyone agrees that the case of Mexico is special, as it is a poor country sharing a 2,000-mile border with the United States. Self-interest alone would suggest that Americans should have a coherent immigration policy toward their southern neighbor. Yet the development of immigration policies for Mexico are more divisive than any other.

Further complicating the issue is the immigrant nature of U.S. cultural identity. Excepting American Indians who compose about 1.5 percent of the population, Americans are recently descended from immigrants. Whether descent was from English Puritans, German redemptioners (indentured servants), Scots-Irish farmers, African slaves, or Mexican *braceros*, most Americans recognize their own immigrant past and pay some homage to it as they consider the nature of current national policies.

Broadly speaking there are two camps in the debate—those favoring an "open" immigration policy and those favoring a more restrictive one. Yet because there is no clear moral imperative, no clear economic advantage, no clear standard for judging appropriate levels of immigration or means of exclusion, both camps are badly fragmented and politically ineffective. Among people who agree that an "open" policy is desirable, there is disagreement over levels of immigration and questions of amnesty for those already in the country illegally. Among those who wish to reduce immigration, there is disagreement over the relative use of border enforcement, reduced caps, and deportations. There is division in every camp regarding the proper roles for federal, state, and local authorities in enforcing immigration law, and there is a rising tide of unprecedented citizen involvement. Anyone in any camp might ask, "what policies provide the best means of preserving the economic vitality and cultural values of the United States?" Until there is substantial agreement in the United States on what constitutes a desirable culture, however, it is impossible to determine how it can be preserved. Do Americans preserve their culture by reinforcing their own immigrant identity, or do they establish a cultural standard from which they will accept only limited deviation?

None of the most contentious issues dividing Americans in 1990 over development of a consistent immigration policy had been resolved by 2006. On the contrary, ongoing immigrant demand and the exponential growth of illegal immigration from Mexico heightened existing divisions. The cost of social services to both legal and illegal immigrants soared into the billions of dollars, raising concerns among average Americans who previously had taken little interest in the subject. State and local officials in the primary magnet states began to demand either federal enforcement of immigration policy or federal funds to support the newcomers. As a result of the terrorist attacks on September 11, 2001, almost all questions related to immigration policy were infused with a national security dimension that further divided those in opposing camps. Out of this combustible mix of cultural, economic, and security concerns, two issues dominated the policy debate by mid-decade: illegal immigration and national security. Together these issues made the crafting of a resolute and coherent immigration policy even more difficult.

The challenge of developing a clear immigration policy in the face of an almost unlimited demand for visas is formidable. The Immigration Act of 1990 increased annual ceilings by about 40 percent, to 675,000. The misleading nature of this figure is evident, however, when one views the U.S. Citizenship and Immigration Services' own numbers showing that the actual annual average of legal immigrants between 1991 and 2005 was about 900,000. Although some categories of immigrants such as family sponsored, employment-based, and diversity lottery are capped, the number of immediate family members allowed to legally enter the United States is not. Since the Immigration and Nationality Act of 1965, family reunification has been the central feature used for determining eligibility for admission. Also, refugee admissions are negotiated annually, and therefore can fluctuate. As a result of the chain migration of families, especially from Mexico and Central America, annual legal immigration is much higher than policy planners had envisioned.

ILLEGAL IMMIGRATION

These higher-than-expected figures are further enhanced by a massive illegal immigration that poses a variety of challenges to the United States. Fundamentally, it raises the specter of a country unable or unwilling to enforce its own laws. If the United States is unable to enforce immigration laws, some argue, it is threatened with destruction from without; if the country is unwilling to enforce them, it is threatened from within. Others argue that it is hypocritical to take a hard public line against illegal immigration while promoting an economic system that cannot and will not do without them.

By 2006 the number of illegal immigrants in the United States topped 10 million, about 28 percent of the total immigrant population. Though illegal immigration has always been an issue, its dramatic growth during the 1990s brought it to the fore of the immigration debate. As long as the percentage of illegal immigrants among the total immigrant population remained relatively low, illegal immigration could to some extent be treated as an issue distinct from regular immigration policy. Between 2000 and 2005, however, some 47 percent of all new immigrants were undocumented (3.7 of 7.9 million). In 1990 the Immigration and Naturalization Service estimated the illegal immigrant population to be 3.5 million; by 2000 they estimated the figure to be 7 million and growing by half a million a year. According to the Census Bureau, the number was a million higher. The federal government's most accurate sample, the Current Population Survey, supports these figures and suggests that the rate of illegal immigration continues to grow.

The most immediate direct effect of this growth is its impact on the U.S. economy, an issue complicated by the unequal distribution of benefits and costs among the states and between various governing agencies in the states and federal government. Four states account for 58 percent of the country's foreign-born population and thus bear the brunt of expenses associated with federal immigration policy. California's nearly 10 million immigrants in 2005 accounted for 28 percent of the nation's total immigrant population; New York, Texas, and Florida accounted for 11 percent, 10 percent, and 9 percent, respectively. With the net fiscal cost of immigration reaching as much as $22 billion per year, it is not surprising that these and other states in which immigration is rapidly growing are clamoring for a more equitable immigration policy and for greater border controls. Critics of illegal immigration argue that job competition leads to the reduction of wages; fewer jobs for citizens; and higher social-welfare costs. Those who favor a more inclusive immigration policy, including amnesty for many illegal immigrants now in the country, argue that immigrants generally take jobs that U.S. citizens are not willing to perform at current wage levels, thus meeting a market need and reducing costs to consumers. They also argue that as immigrants become more assimilated, they will begin to pay taxes necessary to support the aging U.S. population.

The economic debate frequently turns on the cost of social services for immigrants. As of 2005, almost 29 percent of immigrants were enrolled in one or more federal welfare-benefits programs (public assistance, supplemental security income, food stamps, Medicaid, public or subsidized housing, WIC [Women, Infants and Children]), a figure almost 10 percent higher than the native population; and 30 percent were eligible for earned income tax credits. As long as the gap between native and immigrant poverty rates continues to increase—it tripled between 1979 and 1997—there will continue to be significant pressure on social-welfare providers, particularly at the state level. In 2005, for instance, more than one-third of all immigrants had no health insurance, and some 10.3 million immigrant children were eligible for public education. Though illegal immigrants are prohibited from access to most forms of welfare, the costs associated with social services for immigrants, including education, emergency medical care, and law enforcement, are substantial. Estimates place California's cost of services to illegal aliens at more than $3 billion per year and Florida's at more than $2 billion. In August 2005, the governors of New Mexico and Arizona declared states of emergency in border areas, concerned over the federal government's lack of support in law enforcement and interdiction of illegal aliens.

Because Mexicans composed 31 percent of all immigrants in 2005—and 70 percent of all illegal immigrants—and because 62 percent of them live in or near poverty, control of the Mexican border is by far the largest issue related to control of the immigrant population generally. The issue is complicated by the integrated economies of the United States and Mexico—annual U.S. exports of $110 billion to Mexico are second only to Canada. This trade requires millions of border crossings each way, including 4 million trucks coming into the United States from Mexico each year. Though most crossings represent the natural product of legitimate trade or migration, thousands of illegal immigrants, mostly from Mexico and Central America, are smuggled into the United States each year, often with little regard for the safety of those being smuggled and sometimes with fatal results. The humanitarian aspect of the problem was highlighted by the May 2003 case in which 19 illegal immigrants from Mexico, Guatemala, and El Salvador died after being placed in the air-tight container of a truck that was abandoned by its driver in South Texas. More than 70 immigrants had been crammed into the vehicle on the last leg of a trip that was to finally deposit them in Houston. Subsequent inquiries discovered that the illegal immigration pipeline, including both U.S. and Mexican citizens, was netting smugglers more than $1 billion annually. While the United States was active in global anti-trafficking efforts from 2000, when Congress passed the Victims of Trafficking and

Violence Protection Act—seeking to protect poor laborers, women, and children from exploitation—the Mexican migrant labor issue outweighed all others in terms of direct implications for immigration policy.

Proponents of a more restrictive immigration policy also cite the frequent trafficking in drugs across the border and the potential danger of terrorist entry as reasons for greater control. The most immediate issue regarding control of the U.S.-Mexican border, however, is economic. The drastic disparity in wages between the United States and Mexico (often a tenfold difference), coupled with a 2,000-mile common border, means that as long as low wages and a weak economy persist in Mexico, U.S. jobs will be in high demand. The willingness of Mexican workers to pay up to $2,000 for guides (coyotes) to lead them in an illegal border crossing, and to work for low wages when they arrive in the United States, has proven irresistible to many employers, who find Mexican labor to be an incredible value. There is still enormous debate in both the United States and Mexico over punishments that should be meted out to U.S. employers who hire illegal Mexican laborers.

Every attempt to account for these factors through legislation as a means of reducing illegal immigration has failed. The Immigration Reform and Control Act of 1986 that granted citizenship to undocumented Mexicans who could demonstrate long-term continuous residency; the North American Free Trade Agreement (NAFTA) of 1994 that shifted thousands of jobs from the United States to Mexico; the Illegal Immigration Reform and Immigrant Responsibility Act of 1996 that doubled the size and budget of the Border Patrol; and the USA PATRIOT Act that enhanced border security all failed to stem illegal immigration from Mexico. With the discovery in January 2006 of two large and sophisticated tunnels running under the Mexican border with California, critics were given new ammunition for arguing that more must be done to regain control of the border. While most Americans supported the idea of a larger Border Patrol, other methods of controlling immigration were more divisive. Many were troubled by proposals for building a continuous permanent barrier between the two countries and opposed to the activities of private patrols such as the Minutemen. In July 2005, President George W. Bush declared himself "against vigilantes in the United States of America." Though favoring enforcement of immigration law "in a rational way," his attempt to introduce a new guest-worker program between 2004 and 2006 met with substantial opposition, much of it coming from within his own Republican Party.[2]

NATIONAL SECURITY

In the midst of a period of unprecedented growth in both legal and illegal immigration that had already deeply divided the United States, the attacks of September 11, 2001, suggested a new and urgent dimension to the policy debate. Even those who had previously supported an open policy recognized that terrorists or other undesirable aliens might easily take advantage of the immigration system as it was being administered, a view reinforced by two national events in 2002. In March it was reported that visas for two of the hijackers had been posthumously renewed. In October it was learned that the Beltway sniper killings were carried out by an undocumented alien from Jamaica who was scheduled for a deportation hearing at the time of the killings and a U.S. born adherent to the Nation of Islam. In 2004 the 9/11 Commission produced evidence that many of the 19 hijackers had entered the United States on altered passports, had provided false information to authorities, or were in violation of visa provisions, suggesting how easily the immigration bureaucracy could be exploited. The commission concluded by suggesting that "disrupting terrorist mobility globally" was of significant importance in the war on terror, a conclusion that the Bush administration adopted in the immediate aftermath of the 9/11 attacks.[3]

Although there was no systematic overhaul of immigration law, the oversight agencies were reorganized and brought under the direction of a new Department of Homeland Security (2003). The federal government placed more than 300,000 aliens scheduled for deportation on a criminal list; more than doubled the number of border patrol agents; provided high-tech equipment for detecting weapons that might be smuggled across the Canadian or Mexican borders; enhanced the tracking capability of visitors to the United States; required biometric passport upgrades; established the SEVIS database for tracking students in the United States; gave the U.S. attorney general authority to expel anyone suspected of terrorist links; and introduced a more rigorous application and extended waiting period for visa applications from men from predominantly Muslim countries. In 2001 and 2002, there was widespread bipartisan support for many anti-terror measures affecting immigration into the country, but as time passed, natural divisions resurfaced. Critics of these measures argued that few of those affected had any terrorist links and that many of the measures infringed upon civil liberties, particularly of those from Muslim countries. Supporters suggested that immigration policy is a significant, and necessary, tool in the war on global terrorism. "If a loophole can be exploited by an immigrant," observed Jim Chaparro, acting director for immigration enforcement in 2003, "it can also be exploited by a terrorist."[4]

Americans remain deeply divided over almost every aspect of immigration policy. While virtually everyone agreed that security had to be tightened after the 9/11 attacks, there was no consensus on how best to achieve that end. While almost everyone agreed that immigration law should be enforced, assent from many quarters was qualified by stipulating some appropriate changes to the law as it then existed. The great challenge for the

United States is to simultaneously address three fundamental issues: legal immigration, illegal immigration, and border security; and to develop a coherent response that recognizes the distinct requirements of each. The stakes could scarcely be larger.

---

[1] Steven A. Camarota, "Immigrants at Mid-Decade: A Snapshot of American Foreign-Born Population in 2005," December 2005, Center for Immigration Studies, http://www.cis.org/articles/2005/back1405.html (accessed on March 10, 2006).

[2] "President Meets with President Fox and Prime Minister Martin," 23 March 2005, White House web site, http://www.whitehouse.gov/news/releases/2005/03/20050323-5.html (accessed on March 10, 2006).

[3] "Entry of the 9/11 Hijackers into the United States," Staff Statement No. 1, p. 10; 9/11 Commission, http://www.9-11commission.gov/staff statements/staffstatement1.pdf (accessed on March 10, 2006).

[4] "US Threatens Mass Expulsions," BBC News, Internationa Version, 10 June 2003, http://news.bbc.co.uk/2hi/americas/2974882.stm (accessed on March 10, 2006).

CHAPTER 2

THE LAW AND IMMIGRATION

CONSTITUTIONAL FOUNDATIONS AND GENERAL IMMIGRATION AND NATURALIZATION LEGISLATION

The legal regulation of immigration is a complicated process that involves the establishment of standards, processes, and quotas regarding admission; the administration of immigration laws; the enforcement of immigration laws; and the rights, privileges, and protections afforded immigrants from the time they enter the country until the time they become naturalized and enjoy the full benefits of U.S. citizenship. Complicating routine immigration law are both special circumstances that fall outside the ordinary scope of legislation (such as decisions regarding the granting of asylum and refugee status, or the internment of Japanese Americans during World War II) and illegal immigration. Both of these are immigration issues in which the wider international context often dictated some deviation from ordinary immigration policy.

The authority to regulate immigration is rooted in the doctrine of the inherent sovereignty of every nation to define and preserve itself. A number of provisions in the U.S. Constitution support this doctrine, and the courts have consistently upheld it against various challenges by states and individuals based upon other implied powers in the Constitution. Within this broad context, the U.S. Congress has unlimited authority (plenary power) to legislate in matters regarding immigration. Because of inherent sovereignty issues and their international ramifications, the Supreme Court has been reluctant to interfere with immigration legislation, though they have made some important rulings across time. Most decisions have related to questions of statutory interpretation. The executive agencies of the government (such as the Bureau of Customs and Border Protection or Immigration and Customs Enforcement) have no authority in making determinations regarding immigration and therefore must operate within the scope of powers granted by Congress through legislation.

Immigration

Throughout U.S. history, Congress has granted immigration oversight to a variety of governmental departments, including the Department of the Treasury, the Department of Labor, the Department of Justice, and the Department of Homeland Security. Under these departments, immigration law has been more directly executed by an even larger variety of agencies, including the Bureau of Immigration, the Immigration and Naturalization Service, and Citizenship and Immigration Services. Duties and responsibilities have been shifted among a variety of departments and agencies and, undoubtedly, will be again in the future, though at least for the time being most immigration executive functions are performed by three subdivisions of the Department of Homeland Security: U.S. Citizenship and Immigration Services, U.S. Immigration and Customs Enforcement, and the U.S. Customs and Border Protection. Additionally, some executive functions regarding immigration are performed by the Department of State, the Department of Justice, the Department of Labor, and the Department of Health and Human Services. For a concise explanation of the responsibilities of each department and agency, see David Weissbrodt and Laura Danielson's *Immigration Law and Procedure in a Nutshell* (5th edition, Thomson West, 2005).

Immigration law begins with a bill introduced in Congress, and processed through committees and debates in the House and Senate, before it is eventually enacted. Only a small percentage of measures dealing with immigration are comprehensive acts (such as the Immigration Act of 1917 and the McCarran-Walter Act of 1952). The basic body of immigration law in the United States is the Immigration and Nationality Act of 1952, popularly known as the McCarran-Walter Act. The law collected and organized most of the scattered provisions affecting immigration. Most legislative measures are amendments to the McCarran-Walter Act, or another comprehensive act in a previous era. Some of these involve minor amendments—the striking or adding of a few words, phrases, or sections; some substantially revise previous comprehensive acts—as in the case of the pathbreaking Immigration and Naturalization Act of 1965, which was actually a systematic amending of the McCarran-Walter Act. In addition to this ongoing process of revision, direct executive actions embodied in orders, proclamations, and treaties can also substantially affect immigration, though they cannot supersede the authority embodied in congressional legislation. Also, the provisions of an act must be translated into executive action by regulating instructions issued within the various agencies. Finally, where there are interpretive differences, administrative decisions are sometimes made that are published and become part of immigration law. Judicial decisions may also help refine an understanding of immigration law, particularly in reference to questions of constitutional protections and matters of deportation.

When researching immigration law, two final concerns should be addressed. First, legislation is often referenced in more than one way. This is because various enacted measures might be referenced to either their stand-alone form as Public Law (Pub.L.) or as part of the United States Code (U.S.C.), the formal codification by subject matter of the "general and permanent laws of the United States." Thus the section of the McCarran-Walter Act dealing with asylum might be referenced as Pub.L. 414, Sec. 208 or as 8 U.S.C.1158. The U.S. Code, published by the Office of the Law Revision Counsel of the U.S. House of Representatives, is arranged in 50 subject titles, of which laws relating to "Aliens and Nationality" are included in Title 8. The full U.S. Code is published every six years, with annual cumulative supplements containing the most current information. A searchable U.S. Code can be found at the Office of the Law Revision Counsel, http://uscode.house.gov/search/criteria.shtml.

Public laws can be researched through the U.S. Citizenship and Immigration Service at http://uscis.gov/lpBin/lpext.dll/inserts/publaw/publaw-1?f=templates&fn=document-frame.htm#publaw-begin. The U.S. Code does not include executive regulations, federal court decisions, treaties, or laws enacted by state or local governments. Regulations issued by executive branch agencies are available in the Code of Federal Regulations.

Second, there can be a baffling array of legislation titles attached to various measures. In recent scholarly publications, for instance, the comprehensive legislation of 1952 that serves as the current basis of U.S. immigration law is regularly referred to as the Immigration and Nationality Act and the McCarran-Walter Act and less frequently referred to as the McCarran-Walter Immigration and Nationality Act and the McCarran-Walter Immigration and Naturalization Act. The 1965 revision of the 1952 legislation is routinely referred to as the Immigration and Nationality Act of 1965 and the Immigration Act of 1965 and less frequently as the Immigration and Naturalization Act of 1965, the Immigration Act Amendments of 1965, the Immigration Amendments of 1965, and the Hart-Cellar Act. Generally, there is no formal name attached to the legislation, so the title is derived from the authors of the legislation, the function of the legislation, or in reference to previous legislation that is being amended. Usually, but not always, one form of the title becomes generally accepted. In any case, the multiple titles seldom present an insurmountable problem, as the date and title in any form are usually sufficient to identify the precise measure.

U.S. CONSTITUTION (1788)

One of the weaknesses of the Articles of Confederation, agreed to by the newly independent colonies in 1777, was its lack of attention to questions of immigration and naturalization. The new Constitution of 1788 only indirectly dealt with immigration itself. It provided in Article 1, Section 9 that Congress could not prohibit the importation of slaves prior to 1808, but it otherwise said nothing regarding immigration. In Article 1, Section 8, however, Congress was empowered to "establish an uniform Rule of Naturalization." Because no specific standards were established, much room was left for interpretation according to the particular attitudes of the day. The Constitution did draw some distinctions between native-born and naturalized citizens, including a residency requirement for service as a representative or senator (Article 1, Section 2) and prohibition of immigrants from serving as president and vice president (Article 2, Section 1).

NATURALIZATION ACT (1790)

The Naturalization Act of 1790 was the first piece of federal legislation regarding immigration, designed to provide a "national" rule for the process of naturalization. As a result of varying policies among the states for naturalizing citizens during the 1780s, the U.S. government passed "an act to establish an uniform rule of naturalization" on March 26, 1790. Under provisions of Article 1, Section 8 of the Constitution, the measure granted citizenship to "all free white persons" after two years' residence and provided that the children of citizens born outside the borders of the United States would be "considered as natural born citizens."

A new Naturalization Act was passed on January 29, 1795, repealing the old act, raising the residency requirement to five years, and requiring three years' notice of intent to seek naturalization. This greater stringency regarding the naturalization of immigrants was continued in the Alien and Sedition Acts of 1798.

ALIEN AND SEDITION ACTS (1798)

The Alien and Sedition Acts is the collective name given to four laws enacted by the U.S. Congress in the midst of the French Revolution. The laws were ostensibly a reaction to French diplomacy and depredations on the high seas but were mainly aimed at undermining the growing strength of Thomas Jefferson's Republican Party. With Irish, French, and other newly arrived immigrants strongly supporting the Republican Party, Federalists were intent on neutralizing the potential political value of "new" Americans.

• The Naturalization Act extended the residency qualification for full citizenship from five to 14 years.

• The Aliens Act, limited to two years, enabled the president to expel any alien deemed "dangerous to the peace and safety of the United States."

• The Alien Enemies Act gave the president wartime powers to deport citizens of countries with whom the United States was at war.

The Law and Immigration

• The Sedition Act proscribed criticism of the government by both immigrants and native-born citizens.

The main result of the Alien and Sedition Acts was to unify the Republican Party. After Jefferson's election as president in 1800, the Naturalization Act was repealed in 1802. Other measures were allowed to expire in 1800–01, and a new Naturalization Act was passed in 1802.

NATURALIZATION ACT (1802)

With Thomas Jefferson becoming president in 1801, there was a relaxation of the hostility toward immigrants that had prevailed during the administration of John Adams (1797–1801). Jefferson campaigned for a more lenient naturalization law, observing that, under the "ordinary chances of human life, a denial of citizenship, under a residence of fourteen years, is a denial to a great proportion of those who ask it." On April 14, 1802, a new naturalization measure was enacted, reducing the period of residence required for naturalization from 14 to five years. In addition the new law required that prospective citizens give three years' notice of intent to renounce previous citizenship; that they swear or affirm support of the Constitution; that they renounce all titles of nobility; and that they demonstrate themselves to be of "good moral character." The Naturalization Act was supplemented on March 26, 1804, by exempting aliens who had entered the United States between 1798 and 1802 from the declaration of intention. The three years' notice was reduced to two years on May 26, 1824.

MANIFEST OF PASSENGERS ACT (1819)

The Manifest of Passengers Act was the first piece of American legislation regulating the transportation of migrants to and from America, and the first measure requiring that immigration statistics be kept. The United States maintained uninterrupted data on individuals coming into the country from the time this act was passed. Concerned with the dramatic increase in immigration during 1818, and responding to several instances of high mortality on trans-Atlantic voyages, on March 2, 1819, Congress passed "an Act regulating passenger-ships and vessels." It required:

• a limit of two passengers per every five tons of ship burden;

• provision of at least 60 gallons of water, 100 pounds of bread, 100 pounds of salted provisions, and one gallon of vinegar for every passenger on ships departing the United States; and

- reports by ship captains or masters, including names, sexes, ages, and occupations of all passengers taken on board, as well as the number of passengers who had died on board the ship during the voyage.

Six acts and a number of amendments gradually modified the requirements of the 1819 act until it was finally repealed by the Carriage of Passengers Act in 1855.

CARRIAGE OF PASSENGERS ACT (1855)

With the rapid influx of Irish, German, and Chinese immigrants after 1845, a series of steamship disasters, and the prevalence of cholera, typhus, and smallpox among arriving immigrants, in late 1853 Senator Hamilton Fish (R-N.Y.) called for a select committee to "consider the causes and the extent of the sickness and mortality prevailing on board of emigrant ships" and to determine what further legislation might be necessary. With the support of President Franklin Pierce, Congress repealed the Manifest of Passengers Act (1819) and subsequent measures relating to transportation of immigrants, replacing them on March 3, 1855, with "an act to extend the provisions of all laws now in force relating to the carriage of passengers in merchant-vessels, and the regulation thereof." Its main provisions:

- limited passengers, with no more than one person per two tons of ship burden;
- required adequate berths and 14–18 square feet of deck space per passenger, depending upon the height between decks;
- required ample foodstuffs, including the following per each passenger: 20 pounds of "good navy bread," 15 pounds of rice, 15 pounds of oatmeal, 10 pounds of wheat flour, 15 pounds of peas and beans, 20 pounds of potatoes, one pint of vinegar, 60 gallons of fresh water, 10 pounds of salted pork, and 10 pounds of salt beef (with substitutions allowed where specific provisions could not be secured "on reasonable terms");
- required sanitary conditions on board; and
- extended all provisions to steamships.

With advances in shipbuilding technology greatly increasing the size of ships, modifications in the space and food requirements were made in a Carriage of Passengers Act of July 22, 1882.

IMMIGRATION ACT (1864)

After almost a century of relatively unrestricted immigration, Congress asserted its paramount role in regulating the flow of immigrants into the country. The 1864 Immigration Act was designed to increase the flow of laborers to the United States following the disruptions of the Civil War (1861–65). In his message to Congress in December 1863, President Abraham Lincoln urged "the expediency of a system for the encouragement of immigration," noting "the great deficiency of laborers in every field of industry, especially in agriculture and our mines." After much debate, Congress enacted legislation on July 4, 1864, providing for appointment by the president of a commissioner of immigration—operating under the authority of the secretary of state—and for immigrant labor contracts, up to a maximum of one year, pledging wages against the cost of transportation to America.

PAGE ACT (1875)

The Page Act was the first piece of legislation to directly regulate immigration. Aimed at two abuses emanating from Chinese immigration—prostitution and forced labor—it also reflected a growing anti-Asian sentiment that was rising as the economy worsened. The measure:

- prohibited contracted labor from "China, Japan, or any Oriental country" that was not "free and voluntary";
- prohibited immigration of Chinese prostitutes; and
- excluded from all countries convicts and women "imported for the purposes of prostitution."

Screening was so rigorous that most wives and other non-prostitutes were prohibited from entering the country. It is notable that in excluding convicts, an exception was made for "political offenses," providing a basis for future refugee policies.

CHINESE EXCLUSION ACT (1882)

The Chinese Exclusion Act was the first measure specifically to exclude an ethnic group from immigrating to the United States. With the economic depression of the 1870s, many westerners blamed Chinese immigrants for taking jobs and depressing wages, leading to passage of the Page Act (1875) and appointment of a Senate committee to investigate the question of Chinese immigration (January 1876). In 1879 Henry George published *Progress and Poverty*, in which he concluded that the Chinese were economically backward and "unassimilable." In the same year, President Rutherford B. Hayes encouraged Congress to examine ways of limiting Chinese immigration. After much debate and many abortive bills, the United States and China signed the Angell Treaty (1881), which modified the Burlingame

Immigration

Treaty (1868) and gave the United States authority to regulate the immigration of Chinese laborers. A bill was quickly brought forward to exclude Chinese laborers for 20 years, but it was vetoed by President Chester A. Arthur, who argued that such a long period of exclusion would contravene the articles of the Angell Treaty. Arthur reluctantly signed a revised measure on May 6, 1882. Its major provisions:

- excluded all Chinese laborers for 10 years, starting 90 days from enactment;
- denied naturalization to Chinese aliens already in the United States; and
- required registration of all Chinese laborers already in the United States, who were still allowed to travel freely to and from the United States.

Chinese officials and their domestic servants were exempted from the prohibition.

IMMIGRATION ACT (1882)

Responding to dozens of petitions from states worried about the maintenance of indigent immigrants, Congress enacted the Immigration Act on August 3, 1882, the first general measure addressing the question of immigration. Provisions included:

- a head tax of 50 cents per immigrant to be used to create a Treasury-administered fund for the care of immigrants upon arrival;
- expansion of Page Act exclusions of convicts and women "imported for the purposes of prostitution," to also prohibit the immigration of any "lunatic, idiot, or any person unable to take care of himself or herself without becoming a public charge"; and
- authorization for the secretary of the Treasury to contract with state boards for the processing of immigrants.

The language of the exclusionary clauses, originally intended to restrict immigration of those physically or mentally unable to provide for themselves, was changed in 1891 to prohibit "paupers or persons likely to become a public charge." This "LPC clause" enabled immigration officials to refuse entry simply because of an immigrant's poverty.

ALIEN CONTRACT LABOR ACT (FORAN ACT, 1885)

Reflecting a growing concern over the effects of organized labor, Congress enacted the Alien Contract Labor Law on February 26, 1885, the first of

The Law and Immigration

a series of measures designed to undermine the practice of importing contract labor. Although concern over the negative impact of contract labor had become prevalent as early as 1868, it gained new force during debate surrounding the Chinese Exclusion Act (1882). In 1883 and 1884, Congress received more than 50 anti-contract petitions from citizens in 13 states as well as from state legislatures and labor organizations. The result was the Alien Contract Labor Law of February 26, 1885, which:

- prohibited transportation or assistance to aliens by "any person, company, partnership, or corporation . . . under contract or agreement . . . to perform labor or services of any kind";
- voided employment contracts agreed to prior to immigration; and
- levied fines for employers ($1,000 per contract laborer) and ship captains ($500 per contract laborer).

Exempted from the provisions were aliens and their employees temporarily residing in the United States; desirable skilled laborers engaged in "any new industry" not yet "established in the United States"; and "professional actors, artists, lecturers, or singers," personal or domestic servants, ministers of "any recognized religious denomination," professionals, and "professors for colleges and seminaries."

SCOTT ACT (1888)

In response to growing antagonism toward immigrants generally and to Chinese immigrants specifically, William Scott (D-Pa.) introduced legislation to extend restrictions in the Chinese Exclusion Act. The measure:

- excluded "all persons of the Chinese race," excepting "Chinese officials, teachers, students, merchants, or travelers for pleasure or curiosity," and
- excluded the return of Chinese laborers who had come to the United States prior to 1882 unless they had "a lawful wife, child, or parent in the United States, or property therein of the value of one thousand dollars."

The measure was signed by President Grover Cleveland on October 1, 1888.

IMMIGRATION ACT (1903)

In the wake of the assassination of President William McKinley by anarchist Leon Czolgosz in 1901, Congress began a thorough review of American immigration policy. The Immigration Act provided a codification and

65

extension of previously enacted immigration policy and included one of the few restrictions based upon political beliefs. In his first annual message following McKinley's assassination, in December 1901, President Theodore Roosevelt called for a thorough review of America's immigration policy. The Industrial Commission presented its findings to Congress, including a draft bill and 18 recommendations for the codification of immigrant policy. The bill was debated for 14 months, with considerable disagreement over the use of literacy tests and the proper level of the head tax. Finally enacted on March 3, 1903, the measure:

- reaffirmed all immigration and contract labor laws made after 1875;
- expanded excludable classes of immigrants to include anarchists, prostitutes, epileptics, those who had "been insane within five years," and those who had ever had two or more "attacks of insanity";
- provided for deportation within two years of arrival of "any alien who becomes a public charge by reason of lunacy, idiocy, or epilepsy," unless they could clearly demonstrate that the condition had begun after arrival; and
- levied a head tax of $2 per immigrant.

In 1907 excludable groups were expanded to include "imbeciles, feeble-minded [persons], and persons with physical or mental defects which might affect their ability to earn a living."

IMMIGRATION ACT (1907)

Both the general increase in the number of immigrants and the assassination of President William McKinley in 1901 fueled a growing nativism in the United States and in Congress during the first decade of the 20th century. The Immigration Act of February 20, 1907, consolidated earlier legislation and raised the head tax to $4 per immigrant, excepting aliens from Canada, Newfoundland, Cuba, and Mexico. It also created the Dillingham Commission, consisting of three senators, three representatives, and three presidential appointees, to review U.S. immigration policy.

IMMIGRATION ACT (1917)

The Immigration Act of 1917, popularly known as the Literacy Act, marked a turning point in American immigration legislation. Prohibiting entry to aliens over 16 years of age who could not read 30–40 words in their own language, it was the first legislation aimed at restricting, rather than regulating, European immigration. It further extended the tendency toward a "white" immigration policy, creating an "Asiatic barred zone" that prohibited entry of most Asians. The idea of imposing a literacy test to restrict the tide of "undesirable" Europeans was first widely proposed by progressive economist Edward W. Bemis in 1887. It found relatively little political support until the cause was taken up by the Immigration Restriction League. Measures incorporating a literacy test came near success in 1895, 1903, 1912, and 1915, only to be vetoed by presidents Grover Cleveland, William Taft, and Woodrow Wilson. With the United States moving ever closer to joining the war in Europe, however, hostility increased toward Germany, Ireland, and Austria-Hungary, leading to increasing support for policies supporting "one hundred percent Americanism." Representative John L. Burnett (D-Ala.) revived a bill first introduced in 1913 and vetoed by Wilson in 1915. Wilson again vetoed the bill but was overridden by both the House (287 to 106) and the Senate (62 to 19), and the Immigration Act was formally passed on February 5, 1917. The main provisions of the act:

- raised the head tax on immigrants from $4 to $8;
- broadened excludable aliens to include all Asians except Japanese and Filipinos; and
- excluded all aliens 16 or older who, if physically capable of reading, were unable to read 30–40 words "in ordinary use, printed in plainly legible type in some one of the various languages or dialects" of the immigrant's choice.

The measure was less restrictive than some had hoped but was clear evidence of a rising nativist sentiment, and it continued to reduce the number of immigrants that had already declined dramatically since the outbreak of World War I in 1914.

EMERGENCY QUOTA ACT (1921)

Signed in May 1921, the Emergency Quota Act established the first ethnic quota system for selective admittance of immigrants to the United States. With widespread concern about the importation of communist and other radical political ideas, Americans widely supported more restrictive legislation. The measure:

- limited immigration to 357,800 annually from the Eastern Hemisphere and
- established quotas for each national origin group at 3 percent of the foreign-born population of that country in 1910.

About 1 percent of the quota was allotted to non-Europeans. Western Hemispheric immigrants were exempted from the quotas.

67

Immigration

JOHNSON-REED ACT (IMMIGRATION ACT, 1924)

Following passage of the Emergency Quota Act in 1921, isolationist opinions hardened in the country, and American politicians determined that a permanent measure to dramatically reduce immigration was needed. The Johnson-Reed Act ensured that the vast majority of future immigrants would "blend thoroughly into our body politic." The Johnson-Reed Act served as the basis for U.S. immigration policy until the McCarran-Walter Act of 1952. The principal provisions included:

- an overall annual quota of 153,700, allotment of visas based upon a formula of 2 percent of the population of each nation of origin according to the census of 1890; and
- prohibition of aliens not eligible for citizenship, formally excluding entry of Japanese, Chinese, and other Asian immigrants.

The 2 percent formula was designed to be temporary, and it was replaced with a similarly restrictive formula in 1927 that provided the same national origin ratio in relation to 150,000 as existed in the entire U.S. population according to the census of 1920.

Countries most favored according to this formula were Great Britain (43 percent), Germany (17 percent), and Ireland (12 percent). Countries whose immigration had increased dramatically after 1890—including Italy, Poland, Russia, and Greece—had their quotas drastically slashed.

MCCARRAN-WALTER ACT (IMMIGRATION AND NATIONALITIY ACT, 1952)

The Immigration and Nationality Act, popularly known as the McCarran-Walter Act, was an attempt to deal systematically with the concurrent cold-war threat of communist expansion and the worldwide movement of peoples in the wake of World War II. It codified various legislative acts and policy decisions, continuing the highly restrictive policy of the Immigrant Act of 1917 and the Emergency Quota Act of 1921 and Immigration Act of 1924, which relied upon national quotas in determining the nature of future immigration. Senator Patrick McCarran (D-N.Y.) argued against a more liberal immigration policy, fearing an augmentation of the "hardcore, indigestible blocs" of immigrants who had "not become integrated into the American way of life." Together with Representative Francis Walter (D-Pa.), they drafted the McCarran-Walter Act, which preserved the national origins quotas then in place as the best means of preserving the "cultural balance" in the nation's population. The main provisions of the measure included:

68

- establishment of a new set of preferences for selecting immigrants under the national quota system:

  - **Non-quota:** spouses and minor children of citizens, clergy; inhabitants of the Western Hemisphere
  - **First preference:** needed skilled workers, up to 50 percent of quota
  - **Second preference:** parents of citizens, up to 30 percent of quota
  - **Third preference:** spouses and unmarried children of resident aliens, up to 20 percent of quota
  - **Nonpreference:** siblings and older children of citizens

- provision of 2,000 visas for countries within the Asia-Pacific Triangle, with quotas applied to ancestry categories (such as Chinese, Korean, and Japanese) rather than countries of birth
- elimination of racial restrictions on naturalization
- authorization in times of emergency for the attorney general to temporarily "parole" into the United States anyone without a visa

Allotment of visas under the McCarran-Walter Act still heavily favored northern and eastern European countries, which received 85 percent of the quota allotment.

IMMIGRATION ACT (1965)

The Immigration Act of 1965 marked a dramatic change in American immigration policy, abandoning the concept of national quotas as a means of selecting immigrants and establishing the basis for extensive immigration from developing nations. Technically, the various parts of the measure were amendments to the McCarran-Walter Act. The provisions of the McCarran-Walter Act reflected the interwar isolationism of the United States, allotting 85 percent of immigrant visas to countries from northern and western Europe. With President John F. Kennedy's election in 1960, government immigration policy began to change. Kennedy believed that immigrants were valuable to the country, and members of his administration argued that both the cold war and the Civil Rights movement dictated a more open policy toward nonwhite immigrants. With President Lyndon B. Johnson's landslide victory in 1964, his administration was in a position to remedy the "unworkability of the national origins quota system." The major provisions of the Immigration Act:

- replaced national origins quotas with hemispheric caps of 170,000 from the Eastern Hemisphere and 120,000 from the Western Hemisphere and

Immigration

- established a new scale of preferences, including first, unmarried adult children of U.S. citizens (20 percent); second, spouses and unmarried adult children of permanent resident aliens (20 percent); third, professionals, scientists, and artists of exceptional talent (10 percent); fourth, married children of U.S. citizens (10 percent); fifth, siblings of U.S. citizens who were over 21 years of age (24 percent); sixth, skilled and unskilled workers in areas where labor was needed (10 percent); and seventh, those who "because of persecution or fear of persecution . . . have fled from any Communist or Communist-dominated country or area, or from any country within the general area of the Middle East" (6 percent).

Unlike the provisions of previous special legislation, the 10,200 visas were allotted annually, to deal with refugee situations without further legislation.

Although the new legislation was designed to diversify immigration, it did so in unexpected ways. Many of the Old World slots expected to go to Europeans were filled by Asians, who tended to fill higher preference categories. Having become permanent residents, and then citizens, a wide range of family members then became eligible for immigration in high-preference categories. The measure was successful in bringing highly skilled professional and medical people to the United States. At the same time, it was not effective in limiting the overall number of immigrants. Exemptions and refugees made overall immigration numbers larger than those permitted under the act.

IMMIGRATION ACT (1976)

This amendatory legislation sought to redress the distinctions between the Eastern and Western hemispheres regarding selection of immigrants. The Immigration Act of 1965 provided that immigrants from countries in the Western Hemisphere should be processed on a first-come-first-served basis. By the mid-1970s, this led to a waiting period of more than two years. The amendment revised the act most importantly by applying the seven-point preference system to immigrants from the Western Hemisphere, just as it had previously been applied exclusively to immigrants from the Eastern Hemisphere.

IMMIGRATION REFORM AND CONTROL ACT (1986)

In the wake of massive refugee crises in Southeast Asia and Cuba, in 1981 a Select Commission on Immigration and Refugee Policy recommended to the U.S. Congress that undocumented aliens be granted amnesty and that sanctions should be imposed on employers who hired them. After years of heated debate involving ethnic and religious groups, labor and agricultural organizations, business interests, and the government, a compromise measure was reached. The main provisions of the Immigration Reform and Control Act:

- provided amnesty to undocumented aliens who had been continuously in the United States, except for "brief, casual, and innocent" absences, from the beginning of 1982;
- provided amnesty for seasonal agricultural workers employed for at least 90 days during the year preceding May 1986;
- required applicants to take courses in English and American government to qualify for permanent residence;
- imposed sanctions on employers who knowingly hired illegal aliens, including civil fines and criminal penalties up to $3,000 and six months in jail;
- prohibited employers from discrimination on the basis of national origins;
- increased the Border Patrol by 50 percent in 1987 and 1988; and
- introduced a lottery program for 5,000 visas for countries "adversely affected" by provisions of the Immigration Act of 1965.

Because the measure was meant as a onetime resolution of a long-standing problem, a strict deadline for application was established, all applications for legalization being required within one year of May 5, 1987. At the insistence of state governments, newly legalized aliens were prohibited from receiving most types of federal public welfare, though Cubans and Haitians were exempted.

IMMIGRATION ACT (1990)

The Immigration Act of 1990 was the first major revision of U.S. immigration policy since the Immigration Act of 1965, which revised the McCarran-Walter Act of 1952 in the midst of the cold war. The act maintained the national commitment to reunifying families, enhanced opportunities for business-related immigration, and made provision for underrepresented nationalities. Its main provisions:

- raised the annual cap on immigration from 270,000 to 675,000 (700,000 for the first three years);
- divided the immigration preference classes into two broad categories—family sponsorship and employment-related, with annual review of the number limits in each category;
- established a limit of family sponsorships of "480,000 minus the number of aliens who were issued visas or adjusted to legal permanent residence

in the previous fiscal year as 1) immediate relatives of U.S. citizens, 2) children born subsequent to the issuance of a visa to an accompanying parent, 3) children born abroad to lawful permanent residents on temporary trips abroad, and 4) certain categories of aliens paroled into the United States in the second preceding fiscal year, plus unused employment preferences in the previous fiscal year";

- established an employment-based preference limit of 140,000, plus unused family preferences from the previous year, with applications ranked according to the following preferences: first preference, priority workers; second preference, professionals with advanced degrees or exceptional abilities; third preference, skilled workers, professionals, or unskilled workers in high demand; fourth preference, special immigrants; and fifth preference, investors;

- granted an 18-month "temporary protected status" for Salvadorans who had fled political violence in their country during the 1980s; and

- reserved 55,000 visas for "diversity immigrants" (40,000 during the first three years).

Numerical caps were relatively ineffective because refugees, asylees, Immigration and Reform Act legalizations, and Amerasians fell outside its provisions.

ILLEGAL IMMIGRATION REFORM AND IMMIGRANT RESPONSIBILITY ACT (1996)

As a part of a 1996 initiative to curb illegal immigration, Congress passed the Illegal Immigration Reform and Immigrant Responsibility Act (IIRIRA). Together with provisions of the Welfare Reform Act (1996), IIRIRA enacted most of the restrictions brought forward in California's controversial Proposition 187. The measure was reluctantly signed into law by President Bill Clinton on September 30, 1996, as he courted conservative votes for the presidential election less than six weeks away. The main provisions of the measure:

- authorized a doubling of the number of Border Patrol agents between 1996 and 2001 (5,000 to 10,000);

- authorized building additional fences along the U.S.-Mexican border south of San Diego;

- provided tougher penalties for those engaged in document fraud and alien smuggling; and

- instituted greater controls on public welfare provided to illegal aliens.

The most controversial aspects of the measure involved the streamlining of detention and deportation hearings. This enabled illegal aliens to be deported without appeal to the courts, unless they could demonstrate a realistic fear of persecution in their home country.

Clinton did not favor many of the harsher elements of the measure and worked effectively to redress them. He strongly supported passage of the Nicaraguan and Central American Relief Act (NACARA) of November 1997, which effectively granted amnesty to many Central American refugees whose status had remained ambiguous since the 1980s civil war in Nicaragua. In August 1997, Congress had passed the Balanced Budget Act, which restored many benefits to "qualified aliens," and in February 1998, it restored food stamp benefits under the NACARA legislation to "qualified aliens" who were disabled, over 65, or under 18. Finally, in December 2000, Congress passed two adjusting measures: the Legal Immigration and Family Equity Act (LIFE), which temporarily allowed sponsored illegal immigrants to apply for visas without first leaving the country, and the Child Citizenship Act, which granted automatic U.S. citizenship to any person under 18 years of age who (1) had at least one parent with U.S. citizenship, (2) was a permanent U.S. resident under legal custody of the citizen parent, or (3) if adopted, met the requirements of the Immigration and Nationality Act of 1952.

EXECUTIVE ACTIONS AND OTHER LEGISLATION AFFECTING GENERAL IMMIGRATION POLICY

BURLINGAME TREATY (1868)

The Burlingame Treaty between the United States and China (1868) granted "free migration and immigration" to the Chinese. Although it did not permit naturalization, it did grant Chinese immigrants most-favored-nation status regarding rights and exemptions of noncitizens. With the United States embarking on a period of rapid development of mines, railroads, and a host of associated industries in the west, Secretary of State William H. Seward sought a treaty with China that would provide as much cheap labor as possible. Negotiating for China was a highly respected former U.S. ambassador to China, Anson Burlingame, whose principal goal was to moderate Western aggression in China. The Burlingame Treaty signed on July 28, 1868, recognized "the inherent and inalienable right of man to change his home and allegiance" and provided nearly unlimited immigration of male Chinese laborers until passage of the Chinese Exclusion Act (1882).

Immigration

GENTLEMEN'S AGREEMENT (1907)

The "Gentlemen's Agreement" was an informal set of executive arrangements between the United States and Japan in 1907–08 that defused a tense disagreement over the status of Japanese laborers in California. By 1906 Japanese immigration reached 1,000 per month, alarming Californians. The great San Francisco earthquake in April heightened tensions. In October the San Francisco school board passed a measure segregating Japanese students that deeply offended the Japanese nation. Between December 1906 and January 1908, three separate but related agreements were reached that addressed both Japanese concerns over the welfare of its immigrants and Californian concerns over the growing numbers of Japanese laborers:

- In February 1907, immigration legislation was amended to halt the flow of Japanese laborers from Hawaii, Canada, or Mexico.
- In March the San Francisco school board rescinded its segregation resolution.
- During discussions in December 1907 and January 1908, the Japanese government agreed to restrict passports for travel to the continental United States to non-laborers, former residents, or the family members of Japanese immigrants.

To demonstrate that America's East Asian policy was not made from a position of weakness, President Theodore Roosevelt followed the "Gentlemen's Agreement" with a world tour of 16 American battleships, with a symbolic stop in Japan.

TYDINGS-MCDUFFIE ACT (1934)

Growing out of widespread opposition to Filipino agricultural laborers, the Tydings-McDuffie Act granted the Philippines commonwealth status and promised independence within 10 years. As a result, Filipinos were reclassified as aliens, with an immigrant quota of only 50 per year. As nonwhites, the 50,000 Filipinos in the country were also ineligible for naturalization and thus prohibited from participating in New Deal work programs. Exemptions to the act did allow Hawaiian employers to import Filipino farm labor and enabled the U.S. government to recruit Filipinos into the military.

EXECUTIVE ORDER 9066 (1942)

Following the bombing of Pearl Harbor, Hawaii, on December 7, 1941, Japanese Americans fell under general suspicion, leading President Franklin Roosevelt to sign Executive Order 9066 on February 19, 1942. Under its

74

provisions, 120,000 Japanese Americans were forcibly interned in 10 hastily constructed camps throughout the west between February 1942 and their closing in December 1944. Two-thirds of internees were born in the United States. The main provisions of the order:

- authorized the secretary of war and designated military commanders to "Prescribe military areas in such places and of such extent as he . . . may determine, from which any and all persons may be excluded" and
- authorized the secretary of war and designated military commanders to provide transportation and housing for those removed under the order.

Though the order was challenged in three cases before the U.S. Supreme Court—*Yasui v. United States* (1942), *Hirabayashi v. United States* (1943), and *Korematsu v. United States* (1944)—the government's authority was upheld. The Evacuation Claims Act of 1948 provided $31 million in compensation, less than one-tenth the value of lost property and wages.

BRACERO AGREEMENT (1942–64)

Following negotiations with Mexican leaders, an executive agreement was reached in 1942 that established the Emergency Farm Labor Program—popularly known as the "*Bracero* Program" (from the Mexican word for "manual laborer")—for the purpose of ensuring the availability of low-cost agricultural labor. The agreement was sanctioned by Congress in 1943.

The program provided for legal entry into the United States for Mexican workers chosen by the Mexican government, subject to the following provisions:

- Mexicans would not engage in military service.
- Mexicans would not suffer discrimination.
- Workers would be provided wages, transportation, living expenses, and repatriation in keeping with Mexican labor laws.
- Workers would not be eligible for jobs that displaced Americans.
- Workers would be eligible only for agricultural jobs and would be subject to deportation if they worked in any other industry.

The original Bracero Program ended in 1947 but was extended in various ways until 1964. During the 22 years of its existence, almost 5 million *braceros* (U.S. laborers) worked in the United States, contributing substantially to the agricultural development of the United States and remitting more than $200 million to relatives in Mexico. The growth of liberal political power in the United States, increased mechanization in agriculture, and a rising

Immigration

demand for labor in Mexico all contributed to the ending of the program in 1964.

WAR BRIDES ACT (1945)

With U.S. servicemen seeking to bring home from World War II more than 130,000 brides and 25,000 children, special legislation was required to sanction their admission. The War Brides Act of December 28, 1945, was the first of a series of measures designed to address the issue. It authorized admission to the United States of alien spouses and minor children outside the ordinary quota system. The Fiancées Act of June 29, 1946, authorized admission of fiancées for three months as nonimmigrant temporary visitors, provided they were otherwise eligible and had a bona fide intent to marry. On July 22, 1947, the War Brides Act was amended to include Asian spouses. All the measures were further amended on April 21, 1949, extending the expiration date of the original measure to September 11, 1949.

DISPLACED PERSONS ACT (1948)

Bills to assist Central European refugees were brought before Congress in 1937 and 1939, but new legislation was not passed because the number of refugees could be accommodated under existing legislation. The magnitude of the refugee problem was so greatly enhanced by World War II, however, that new legislation became imperative. The main provisions of the act included:

* approval of 220,000 visas to be issued for two years without regard to quota, but charged to the appropriate quotas in future years;
* up to 3,000 non-quota visas for displaced orphans; and
* a grant of power to the attorney general, with the approval of Congress, to adjust the status of up to 15,000 displaced persons who entered the country prior to April 1, 1948.

The Displaced Persons Act was amended on June 16, 1950, to add another 121,000 visas, for a total of 341,000, through June 1951, chargeable against future quotas at a maximum rate of one-fourth of quotas for three fiscal years (1951–54) and at one-half of quotas thereafter as needed. The number of visas for orphans was raised to 5,000 and taken as a part of the total authorization of 341,000. The provision for adjusting the status of previously admitted displaced persons was extended to those who had entered the United States prior to April 30, 1949. An additional section was added to the Displaced Persons Act, providing 5,000 additional non-quota visas for orphans under the age of 10 who were coming for adoption, to an agency, or to reside with close relatives. On June 28, 1951, the Displaced Persons Act was again amended to extend the time for issuing the 341,000 visas to the end of 1951 and through the first half of 1952 for displaced orphans.

REFUGEE RELIEF ACT (1953)

Grappling with the implications of cold-war conflict with the Soviet Union, the Refugee Relief Act of August 7, 1953, principally sought to aid three classes of people: refugees (those unable to return to their homes in a communist country "because of persecution, fear of persecution, natural calamity or military operations"); escapees (refugees who had left a communist country fearing persecution "on account of race, religion, or political opinion"); and German expellees (ethnic Germans living in West Germany, West Berlin, or Austria who had been forced to flee from territories dominated by communists). The measure:

- authorized 205,000 special non-quota visas to refugees, escapees, German expellees, and their immediate family members;
- allotted 2,000 visas to indigenous refugees who had taken refuge in U.S. consular offices in East Asia;
- allotted 2,000 visas to Chinese refugees;
- allotted 2,000 visas to those qualifying for aid from the United Nations Relief and Works Agency for Palestine Refugees in the Near East; and
- allotted 4,000 non-quota visas for eligible orphans under 10 years of age who were lawfully adopted by a U.S. citizen and who came from an area where quotas had already been filled.

German expellees (55,000), Italian refugees (45,000), and German escapees (35,000) received the largest numbers of visas.

REFUGEE ACT OF 1980

The massive influx of Vietnamese refugees in the wake of the Vietnam War highlighted the weaknesses of U.S. refugee policies. The Refugee Act of 1980 was crafted to bring U.S. law into compliance with international treaty obligations, particularly the United Nations Protocol Relating to the Status of Refugees, to which the United States had acceded in 1968. The measure:

- accepted the broader United Nations definition of a refugee as "any person who . . . owing to a well-founded fear of being persecuted for reasons of race, religion, nationality, membership of a particular social group or political opinion, is outside the country of his nationality and is unable or, owing to such fear, is unwilling to avail himself of the protection of that country; or who, not having a nationality and being outside the country of his former habitual residence, . . . is unable or, owing to such fear, is unwilling to return to it;"

- allowed for annual entrance of 50,000 persons; and
- provided for annual review of quotas.

According to provisions of the act, refugees were exempted from the immigrant preference system, as were their immediate relatives.

IMMIGRATION MARRIAGE FRAUD AMENDMENTS (1986)

Amending the McCarran-Walter Act of 1952, the Immigration Marriage Fraud Amendments required a two-year residency requirement for alien spouses and children before obtaining permanent resident status. By provisions of the amendment, a couple was required to apply for permanent status within 90 days of the end of the conditional two-year period. The Immigration and Naturalization Service could then interview the couple in order to satisfy themselves that 1) the marriage was not arranged "for the purpose of procuring an alien's entry as an immigrant, 2) the marriage was still legally valid, and 3) that a fee was not paid for the filing of the alien's petition. Punitively, the measure made marriage fraud punishable by up to five years in prison and $250,000 in fines, further grounds for deportation, and a permanent bar to future applications. The amendments also required that aliens contracting marriages after the beginning of deportation proceedings live two years outside the United States before becoming eligible for permanent resident status. The measures were further amended in 1990 to allow for exemptions in the case of wife or child battering, or if clear evidence could be presented to show that the marriage was contracted in good faith and not for the purpose of gaining residency.

PROPOSITION 187 (SAVE OUR STATE INITIATIVE, 1994)

Proposition 187 was an anti-immigrant, California state initiative denying education, welfare benefits, and nonemergency health care to illegal immigrants. It developed in response to a massive influx of illegal Mexican and Central American immigrants into California, which was home to some 40 percent of the 5 million illegal immigrants in the United States. Concern over the cost of providing social services to these immigrants led Californians to approve the measure 59 to 41 percent. Because certain aspects of the measure were almost certainly unconstitutional, it was never formally enacted, though many of its measures were finally enacted in the Welfare Reform Act and Illegal Immigration Reform and Immigrant Responsibility Act, both of 1996.

WELFARE REFORM ACT (1996)

Reflecting the anti-immigration mood of the 1990s and concern over the high cost of social services to both immigrants and citizens, the Welfare Reform Act—more formally and descriptively known as the Personal Responsibility and Work Opportunity Reconciliation Act—replaced Aid to Families with Dependent Children with a new program that limited aid to two consecutive years and five years over a lifetime. Not strictly an immigration measure, the Welfare Reform Act nevertheless contained provisions denying cash welfare, food stamps, Medicaid, and supplemental security income to legal immigrants. President Bill Clinton, who personally opposed many of the more stringent aspects of the measure, nevertheless signed it on August 22, 1996, in part to strengthen conservative support for the November presidential election. In 1998 food stamp benefits were restored to more than a quarter of the immigrants who had previously been declared ineligible to receive them.

USA PATRIOT ACT (2001)

In the wake of the September 11, 2001, terrorist attacks, the administration of President George W. Bush proposed a series of sweepings measures designed to combat terrorism, including strengthened border controls. Although not designed to directly address legal immigration policy, it included a number of important provisions affecting immigration. The Uniting and Strengthening America by Providing Appropriate Tools Required to Intercept and Obstruct Terrorism (USA PATRIOT) Act was quickly passed and signed into law by Bush on October 26, 2001. The main provisions of the PATRIOT Act included:

- greater surveillance of aliens and increased power of the attorney general to identify, arrest, and deport aliens;
- a definition of "domestic terrorism" that included "acts dangerous to human life that are a violation of the criminal laws of the United States or of any State that appear to be intended to intimidate or coerce a civilian population; to influence the policy of a government by intimidation or coercion; or to affect the conduct of a government by mass destruction, assassination, or kidnapping";

- provisions for monitoring some aliens entering on nonimmigrant visas;
- requirements for digitalization of and more extensive background checks of all applications and petitions to the Immigration and Naturalization Service;
- creation of the SEVIS database to track the location of aliens in the country on student visas; and
- authorization for U.S. attorney general to immediately expel anyone suspected of terrorist links.

The State Department also introduced a 20-day waiting period for visa applications from men 16–45 years of age from Afghanistan, Algeria, Bahrain, Djibouti, Egypt, Eritrea, Indonesia, Iran, Iraq, Jordan, Kuwait, Lebanon, Libya, Malaysia, Morocco, Oman, Pakistan, Qatar, Saudi Arabia, Somalia, Sudan, Syria, Tunisia, United Arab Emirates, and Yemen. Any applications considered to be suspicious were forwarded to the Federal Bureau of Investigation (FBI), creating a further delay.

Though widely supported by the American public, the PATRIOT Act remains a focal point of the evolving debate about the nature of terrorism, the means necessary to combat it, and the wisdom of sacrificing civil liberties for security. Although the act specifically affirmed the "vital role" in American life played by "Arab Americans, Muslim Americans, and Americans from South Asia" and condemned any stereotyping and all acts of violence against them, some groups believe that the PATRIOT Act enables the federal government to target their activities and to suppress a variety of activist groups that disagree with the government on a wide array of issues.

A number of provisions in the measure were set to expire on December 31, 2005, including the controversial Section 215, which enabled the government to access "business records," including library requests. After several deadline extensions, more than 20 investigations, and extensive debate, all provisions of the USA PATRIOT Act were reinstated in March 2006. Section 206, approving "roving surveillance," and Section 215 will expire after four years.

HOMELAND SECURITY ACT (2002)

The Homeland Security Act was a sweeping response to the terrorist attacks of September 11, 2001, designed both to restructure the institutional character of American intelligence and counterterrorism operations and to provide new authority for the war on terror. On June 18, 2002, President George W. Bush sent to Congress a proposal for creation of a new Department of Homeland Security. The bill passed the House of Representatives on July 26 by a vote of 295 to 132 and passed the Senate on

November 19 by a vote of 90 to 9. It was signed three days later by Bush. Its main provisions:

• established a new, cabinet-level Department of Homeland Security, which became fully operational on March 1, 2003;

• abolished the Immigration and Naturalization Service, whose functions were transferred to various agencies within the newly created Department of Homeland Security;

• increased authority for agencies to collect and maintain data on individuals and groups, including databases combining personal, governmental, and corporate records;

• limited information citizens could request under the Freedom of Information Act and imposed criminal penalties for government employees who leak information; and

• granted new power to government officials to declare national health emergencies, including quarantines and forced vaccination.

Most important for immigration, the measure completely reorganized the administration of the immigration services and border control. Although most administrative functions related to immigration fall under the Department of Homeland Security, some still are performed by the Department of State, the Department of Justice, the Department of Labor, and the Department of Health and Human Services. The exact relationship between the various departments and agencies was being continually refined between 2002 and 2005.

INTELLIGENCE REFORM AND TERRORISM PREVENTION ACT (IRTPA, 2004)

Following the terrorist attacks of September 11, 2001, a bipartisan National Commission on Terrorist Attacks upon the U.S. (9/11 Commission) was formed to examine the government response. The recommendation of the 9/11 Commission were substantially incorporated in the Intelligence Reform and Terrorism Prevention Act, which completely overhauled the government's intelligence operations. The House of Representatives passed the measure on December 8, 2004, by a vote of 336 to 75, and the Senate followed suit the next day by a vote of 89 to 2. The principal work of the measure was to create a new position of director of national intelligence, in charge of integrating the activities of 15 separate agencies responsible for gathering national intelligence and answerable directly to the president. A number of provisions in IRTPA directly affected immigrants, both alien and naturalized. The most important include:

- strengthening visa application requirements;
- establishing a visa and passport security program within the State Department;
- more stringent passport requirements for travel in the Western Hemisphere;
- development of a biometric data system within the Department of Homeland Security to track people entering and exiting the United States;
- strengthening Mexican border security by adding 10,000 full-time border patrol agents and 4,000 new investigators for Immigration and Customs Enforcement over the next five years;
- increasing by 40,000 the number of detention beds available for housing aliens awaiting deportation;
- requiring federal agencies to establish minimum standards for documents required in boarding airplanes and for issuing driver's licenses and birth certificates;
- federal criminalization of the smuggling of aliens into the United States; and
- requiring the General Accountability Office to study potential weaknesses in the U.S. asylum system.

IRTPA also requires a passport of all U.S. citizens and foreign nationals for air and sea travel between the United States and the Caribbean, Bermuda, Central and South America (from December 31, 2005); for all air and sea travel to or from Mexico and Canada (from December 31, 2006); and for all air, sea, or land travel to the Caribbean, Bermuda, and Central and South America (from December 31, 2007). Although almost all recommendations of the 9/11 Commission were adopted, in early 2006, members of the commission were still concerned with the pace of implementation.

COURT CASES

CHEROKEE NATION V. GEORGIA, 30 U.S. 1 (1831)

Background

The radical cultural distinction between American Indians and European settlers had long enabled American citizens to justify physical and political aggression against Indian tribes. By the 1820s, however, it became clear that many of the remaining southern tribes—the Cherokee, Creek, Seminole, Chickasaw, and Choctow—were settled and had sophisticated cultures. Most southern whites were not satisfied with the pace of Indian removal, and in 1830 Congress passed the Removal Act, which further pressured tribal relocations in the west by opening new negotiations.

Legal Issues

While most tribes acceded to local and federal pressure, the Cherokee appealed to the U.S. Supreme Court for an injunction against removal. The main legal issue upon which the case turned, however, was the standing of American Indians before the Court, and thus their right to seek protection under the U.S. Constitution.

Decision

Though sympathetic to the plight of the Cherokee, Chief Justice John Marshall ruled that as Indians they were aliens who had no standing before the court. He argued that "though the Indians are acknowledged to have an unquestionable, and, heretofore, unquestioned right to the lands they occupy, until that right shall be extinguished by a voluntary cession to our government; yet it may well be doubted whether those tribes which reside within the acknowledged boundaries of the United States can, with strict accuracy, be denominated foreign nations. They may, more correctly be denominated domestic dependent nations. . . . Their relation to the United States resembles that of a ward to his guardian." The decision was modified but not overturned in a companion case the following year. In *Worcester v. Georgia* (31 U.S. 515), the Court held that Georgia state laws related to the Cherokee violated the contract and commerce clauses of the Constitution and the sovereignty of the Cherokee nation. In that decision, Marshall emphasized Cherokee nationality, as opposed to domestic dependence.

Impact

Because Indians were not "free white persons," they were considered aliens who could not be naturalized and thus had no standing before the court. In practice many localities and states granted the rights of citizenship to acculturated Indians. In the Dawes Act of 1887, Congress granted citizenship to American Indians not living on reservations and in 1924 granted citizenship to all American Indians.

HENDERSON V. MAYOR OF NEW YORK, 92 U.S. 259 (1876)

Background

The danger of encouraging the importation of immigrant paupers and the cost of processing immigrants led states to seek financial guarantees against the cost. In some cities, port authorities and commissions were abolished, leaving screening and orientation to private organizations, which were quickly overwhelmed. In New York, vessel masters were required to report the landing of all aliens and to pay on bond against their becoming a public charge.

Legal Issues

The main legal issue was the question of whether the admitted "police power" of the state to protect itself was sufficient to override the constitutional mandate for Congress to regulate all foreign commerce, according to Article 1, Section 8. Revolving around the constitutionality of an act of the New York legislature requiring masters of vessels to post bonds in the event that immigrants on board their ships became public charges, the matter was brought before the U.S. Supreme Court.

Decision

The Court nullified state requirements that vessel masters pay bonds and head taxes, basing their decision on the Commerce Clause of the U.S. Constitution. It also ruled that immigration should be subject to "a uniform system or plan" and that the same laws that "govern the right to land passengers in the United States from other countries ought to be the same in New York, Boston, New Orleans and San Francisco." According to Justice Samuel F. Miller: "It is too clear for argument that this demand of the owner of the vessel for a bond or money on account of every passenger landed by him from a foreign shore is, if valid, an obligation which he incurs by bringing the passenger here, and which is perfect the moment he leaves the vessel. We are of opinion that this whole subject has been confided to Congress by the Constitution; that Congress can more appropriately and with more acceptance exercise it than any other body known to our law, state or national; that by providing a system of laws in these matters, applicable to all ports and to all vessels, a serious question, which has long been matter of contest and complaint, may be effectually and satisfactorily settled."

Impact

This decision marked the end of laissez-faire immigration, in which state and local governments generally administered immigration, shifting the burden of responsibility to the federal government. Because there was no federal bureaucracy established for dealing with immigration, the federal government subsidized New York State with monies raised from the imposition of a head tax that gradually rose from 50 cents in 1882 to $8 in 1917. Shippers challenged the constitutionality of the federal head tax because it did not raise revenue for the general welfare, but the Supreme Court ruled that the measure was more closely associated with regulating immigration—over which Congress had unlimited authority power—than in raising revenue. As the federal government consolidated its powers over immigration, its responsibilities grew, leading to the opening of the first federal reception center on Ellis Island in 1892.

MULLER V. OREGON, **208 U.S. 412 (1908)**

Background

Women immigrants, especially from the 1880s, were subjected to largely unregulated factory labor. In 1903 Oregon, like a number of other states, passed a Progressive reform measure limiting women working in factories and laundries to 10 hours of work each day. In this case, Portland, Oregon, laundry owner Curt Muller required female employees to work more than the legal maximum of 10 hours. When charged with a violation and fined $10, Muller challenged the ruling, arguing that women workers should have the same right to enter into contracts as men. The Oregon Supreme Court upheld the constitutionality of the Ten-Hour Law in 1906.

Legal Issues

The "single question" observed in Justice David J. Brewer's opinion was "the constitutionality of the statute under which the defendant was convicted so far as it affects the work of a female in a laundry." A second issue, raised by the plaintiff, involved the question of whether women laborers were free to make contracts under the right to "purchase and sell labor" as part of the "liberty guaranteed by the Fourteenth Amendment to the Constitution.

Decision

Arguing for the state, Louis D. Brandeis introduced both legal precedent and sociological data in support of the need for special protections for women—though the sociological data presented in 110 pages dwarfed the legal arguments, presented in two pages. The Court upheld the Oregon measure protecting women in the workplace, ruling that guarantees under the Fourteenth Amendment are not absolute, and that, in the words of Brewer, "a woman's physical structure and the performance of maternal functions place her at a disadvantage in the struggle for subsistence is obvious . . . as healthy mothers are essential to vigorous offspring, the physical well-being of woman becomes an object of public interest and care in order to preserve the strength and vigor of the race." Brewer noted that the Court's decision did not infringe upon the decision in *Lochner v. New York* (1905), in which general daily hour limits in bakeries were struck down by the Court as a violation of freedom of contract.

85

Immigration

Impact

The Supreme Court ruling upheld special protections for women, but at the expense of some rights with regard to liberty of contract. It also gave legal sanction to the prevailing sociological view of the day that men and women were not equal and therefore should not be treated equally in all cases before the law. Although considered progressive at the time, the decision threatened the livelihood of immigrant women, often forcing them into unsafe conditions when they evaded the law. In this case, the "Brandeis brief" was first introduced as a legitimate means of arguing for progressive reform, using sociological, medical, and scientific evidence to demonstrate a reasonable case for the Oregon law. Finally, it laid a foundation for later New Deal protections in the gender-neutral Fair Labor Standards Act of 1938.

OZAWA V. UNITED STATES, 260 U.S. 178 (1922)

Background

Takao Ozawa was born in Japan, arriving in the United States as a student in 1894, graduating from a California high school, and attending the University of California, Berkeley, before joining a U.S. business firm in Honolulu. He raised his children in America and was continuously a resident for 20 years before applying for citizenship. Denied citizenship by the district attorney for Hawaii, he appealed to the U.S. District Court for the Territory of Hawaii for the right to be naturalized.

Legal Issues

The district court ruled that Ozawa was "in every way eminently qualified" for citizenship except he was not white and clearly not of African ancestry. He then appealed to the U.S. Supreme Court, where he argued that he was "at heart . . . a true American" and referred to the general introductory clauses of Section 4 of the 1906 Naturalization Act, which read: "That an alien may be admitted to become a citizen of the United States in the following manner, and not otherwise."

Decision

Although the Court observed that the term *white* was more broadly conceived than Caucasian—taking into account, for instance, character traits that might be linked to race or ethnicity—it also ruled that Ozawa clearly did not qualify under any legislation related to naturalization that had, consistently since 1790, accepted only "free white persons" as eligible candidates, subsequently enlarged in 1870 to include only "aliens of African nativity and persons of African descent." According to Justice George

The Law and Immigration

Sutherland, "if Congress in 1906 desired to alter a rule so well and so long established it may be assumed that its purpose would have been definitely disclosed and its legislation to that end put in unmistakable terms."

Impact

With the matter of naturalization clearly decided against Asians, the Gentlemen's Agreement of 1907 was abrogated and Japanese were excluded from immigration to the United States. The exclusion of immigrants ineligible for citizenship was carried still further in the following year, when Bhagat Singh Thind, a Caucasian Indian and U.S. World War I veteran who had been granted citizenship in Oregon, was denaturalized as an ineligible alien. Although racially "white," the Supreme Court ruled that he was not "white" according to the "understanding of the common man."

KOREMATSU V. UNITED STATES, 323 U.S. 214 (1944)

Background

In 1942 Fred Korematsu was hired in a defense-related job, after failing a physical exam for the military. When Japanese internment began in May 1942 under Executive Order 9066 requiring the removal of Japanese Americans from sensitive military areas, he moved to another town, changed his name, and had facial surgery in order to present himself as a Mexican American. When his secret was discovered, he was convicted to five years in prison, paroled, then sent to a detention camp.

Legal Issues

This case centered on breaching Exclusion Order No. 34, issued on the basis of Executive Order 9066 of 1942 in which President Roosevelt argued that "the successful prosecution of the war requires every possible protection against espionage and against sabotage to national-defense material, national-defense premises, and national-defense utilities. . . ." Korematsu argued that by May 1942, when the order was issued, all threat of Japanese invasion had passed. His loyalty was not called into question. Korematsu's was the third case brought by a Japanese American to reach the Supreme Court. The constitutionality of military judgment in such cases had been upheld in both *Yasui v. U.S.* (1942) and *Hirabayashi v. U.S.* (1943).

Decision

Justice Hugo L. Black, writing for the majority, supported the action of the military authorities on the grounds that "we were at war with the Japanese Empire, because the properly constituted military authorities feared an

87

invasion of our West Coast," and because military authorities believed it necessary "that all citizens of Japanese ancestry be segregated from the West Coast temporarily." While the decision constituted a "hardship," Black argued, "hardships are a part of war." Though Black did not agree that Korematsu had been singled out for racial or ethnic discrimination, in an oft-cited section of his opinion, he wrote that "all legal restrictions which curtail the civil rights of a single racial group are immediately suspect" and must be given "the most rigid scrutiny." According to Black, it only confused the issue "to cast this case into outlines of racial prejudice, without reference to the real military dangers which were presented."

Impact

According to the majority opinion, the nation's power to defend itself took precedence over individual constitutional rights. It was the only case, however, where Black's "rigid scrutiny" test was applied and the restrictive law upheld. Black's judgment that "all legal restrictions which curtail the civil rights of a single racial group are immediately suspect" became the standard by which similar cases based upon race would be decided.

OYAMA V. CALIFORNIA, 332 U.S. 633 (1948)

Background

In 1934 Kajiro Oyama purchased six acres of land in southern California and had the deed placed in the name of his six-year-old son Fred. This was a common means of bypassing provisions of the restrictive Alien Land Laws of 1913 and 1920 that sought to prohibit ownership of land by persons not eligible to become naturalized U.S. citizens. Six months later, Kajiro was granted guardianship, but he did not register with the state as required by the Alien Land Law. The Oyamas were removed in 1942 under Executive Order 9066, and two years later, the state of California filed a petition to recover Oyama's lands on the grounds that they had been purchased in deliberate evasion of the Alien Land Laws. The Supreme Court of California upheld the trial court's ruling, finding it constitutional to exclude ineligible aliens from owning agricultural land.

Legal Issues

Legal issues revolved around whether or not Fred Oyama, born in the United States and thus a U.S. citizen, was guaranteed equal protection before the law. Also, there was the question of whether due process had been breached in taking Kajiro Oyama's property after the legal limitation period had expired.

The Law and Immigration

Decision

Chief Justice Fred N. Vincent ruled narrowly in agreeing that the Alien Land Law deprived Fred Oyama of the equal protection of his privileges as an American citizen. Justice Hugo Black wrote a notable concurring opinion, arguing that "basic provisions of the California Alien Land Law violate the equal protection clause of the Fourteenth Amendment and conflict with federal laws and treaties governing the immigration of aliens and their rights after arrival in this country." In doing so, he observed that the effect of the law, though not its explicit words, discriminated against Japanese residents. Though agreeing that Oyama had been deprived of equal protection, Black went further, arguing that he "would now overrule the previous decisions of this Court that sustained state land laws which discriminate against people of Japanese origin residing in this country."

Impact

The Oyama decision extended the reach of the Fourteenth Amendment. It was clear to many, including Justices Black and Frank Murphy, that California's Alien Land Law was "outright racial discrimination." This was the basis for the decision in *Fujii Sei v. State of California* (1952) that declared the measure unconstitutional and led to its repeal in 1956. The case was unusual, too, in the widely differing opinions rendered by concurring justices.

GRAHAM V. RICHARDSON, 403 U.S. 365 (1971)

Background

This case was originally brought by Carmen Richardson, a Mexican citizen legally admitted to the United States in 1956, against John O. Graham the Arizona commissioner of public welfare, who had denied her public-welfare disability benefits on her failure to meet the 15-year residency requirement for noncitizens. In a class-action suit, she argued that the residency requirement abridged her constitutional right to "equal protection" under the Fourteenth Amendment. The state appealed her victory in the federal court to the Supreme Court.

Legal Issues

The principal legal issue involved the application of state residency requirements for gaining access to welfare programs. "The issue," according to Justice Harry Blackmun, was "whether the Equal Protection Clause of the Fourteenth Amendment prevents a State from conditioning welfare benefits either (a) upon the beneficiary's possession of United States citizenship, or

Immigration

(b) if the beneficiary is an alien, upon his having resided in this country for a specified number of years."

Decision

The Supreme Court ruled that residency requirements did violate the equal protection clause. According to the decision, state interest in protecting its financial resources was not sufficiently compelling to override the promised protections. Additionally, the Court ruled that, because the Constitution granted the federal government authority over the admission of aliens and the condition of their residence, state laws interfering with federal laws violate the Supremacy Clause. According to the Court, the classification of "alien" is suspect under the Fourteenth Amendment. As a "discrete and insular minority," they require a high level of judicial protection. In so ruling, the Court "rejected the concept that constitutional rights turn upon whether a governmental benefit is characterized as a 'right' or a 'privilege.'"

Impact

Although a number of exceptions were subsequently made to *Graham v. Richardson*, including lower burdens of proof for excluding aliens from certain government positions, and employment as public school teachers, the decision established a high burden for establishing cause for limiting alien privileges. Whereas states had argued a public interest in the distribution of limited public resources, the Supreme Court countered that the terms of admitting aliens was an overriding federal charge. By not explicitly clarifying whether states could determine benefits eligibility, however, the case left room for future challenges to the general premise that alienage was suspect as a basis for exclusion.

LAU ET AL. V. NICHOLS, 414 U.S. 563 (1974)
Background

By the 1970s, there was little overt hostility toward Chinese, but there was discrimination. At that time, there were some 3,500 Chinese students in the San Francisco public school system who spoke little or no English, though only about 1,700 of them were receiving special instruction in the English language. According to the Supreme Court, "the failure of the San Francisco school system to provide English language instruction to approximately 1,800 students of Chinese ancestry who do not speak English, or to provide them with other adequate instructional procedures" denied them a "meaningful opportunity to participate in the public educational program."

The Law and Immigration

Legal Issues

At issue was the question of whether instruction in English alone violated protections guaranteed under the Civil Rights Act of 1964, which banned discrimination on the basis of "race, color, or national origin." The court of appeals had denied a remedy, arguing that "every student brings to the starting line of his educational career different advantages and disadvantages caused in part by social, economic and cultural background, created and continued completely apart from any contribution by the school system."

Decision

Justice William O. Douglas, writing on behalf of the Court, argued that although Section 71 of the California Education Code stated that "English shall be the basic language of instruction in all schools," it also stated that it is "the policy of the state" to ensure "the mastery of English by all pupils in the schools," and if explicitly authorized bilingual instruction "to the extent that it does not interfere with the systematic, sequential, and regular instruction of all pupils in the English language." Since the respondent school district was contractually agreed to "comply with Title VI of the Civil Rights Act of 1964 . . . and all requirements imposed by or pursuant to the Regulation" of Health, Education, and Welfare, and the federal government had the "power to fix the terms on which its money allotments to the States shall be disbursed," the judgment of the court of appeals was reversed and appropriate relief called for.

Impact

The unanimous Supreme Court decision established a new standard of enforcement referred to as the "Lau Remedies." The decision paved the way for children with "limited English proficiency" to receive "appropriate instruction," which was generally interpreted to mean bilingual instruction, laying a foundation for future decisions regarding Spanish-language instruction in schools. The Supreme Court argued that a "meaningful education" should be available regardless of language background.

PLYLER V. DOE, 457 U.S. 202 (1982)

Background

The case emanated from a revision to the Texas education laws in 1975 that allowed the state to withhold funds from local school districts for educating children illegally resident in the state. The challenge was based on the right of states with high immigrant populations to apportion limited resources as they saw fit for the purpose of education.

Legal Issues

The central legal question was whether the Texas law violated the equal protection clause of the Fourteenth Amendment. In order to judge the question of equal protection, the Court had to address the meaning of the phrase "within its jurisdiction" in the guarantee that "no State" should "deny to any person within its jurisdiction the equal protection of the laws." Finally, there was the question of whether education was a fundamental right that could not be denied to aliens.

Decision

The Supreme Court ruled that states could not deny the right of public education to aliens based on their parents' immigrant status and that denying enrollment to such children violated the equal protection clause of the Fourteenth Amendment. In severely disadvantaging the children of illegal aliens, Texas could not prove that the action served a "compelling state interest." According to Justice William Brennan, delivering the majority opinion of the Court, it was important in cases regarding equal protection challenges "respecting a State's differential treatment of aliens, the courts must be attentive to congressional policy concerning aliens." In the absence of "any contrary indication fairly discernible in the legislative record," Brennan argued, "no national policy is perceived that might justify the State in denying these children an elementary education." According to Brennan, "the deprivation of public education is not like the deprivation of some other governmental benefit." Such deprivation "takes an inestimable toll on the social, economic, intellectual, and psychological well-being of the individual, and poses an obstacle to individual achievement."

Impact

States were required to provide public funding in order to educate children who were illegally residing in the United States. Chief Justice Warren Burger's argument in dissent, that "by definition, illegal aliens have no right whatever to be here, and the state may reasonably, and constitutionally, elect not to provide them with governmental service at the expense of those who are lawfully within the state," formed a basis for later challenges seeking reimbursement from the federal government for costs connected with the legalization of Immigration Reform and Control Act applicants and illegal aliens applying for welfare benefits, health services, and other costs.

The Law and Immigration

IMMIGRATION AND NATURALIZATION SERVICE V. CHADHA, 462 U.S. 919 (1983)

Background

Jagdish Chadha, born in Kenya of Asian Indian parents and holding a British passport, came to the United States as a student in the mid-1960s. Overstaying his visa, he was threatend with deportation. Neither Kenya nor Great Britain would allow him to return, despite the expiration of his visa. Opponents of the legislative veto used Chadha's case to test the constitutionality of congressional oversight. At the deportation hearing, Chadha argued that he "had resided continuously in the United States for over seven years, was of good moral character, and would suffer 'extreme hardship' if deported." The Immigration and Naturalization Service judge ruled in Chadha's favor, but the House of Representatives vetoed the approval and in 1976 ordered his deportation, based on a section of the Immigration and Nationality Act that authorized either house of Congress to invalidate and suspend deportation rulings by the U.S. attorney general. As a result, Department of Justice attorneys in both the Jimmy Carter and Ronald Reagan administrations joined the INS in arguing against the constitutionality of the legislative veto.

Legal Issues

Most narrowly the case involved the right of Congress to determine when a person fails to meet the statutory requirements for permanent residence. More broadly it involved the constitutional issue of separation of powers regarding the legislative veto, a device drafted in agreement between Congress and the Herbert Hoover administration in 1932, enabling a presidential action in return for the right of either house of Congress to veto the action if dissatisfied. In the Chadha case, Department of Justice attorneys challenged the legislative veto, in essence setting up a battle between congressional and presidential powers.

Decision

The Court held that legislative vetoes represented a subversion of the "single, finely wrought and exhaustively considered procedure" for enacting legislation, ruling that one house of Congress did not have the constitutional power to veto an INS decision. According to Chief Justice Warren Burger, the promise of greater governmental efficiency was not sufficient to offset the "explicitly constitutional standards" regarding the lawmaking process. "The choices we discern as having been made in the Constitutional Convention impose burdens on governmental processes that often seem clumsy, inefficient, even unworkable, but those hard choices were consciously made by men who had lived under a form of government that permitted arbitrary governmental acts to go unchecked. There is no support in the Constitution or decisions of this Court for the proposition that the cumbersomeness and delays often encountered in complying with explicit constitutional standards may be avoided, either by the Congress or by the President. With all the obvious flaws of delay, untidiness, and potential for abuse, we have not yet found a better way to preserve freedom than by making the exercise of power subject to the carefully crafted restraints spelled out in the Constitution."

Impact

The decision invalidated the legislative veto that had enabled the U.S. Congress, often in negotiation with the executive branch, to veto certain executive actions on grounds of efficiency. It is still unclear the degree to which the courts might be called upon to referee future contests of power between the executive and legislative branches of government, though it appears that informal agreements of various kinds will be allowed to continue. The decision did suggest an implicit right of the executive branch to execute immigration law.

RUMSFELD V. PADILLA, 542 U.S. 426 (2004)

Background

Jose Padilla, an American citizen returning from Pakistan in 2002, was detained as a material witness in a government investigation of the al-Qaeda terrorist network. Eventually, he was declared an "enemy combatant" by the Department of Defense, which enabled the government to hold him indefinitely without access to the courts. He was then transferred to a military brig in South Carolina. In response to a petition for a writ of habeas corpus, the U.S. District Court for the Southern District of New York found that the Department of Defense had the power to detain Padilla as an enemy combatant. Padilla's attorney argued that the detention was prohibited by the federal Non-Detention Act, which prohibited the imprisonment of a citizen "except pursuant to an Act of Congress." On appeal the Second Circuit Court of Appeals panel reversed the district court's ruling, finding that the president could not declare American citizens captured outside a combat zone as enemy combatants.

Legal Issues

The principal legal question was whether the president was authorized by Congress's "Authorization for Use of Military Force" to detain a U.S. citizen based on a determination that he is an enemy combatant, or whether that power is precluded by the Non-Detention Act. According to Chief Justice William Rehnquist, "the question whether the Southern District has jurisdiction over Padilla's habeas petition breaks down into two related sub-questions. First, who is the proper respondent to that petition? And second, does the Southern District have jurisdiction over him or her?"

Decision

The Supreme Court did not rule on the merits of this case, but, in a 5 to 4 decision, announced that the suit could not be considered because it had not been filed against the person with the direct power (the brig commander) to release the prisoner, in the state of his residence (South Carolina). According to Rehnquist, "Padilla's argument reduces to a request for a new exception to the immediate custodian rule based upon the 'unique facts' of this case. While Padilla's detention is undeniably unique in many respects, it is at bottom a simple challenge to physical custody imposed by the Executive . . . his detention is thus not unique in any way that would provide arguable basis for a departure from the immediate custodian rule. Accordingly, we hold that Commander Marr, not Secretary Rumsfeld, is Padilla's custodian and the proper respondent to his habeas petition."

Impact

On November 17, 2005, Padilla and four others were indicted for conspiracy to murder, kidnap, and maim persons in a foreign country and conspiracy to provide material support for terrorists, among other charges. Three days later, President George W. Bush ordered that Padilla be turned over to the U.S. attorney general for the purpose of initiating criminal proceedings. Some people argued that Bush had abused presidential power in cases against suspected terrorists, though it was generally conceded that he had until 2006 used the power sparingly. On April 3, the U.S. Supreme Court declined to hear Padilla's appeal regarding Bush's authority to hold him as an enemy combatant.

CHAPTER 3

CHRONOLOGY

Included here are some of the key events regarding the history of immigration and immigration policy development in the United States.

1607

■ Jamestown (in modern-day Virginia) is founded, becoming the first permanent English settlement in the Americas.

1619

■ The first American legislative assembly meets at Jamestown.
■ The first shipload of African slaves to reach America lands at Jamestown.

1620

■ Pilgrims, diverted by weather from their original destination in Virginia, voyage to America on the *Mayflower* and establish the Plymouth Colony in Massachusetts.

1623

■ The Dutch West India Company begins settlement of the New Netherlands.

1630–40

■ 16,000 Puritans migrate to New England, establishing a religious and cultural foundation for the region.

1634

■ The colony of Maryland is founded by Lord Baltimore as a haven for English Roman Catholics.

Chronology

1642–49

- The English Civil War leads to a largely Puritan government under Oliver Cromwell and a larger Puritan influence in America.

1649

- The Maryland Toleration Act extends freedom of worship to all who accept the divinity of Christ.

1654

- The first Jewish immigrants in America arrive at New Amsterdam.

1660

- With the restoration of the Stuart monarchy, emigration from England is officially discouraged.

1663

- Eight loyal courtiers of Charles II are granted proprietary control of all lands between Virginia and Florida, and they establish the Carolina colonies.

1664

- English victories in the Anglo-Dutch wars lead to the transfer of New Netherlands to the English Crown, which is then divided into the colonies of New York and New Jersey.

1681

- Pennsylvania is founded by William Penn as a haven for Quakers and a "holy experiment" in religious toleration.

1683

- The first German settlers in America arrive in Pennsylvania.

1685

- Revocation of the Edict of Nantes by French emperor Louis XIV drives 15,000 Protestant French Huguenots into British North America.

1697

- The Royal African Company's monopoly ends, and the slave trade expands rapidly.

Immigration

1707
- The Act of Union between England and Scotland creates the new state of Great Britain.

1709
- A combination of religious persecution, high taxes, and poor crops drive thousands of Germans from the Palatinate.

1717
- Transportation of felons to the American colonies is authorized by the British Parliament, leading to the expulsion of rebellious Scots-Irish.

1718
- Parliament prohibits the emigration of skilled artisans from Great Britain.

1720
- The redemptioner trade becomes systematized, leading to widespread opportunities for emigration from Europe.

1727
- Pennsylvania requires alien immigrants to swear allegiance to the Crown upon their arrival.
- Religious persecution drives the first Amish settlers to Pennsylvania.

1730
- German and Scots-Irish immigrants from Pennsylvania begin to colonize the southern backcountry.

1732
- Georgia is founded as a penal colony for the "worthy" poor and also to serve as a buffer against expansion from Spanish Florida.

1740
- Parliament passes the Naturalization Act, conferring British citizenship on alien immigrants to America.

1745
- The Jacobite rebellion in Scotland is quelled, leading to the exodus of more rebellious Scots.

Chronology

1754

■ Conflict between Britain and France in the Ohio River valley leads to the French and Indian War.

1755

■ Acadians loyal to France are expelled from Nova Scotia; by 1760 some 4,000 have migrated to Louisiana, establishing "Cajun" culture there.

1756

■ The population of British America reaches 1.5 million.

1763

■ In western Pennsylvania, the Paxton Boys demand tax relief and money, expressing the concerns of many frontier settlers.

1768–71

■ The Regulator movement in North Carolina leads to small-scale civil war, as underrepresented frontier areas rise up against royal control.

1771–73

■ Depression in the Ulster linen trade leads to extensive Scots-Irish immigration to America.

1775

■ The British government suspends emigration as war breaks out in the American colonies.

1783

■ Some 80,000 United Empire Loyalists from the newly formed United States of America begin to immigrate to Canada.
■ Noah Webster's *American Spelling Book* introduces an Americanized system of spelling and goes on to be one of the best-selling books in American history.

1788

■ The U.S. Constitution is ratified, including Article 1, Section 8, empowering Congress "to establish a uniform Rule of Naturalization"; all powers regarding the administration of immigration are implicitly granted to Congress.

Immigration

1789

■ The outbreak of revolution in France leads to the exodus of 10,000 political refugees, including 3,000 African French Creoles who settle in Philadelphia.

1790

■ The U.S. Congress passes the Naturalization Act, imposing a two-year residency requirement for "free white" aliens of good moral character.
■ The first U.S. census counts 3.9 million people in the United States.

1791

■ A slave revolt in Santo Domingo leads to the establishment of the first black-controlled state in the Western Hemisphere in 1804.

1793

■ The Wars of the French Revolution begin; over the next 12 years, Napoleon redraws the boundaries of Europe, leading to the emigration of thousands.

1798

■ An unsuccessful Irish rebellion leads to more direct British control and the creation of the United Kingdom of Great Britain and Ireland in 1801.
■ U.S. Congress passes the Alien and Sedition Acts, raising residency requirements for naturalization and enhancing the president's power to expel alien residents.

1802

■ War between England and France resumes.
■ The Naturalization Act of 1790 is revised to require a five-year residency requirement.

1803

■ The British Passenger Act limits the number of immigrants that can be carried on transatlantic voyages.
■ Supreme Court chief justice John Marshall, in *Marbury v. Madison*, establishes the principal of judicial review, one of the few checks on Congress's power to regulate immigration.
■ President Thomas Jefferson purchases Louisiana from France, doubling the size of the country and providing huge tracts of good agricultural land that would attract immigrants into the 20th century.

Chronology

1807

- Congress prohibits the importation of African slaves into the United States.
- President Thomas Jefferson attempts to avert war with Great Britain by imposing an embargo on all ships leaving U.S. ports for foreign ports.

1814

- The Treaty of Ghent ends the War of 1812, leading to improved relations with Britain.

1818

- The Black Ball Line of sailing packets begins regular Liverpool–New York Service.

1819

- The Manifest of Immigrants Act requires numeration of immigrants and is the first U.S. measure to regulate immigration.

1825

- Great Britain repeals laws prohibiting emigration, leading to a major movement of immigrants from England and Ireland.

1830

- A Polish revolution leads to the immigration of lesser nobles and members of the intelligentsia from the Russian Empire.

1834

- The Ursuline Convent at Charlestown, Massachusetts, is burned in an outburst of anti-Catholic nativism.
- Samuel F. B. Morse, inventor of the telegraph, publishes his anti-Catholic diatribe, *A Foreign Conspiracy against the Liberties of the United States.*

1836

- Maria Monk's *Awful Disclosures of the Hôtel Dieu Nunnery of Montreal* heightens American nativist tendencies.
- The Republic of Texas gains independence from Mexico.

1837

- Financial panic in the United States undermines the economic situation of recently arrived immigrants.

- An abortive rebellion in Canada leads to greater British control.

1838

- The British Parliament passes the Irish Poor Law Act, establishing workhouse relief and some state-assisted emigration as a means for addressing overpopulation and poverty in Ireland.

1840

- The Cunard Line is founded, becoming one of the largest oceanic carriers of transatlantic immigrants.
- Congress requests census information on mental illness and "idiocy," categories that will later be used to exclude immigrants.

1844

- Anti-Catholic riots break out in Philadelphia, as nativist workers protest the depression of wages by Irish laborers.

1845

- Nativism finds political expression in the founding of the Native American Party.
- The Republic of Texas, with its large Hispanic population, joins the United States.

1845–49

- Potato famine in Ireland leads to a million deaths and the immigration of 1.7 million Irish to the United States by 1860.

1846

- Crop failures in Germany and Holland lead to further increases in immigration.

1848

- The Treaty of Guadalupe Hidalgo, ending the U.S.-Mexican War, guarantees citizenship to Mexican citizens remaining in territory ceded to the United States.
- In Germany revolution, crop failures, and religious persecution lead to the emigration of almost a million German speakers to the United States by 1860.

Chronology

- Emancipation of the peasants in Germany and Austria-Hungary provides greater legal opportunities for emigration.
- The collapse of the Young Ireland independence movement adds political motivations to Irish immigration.

1849

- The Supreme Court rules in the *Passenger* cases that states may exercise "police power" over immigrants but that the power of taxing them is that of Congress alone.

1851–64

- As many as 30 million Chinese are killed in the Taiping Rebellion, devastating southeastern China and driving thousands of Chinese to immigrate to North America.

1853

- Demonstrations in Cincinnati against papal legate Monsignor Bedini reflect growing anti-Catholic sentiment in the United States.

1854–56

- The nativist Know-Nothing political movement reaches its height.

1855

- The Carriage of Passengers Act codifies all existing measures relating to the transportation of immigrants, limiting the number of passengers per ship and requiring sanitary conditions and ample foodstuffs.
- The Castle Garden immigrant depot in New York City opens.

1856

- The Irish Catholic Colonization Convention is held in Buffalo, New York.

1857

- Financial panic in the United States heightens resentment against Irish workers.

1861–65

- The U.S. Civil War ends slavery, brings immigration to a standstill, and serves as a training ground for Irish nationalists.

Immigration

1862

■ The Homestead Act provides 160 acres of free land to settlers who improve the land and remain there for five years, spurring immigration and westward migration.

1864

■ The Immigration Act legalizes contract labor and encourages immigration as a means of developing the country.

1868

■ Ratification of the Fourteenth Amendment to the Constitution guarantees citizenship, due process, and equal protection before the law to all persons born or naturalized in the United States.

1870

■ Congress passes the Naturalization Act, granting citizenship rights to "persons of African descent."

1871–77

■ Irish-Catholic Molly Maguires attack and intimidate mine owners in eastern Pennsylvania coalfields.

1875

■ The Page Act, prohibiting the importation of prostitutes, alien convicts, and forced laborers from Asia, is the first U.S. legislation to directly regulate the influx of immigrants.

1882

■ Congress passes an Immigration Act establishing a head tax of 50 cents per immigrant and extending Page Act exclusions to include "lunatics, idiots," or any person likely to become a public charge.
■ The Chinese Exclusion Act ends the era of open immigration and is the first immigration legislation to exclude a specific ethnic group.
■ Anti-Semitic pogroms in Russia lead to widespread immigration to the United States.

1885

■ The Foran Act (Alien Contract Labor Act) prohibits the importation of contract labor and assesses fines on employers and ship captains.

Chronology

1886

- The Statue of Liberty is dedicated in New York City and becomes the most visible symbol of the personal freedoms that attracted most immigrants.
- The Haymarket Riot in Chicago rekindles nativist fears of foreign radicalism.

1887

- The secret, anti-Catholic American Protective Association is founded.

1889

- Jane Addams opens Hull House in Chicago in order to assist the urban poor.

1890

- The superintendent of the Census suggests the disappearance of the American frontier.

1891

- The federal government formally assumes supervision of the immigration process.

1892

- Ellis Island opens, becoming the first major federal immigration reception facility.
- Financial panic in the United States leads to a rise in nativism.

1894

- The Immigration Restriction League is organized, and it proposes a literacy test for the purpose of restricting immigration.

1894–95

- The American Protective Association reaches its peak of influence, though a reviving economy and popular politics soon make it difficult to be openly hostile toward Catholics.

1894–96

- Massacres in the Ottoman Empire drive 100,000 Armenians to immigrate to the United States.

Immigration

1903

■ Congress passes an immigration act, expanding the list of excluded immigrants to include polygamists, anarchists, and other radicals.

1905

■ The Japanese and Korean Exclusion League is organized.

1906

■ The American Jewish Committee is formed to protect Jewish civil rights around the world.

1907

■ Congress passes an Immigration Act raising the head tax on immigrants and adding to the excluded list persons with physical or mental defects that might affect their ability to earn a living, those with tuberculosis, and children unaccompanied by their parents.
■ The United States and Japan diffuse tensions through a series of accords known as the Gentlemen's Agreement, voluntarily restricting immigration from Japan.

1908

■ The Immigrants' Protective League is founded by Hull-House progressives.

1910

■ The Angel Island Immigrant Detention Center is established in San Francisco for processing most west coast immigrants.

1911

■ The Dillingham Commission Report reinforces the idea that immigrants from eastern and southern Europe are less desirable than those from northern and western Europe and recommends a literacy test as the best means of screening immigrants.

1912

■ Mary Antin publishes the autobiographical *The Promised Land*, ardently supporting immigrant conformity to Anglo societal norms.

1913

■ The California legislature passes the Alien Land Act, prohibiting non-citizens from owning land in California.

Chronology

1914–18

- World War I leads to the displacement of millions and the breakup of the multinational Austro-Hungarian, Ottoman, and Russian empires.

1916

- Madison Grant publishes *The Passing of the Great Race in America*, utilizing eugenics to encourage nativist opposition to immigration.

1917

- Congress passes the Literacy Act, prohibiting entry to aliens over 16 years of age who could not read 30–40 words in their own language.

1917–22

- A temporary labor program brings 80,000 Mexican laborers to the American Southwest.

1919

- Fear of radical communist and anarchist elements following the Bolshevik Revolution in Russia leads to a Red Scare and the arrest of 4,000 suspects and the deportation of 200.

1921

- Congress passes the Emergency Quota Act, setting a limit on European immigration of approximately 358,000, with national quotas based on a formula allowing each nation 3 percent of foreign-born persons of that nationality who lived in the United States in 1910.

1922

- In *Ozawa v. United States*, the U.S. Supreme Court rules that Japanese immigrants cannot become naturalized citizens because they are not white.

1923

- In *United States v. Bhaghat Singh Thind*, the U.S. Supreme Court rules that Asian Indians cannot become naturalized citizens because they are not commonly perceived to be "white."

1924

- Congress passes the Johnson-Reed Act (Immigration Act of 1924, National Origins Act), establishing annual quotas of all nationalities at 2 percent the number of foreign-born of each nationality resident in the United States according to the 1890 census.

1927

- The Johnson-Reed Act quota is replaced with the national origins provision, basing each nationality quota on its proportion of the population according to the 1920 census. Proportions are based on a figure of 153,714 annually from Europe.
- The Oriental Exclusion Act bans most immigration from Asia.
- The U.S. Border Patrol is established.

1929

- The provisions of the Johnson-Reed Act become operative.
- The stock-market crash ruins the economy and dramatically undermines immigration throughout the 1930s.

1930

- President Herbert Hoover directs consuls to enforce strictly the provisions of the immigration acts barring "those likely to become a public charge."

1933

- Adolf Hitler becomes German chancellor and begins an escalating anti-Semitic campaign.

1934

- Congress passes the Tydings-McDuffie Act, granting the Philippines commonwealth status, promising independence within 10 years, and limiting Filipino immigration to 50 per year.

1937

- Japan invades China, initiating World War II in Asia.

1939

- Germany invades Poland, initiating World War II in Europe.

1940

- Congress passes the Alien Registration Act, requiring registration of all aliens over 14 years of age in the United States.

Chronology

1941

- Japanese aircraft attack the U.S. naval base at Pearl Harbor, Hawaii, leading to a U.S. declaration of war against Japan.

1942

- President Franklin D. Roosevelt issues Executive Order 9066, leading to the forcible internment of 120,000 Japanese Americans between 1942 and December 1944.
- The United States and Mexico agree to the Emergency Farm Labor Program (Bracero [U.S. laborer] Program), permitting Mexican farm laborers to legally work in the United States; eventually, more than 5 million enter the country legally and several million more illegally.

1943

- Clashes, known as the "zoot-suit" riots, between U.S. servicemen and Hispanic citizens of Los Angeles demonstrate ethnic tensions in the country.
- Congress repeals the Chinese Exclusion Act and, with it, the ban on Chinese immigration.

1944

- In *United States v. Korematsu*, the U.S. Supreme Court upholds the constitutionality of Japanese internment.

1945

- World War II ends and prisoners in Nazi death and labor camps are liberated.
- Congress passes the War Brides Act, facilitating the entry of more than 150,000 alien wives, husbands, and children of members of the U.S. armed forces.

1946

- Congress passes the Luce-Cellar Act, allowing Filipinos and Asian Indians to become naturalized citizens of the United States.
- Congress amends the War Brides Act to allow alien fiancées to enter the United States under certain conditions.

1948

- Congress passes the Displaced Persons Act, allowing the entrance of 220,000 displaced persons in addition to those admitted under the annual quotas.
- The new state of Israel is created.

Immigration

1950

- Congress amends the Displaced Persons Act, adding 134,000 to the numbers that may be admitted under its provisions.
- Congress passes the Internal Security Act, barring admission to foreign communists or anyone involved in activities "which would be prejudicial to the public interest."

1952

- Congress passes the McCarran-Walter Act (Immigration and Naturalization Act), eliminating race as a bar to immigration and naturalization; reaffirming the national origins system with quotas; providing more thorough screening of immigrants; and establishing preference for those with relatives in America or those with work-related skills.

1953

- Congress passes the Refugee Relief Act, authorizing the admission of 205,000 special non-quota refugees.

1954

- Ellis Island closes after 62 years, with more than 12 million immigrants having passed through its gates.
- Operation Wetback leads to the repatriation of undocumented workers to Mexico.

1956

- Soviet repression of the revolution in Hungary leads to the immigration of 36,000 Hungarians to the United States.

1957

- Congress passes the Refugee-Escape Act, liberalizing provisions of the McCarran-Walter Act and allowing more non-quota immigrants to enter the United States.

1959

- Fidel Castro gains control of Cuba, consolidating his power through the Communist Party and leading to the emigration of more than 700,000 Cubans by the mid-1960s.

1960

- Congress passes the World Refugee Year Law, permitting the entrance of additional refugees.

Chronology

1961

■ Cuban émigrés assisted by the United States unsuccessfully attempt to invade Cuba at the Bay of Pigs.

1962

■ Congress passes the Migration and Refugee Assistance Act, facilitating the admission of refugees.
■ A Soviet attempt to place nuclear weapons in Cuba leads to a U.S. blockade and the threat of a nuclear exchange.

1964

■ The Emergency Farm Labor Program (Bracero Program) is terminated.
■ The Gulf of Tonkin incident leads to widespread U.S. military involvement in Vietnam, lasting until withdrawal in 1975.

1965

■ Congress passes the Immigration Act, abolishing the national origins system; establishing a limit of 170,000 outside the Western Hemisphere while placing a limit of 20,000 on any one country; admitting immigrants on a first-come, first-qualified basis; establishing preferences for close relatives as well as refugees and those with occupational skills needed in the United States; and placing a ceiling of 120,000 on immigration from the Western Hemisphere.

1970

■ The U.S. Census for the first time asks people of Hispanic or Spanish descent to identify themselves.

1975

■ A communist regime is established in Vietnam, as the U.S. military withdraws; 125,000 refugees, including most top political and military figures and their families, are brought to the United States.

1975–81

■ Hundreds of thousands of "boat people" flee Vietnam, with almost 250,000 arriving in the United States via Thailand, Malaysia, or Indonesia.

1976

■ Congress extends the limit of 20,000 immigrants per country to the Western Hemisphere and establishes a modified preference system for the hemisphere.

Immigration

1978

- Congress establishes a single worldwide ceiling of 290,000 for the admission of immigrants and a uniform preference system.
- Congress creates a Select Commission on Immigration and Refugee Policy to study and evaluate existing immigration policy.

1979

- The Orderly Departure Program is established to enable Vietnamese immigrants to leave Vietnam legally.

1980

- The Mariel Boatlift occurs, in which Fidel Castro allows 125,000 emigrants to leave Cuba for the United States, including 24,000 with criminal records.
- Congress passes the Refugee Act of 1980, increasing the number of refugees from 17,400 to 50,000 annually and the total annual immigration to 320,000; it defines *refugee* to include persons from any part of the world and not just the Middle East or communist countries and also creates the office of U.S. Coordinator for Refugee Affairs.

1982

- In *Plyler v. Doe*, the Supreme Court rules that states cannot deny public education to aliens based on their parents' immigrant status.

1986

- Congress passes the Immigration Reform and Control Act, prohibiting employers from knowingly employing undocumented aliens, granting amnesty to those residing illegally in the United States since 1982, and providing for the admission of temporary farm workers.

1988

- The Civil Liberties Act provides a monetary compensation of $20,000 and a presidential apology to surviving Japanese Americans interred during World War II.

1990

- The Immigration Act increases annual immigration to 700,000, excluding refugees, until 1995, when the limit becomes 675,000.
- The Ellis Island immigration station reopens as the National Immigration Museum.

Chronology

1992

- The Chinese Student Protection Act permits Chinese students in the United States between June 1989 and April 1990 to adjust to immigrant status.

1994

- The North American Free Trade Agreement reduces tariffs on trade between the United States, Canada, and Mexico and guarantees business rights among the countries.

1995

- California voters approve Proposition 187, denying public education, welfare, and nonemergency health-care services to illegal aliens; most of its provisions are declared unconstitutional by the courts.

1996

- Congress passes the Illegal Immigration Reform and Immigrant Responsibility Act, strengthening border defenses, easing restrictions on deportation, and tightening procedures for granting asylum.
- Congress passes the Personal Responsibility and Work Opportunity Act (Welfare Reform Act), denying most welfare benefits to noncitizens.

1998

- Congress passes the Agricultural Research, Extension, and Education Reform Act and the Noncitizen Benefit Clarification and Other Technical Amendments Act, restoring some public benefits previously denied to noncitizens.

2000

- *January–June:* Cuba and the United States wage an international legal battle over the child Elián González, who in the previous year had escaped to the United States via raft with his mother, who had died in the process.
- *February:* The American Federation of Labor and Congress of Industrial Organizations reverses its position on immigration, supporting the Restoration of Fairness in Immigration Act.
- *December:* Congress passes the Legal Immigration and Family Equity Act and the Child Citizenship Act, both ameliorating some of the harsher provisions of the restrictive legislation of 1996.

2001

- *September 11:* Terrorists attack New York City and Washington, D.C., killing almost 3,000.

Immigration

- *October 26:* President George W. Bush signs the USA PATRIOT Act into law, providing sweeping measures for protecting borders and monitoring potential terrorists.

2002

- *March:* September 11 hijackers Mohamed Atta and Marwan al-Shehhi posthumously receive notice from the Immigration and Naturalization Service that they have been approved for student visas.

2003

- *March 1:* The newly established Department of Homeland Security becomes operational, taking over most immigration administration and services from the Immigration and Naturalization Service, which is disbanded.
- *April 25:* The Bureau of Citizenship and Immigration Services grants asylum to Mohammed Odeh al-Rehaief, an Iraqi citizen who assisted U.S. Marines in rescuing Private Jessica Lynch.

2004

- The illegal immigrant population in the United States tops 10 million.

2005

- *November 28:* President George W. Bush proposes comprehensive immigration reform based upon tightening borders and creating a temporary guest-worker program with Mexico.
- *December 17:* President George W. Bush signs the Intelligence Reform and Terrorism Prevention Act, strengthening passport requirements for travel in the Western Hemisphere, adding 10,000 new border patrol agents, and increasing by 40,000 the number of detention beds available for housing aliens awaiting detention.
- More than 870,000 foreign students are tracked through the Student and Exchange Visitor Information System (SEVIS) database.

2006

- *March 31:* U.S. Senate opens debate on comprehensive revision of immigration policy.
- *April 7:* Compromise immigration bill that would legalize millions of illegal immigrants fails in the U.S. House of Representatives.
- *April 20:* President George W. Bush unveils a new strategy targeting companies employing illegal immigrants.

Chronology

- *April 26:* U.S. Senate approves $2 billion appropriation to stop illegal immigration
- *May 1:* "A Day Without Immigrants" protests draw more than a million immigrant rights supports across the United States.
- *May 15:* President George W. Bush addresses the nation, discussing his plan for comprehensive immigration reform.
- *July–August:* Congressional field hearings on immigration are held in California, Texas, and Arizona.
- *September 19:* The House of Representatives passes a measure authorizing the construction of a 700-mile border fence between the United States and Mexico.

CHAPTER 4

BIOGRAPHICAL LISTING

This chapter consists of brief profiles of key men and women who helped shape American attitudes toward immigration, crafted American immigration policy, and assisted immigrants who came to the United States.

Grace Abbot (1878–1939), social reformer who worked extensively to improve government services to urban immigrants. She served as secretary of the Immigrants Protective League, secretary of Massachusetts Immigration Commission, director of the Illinois State Immigrants Commission, and head of the Children's Bureau of U.S. Department of Labor. She also taught public-welfare administration at the University of Chicago's School of Social Service from 1934 to 1939.

Jane Addams (1860–1935), social reformer, founder of Hull House, and the first woman to be awarded the Nobel Peace Prize (1931). Based upon her observations of Toynbee Hall in London, Addams and Ellen Gates Starr established Hull House in Chicago in 1889, a settlement house enabling middle–class women to help impoverished West Side women. She helped establish the Immigrants Protective League in 1908. A committed suffragist, she supported Theodore Roosevelt's Progressive Party in 1912. Addams was active in the international peace movement and served as president of the Women's International League for Peace and Freedom from 1919 to 1935.

Mary Antin (1881–1949), Russian immigrant and author who argued for immigrant conformity to Anglo social norms. After immigrating to the United States in 1894, Antin quickly learned English and began to support Progressive measures. Her books include *From Plotzk to Boston* (1899) and her memoir *The Promised Land* (1912), which was serialized in the *Atlantic Monthly*.

John Ashcroft (1942–), U.S. attorney general (2000–05) who worked hand in hand with President George W. Bush in the wake of the September 11 attacks to create more secure American borders, often at the expense of previous immigrant privileges. After a distinguished career in Missouri as auditor, attorney general, governor, and U.S. senator, Ashcroft was appointed U.S. attorney general by Bush in 2000. As a senator, he was active on the Senate Judiciary Committee, and as attorney general, he vigorously promoted new immigration regulations that would expedite hearings, particularly those related to removal proceedings. Ashcroft was a leading proponent of the USA PATRIOT Act and creation of the Department of Homeland Security.

Emily Greene Balch (1867–1961), educator and social reformer. After earning her B.A. from Bryn Mawr and completing postgraduate work at Harvard Annex, the University of Chicago, and the University of Berlin, she joined the faculty of Wellesley College (1896–1918). Balch worked widely for progressive reform, most notably for world peace, helping to found the Women's International League for Peace and Freedom in 1919; she shared the Nobel Peace Prize with John R. Mott in 1946. Her academic specialty was Slavic immigration, and she notably published *Our Slavic Fellow Citizens* (1910).

Lyman Beecher (1775–1863), evangelical Presbyterian minister. As president of Lane Seminary (1832–52), he spoke out vigorously against Catholicism and in favor of government limitations on certain types of immigration. Although he urged respect for "industrious foreigners," he wanted "an immediate and energetic supervision" of the government "to check the influx of immigrant paupers, thrown upon our shores by the governments of Europe, corrupting our morals, quadrupling our taxation, and endangering the peace of our cities, and of our nation."

Irving Berlin (1888–1989), composer who helped establish popular music in the early technological age and reflected assimilationist tendencies among immigrants prior to WWII. Born Israel Baline in Temun, Russia, Berlin immigrated to the United States with his family at age four and began singing and playing in New York City bars and restaurants. Becoming famous principally as a composer in the 1920s and 1930s, he reached his peak of popularity with musical scores and lyrics for both Broadway and Hollywood. Among his most famous works are "Alexander's Ragtime Band," "God Bless America," and scores for *Annie Get Your Gun, In Your Easter Bonnet,* and *White Christmas.*

Franz Boas (1858–1942), anthropologist and educator who combined anthropology, ethnology, archaeology, and linguistics to reject contemporary eugenic theories of race. Born in Germany, he immigrated to the United States in 1886, most notably making his mark as a professor at Columbia University. Boas demonstrated that the restrictive immigration legislation of the 1920s was founded upon false assumptions regarding the ability of peoples to assimilate. His principal books included *The Mind of Primitive Man* (1911), *Anthropology and Modern Life* (1928), and *Race, Language and Culture* (1940).

Immigration

Evangeline Cory Booth (1865–1950), social reformer and general of the International Salvation Army who helped transplant the organization from its birthplace in England to the United States. The daughter of Salvation Army founder William Booth, Evangeline began preaching at age 17. After serving as commander of the Salvation Army in Canada (1895–1904), Booth became commander in the United States (1904–34) and, eventually, international general (1934–39). A gifted organizer, Booth promoted a Salvation Army presence on Ellis Island to help protect newly arrived immigrants from being taken advantage of, and she generally promoted their welfare once they had arrived in American cities.

Pat Buchanan (1938–), political commentator, presidential candidate, and founder of The American Cause. After representing the right-wing of the Republican Party in the Richard Nixon, Gerald Ford, and Ronald Reagan administrations, Buchanan unsuccessfully campaigned for the presidential nomination in 1992 and 1996, in large part on a commitment to policies encouraging self-reliance, limited government, and legal immigration based upon assimilation and national unity. Through his political organizations, he continues to argue that the United States' ability to assimilate immigrants has been overwhelmed since 1966 and that "if America is to survive as one nation, we must stem this tide to mend the melting pot and assimilate the 28 million foreign-born already living within our borders."

George Walker Bush (1946–), 43rd president of the United States (2001–09). Son of George Herbert Walker Bush (41st president of the United States), Bush took an M.B.A. from Harvard Business School in 1975 and founded an oil and gas exploration company. He was twice elected governor of Texas (1994, 1998), in which capacity he developed a close relationship with Mexican president Vicente Fox. After the terrorist attacks of September 11, 2001, he worked vigorously to tighten access through U.S. borders, most notably through creation of a new Department of Homeland Security and a restructuring of immigration services within the new department. Early in 2005 Bush proposed a guest-worker program that became central to the broader issue of immigration reform, still being debated by Congress during the summer of 2006.

Frances Xavier Cabrini (1850–1917), Roman Catholic nun and missionary. Born in Italy, Cabrini founded the Missionaries of the Sacred Heart (1880). She immigrated in 1889 to minister to Italian immigrants. Her wide-ranging efforts included work in education, health care, orphanages, and ministry to immigrant families and prisons. She was known as "Mother Cabrini"; Pope Pius XII proclaimed her patroness of immigrants. She was canonized in 1946, becoming the first American saint.

Abraham Cahan (1860–1951), journalist and immigrant organizer. Born in Podberezya, Russia, Cahan immigrated to New York City in 1882, where he founded the influential *Jewish Daily Forward* (1897). Cahan was also a teacher, and he participated in socialist and union politics. He was a highly respected novelist, known for his depictions of Jewish life in America. His most famous works were *Yekl: A Tale of the New York Ghetto* (1896) and *The Rise of David Levinsky* (1917).

Andrew Carnegie (1835–1919), immigrant and industrialist. Carnegie immigrated to the United States from Scotland in 1848 and eventually created the largest iron and steel works in the world. With the ultimate rags to-riches story, he suggested to many Americans the value of full assimilation, and the risk in allowing too many immigrants from outside western Europe. Known for his philanthropy, Carnegie eventually provided hundreds of millions of dollars for a variety of humanitarian purposes.

Jimmy Carter Jr. (1924–), 39th president of the United States (1977–81). After a career in the U.S. Navy, Carter was elected to the Georgia Senate in 1962 and became governor in 1970. Following the Watergate scandal, he was elected to the presidency as a Washington outsider. With Congress he established the Select Commission on Immigration and Refugee Policy, whose recommendations eventually led to provisions of the Immigration Reform and Control Act (1986). In retirement he worked actively on humanitarian and refugee issues.

Cesar Chavez (1927–93), social activist and labor leader who became the most visible spokesman for the rights of migrant farm workers during the 1960s and 1970s. A second-generation Mexican whose family had emigrated from Chihuahua in 1888, his family was displaced by the Great Depression, becoming migrant farm workers. During the 1950s, he worked with the Community Services Organization. By 1958 he became actively involved in labor organization and in 1962 founded the Farm Workers Association (FWA). Chavez gained national prominence in 1965 when he led the FWA into a Delano, California, grape workers' strike that had been initiated by the Agricultural Workers Organizing Committee on behalf of Filipino laborers. Although he remained active in the 1970s, he was increasingly attacked by members of the Hispanic community for his opposition to employment of both legal and illegal Mexican labor.

William Jefferson Clinton (Bill Clinton) (1946–), 42nd president of the United States (1993–2001). Clinton made his reputation in Arkansas politics, serving as Arkansas attorney general and governor (elected in 1982, 1984, 1988). He was elected U.S. president in 1992 and reelected in 1996. During his administration, Clinton opposed the harsher provisions of the Illegal Immigration Reform and Immigrant Responsibility Act (1996); supported the Nicaraguan Adjustment and Central American Relief Act; and generally favored pluralistic multiculturalism.

John Rogers Commons (1862–1945), economist and political activist who provided a wide range of data to the U.S. government and other

119

Immigration

organizations concerned with the economic impact of immigration. He wrote a report on immigration for the U.S. Industrial Commission (1902–04) and edited numerous volumes for *A Documentary History of American Industrial Society* (1910–11) and the *History of Labor in the United States* (1918). His *Races and Immigrants in America* (1907) supported the idea that immigrant assimilation was unlikely, thus contributing to the restrictive legislation of the 1920s.

William Paul Dillingham (1843–1923), Republican senator from Vermont who chaired an important government commission (commonly known as the Dillingham Commission) to study immigration, launched in 1907 at the peak of the wave of immigration from eastern and southern Europe. As part of the Immigration Act of 1907, the commission was established to evaluate U.S. immigration policy. In 1911 the full, 42-volume report of the commission was published, clarifying the now commonplace assumption that the "new immigration" from the early 1880s was marked by an increase in transient laborers that resisted assimilation. Under Dillingham's guidance, the committee recommended a wide range of immigration restrictions, including a literacy test.

Albert Einstein (1879–1955), scientist and pacifist who represented to many the ongoing benefit of a relatively open policy of immigration. Born in Ulm, Germany, he became one of the most brilliant scientists of his day, winning the Nobel Prize in Physics in 1921. In 1933, during a visit to the United States, he announced that he would not return to Nazi Germany, where his Jewish ethnicity and Zionist politics were unwelcome. Einstein's warnings helped spur the U.S. nuclear development program.

Henry Ford (1863–1947), entrepreneur and founder of Ford Motor Company who became almost as well known for his anti-Semitism as for his engineering and business achievements. Born in Greenfield, Michigan, Ford was apprenticed to a machinist at age 15 and produced his first gas-powered car in 1893. In 1903 he founded the Ford Motor Company, pioneering the assembly line process and making the automobile affordable to the masses. Because he generally paid his workers above scale, he often found himself at odds with other industry and governmental leaders, including President Franklin D. Roosevelt. Ford's belief that the "international Jew" was at the heart of world conflict led him to purchase the *Dearborn Independent* (1919), where he began to run a series of articles outlining their activities. His articles, reflective of a common xenophobia of the time, enjoyed wide circulation in newspapers, pamphlets, and books.

Marcus Garvey (1887–1940), political activist who was one of the earliest exponents of African racial consciousness. Leaving his Jamaican home in 1907, he traveled widely and gained a strong sense of the potential unity within the African diaspora. In 1914 he formed the Universal Negro Improvement Association, and two years later, he established a branch in

New York City. Believing that blacks would never be treated justly in pre-dominantly white societies, he urged them to return to Africa, where they could create "a place in the sun." Garvey was charged with fraud in 1922 in connection with the financing of the Black Star Line of ships designed to take blacks back to Africa. After President Calvin Coolidge commuted his sentence in 1927, Garvey was deported to his homeland.

Nathan Glazer (1923–), sociologist and one of America's leading schol-ars of race and ethnicity. After working briefly in the John F. Kennedy administration, he was a professor of education and sociology at Har-vard University (1968–93), and from 1973 to 2002, he was coeditor of *The Public Interest.* Although initially supportive of President Lyndon Johnson's Great Society programs, he became progressively disenchanted with them, writing the scathing *Affirmative Discrimination: Ethnic Inequal-ity and Public Policy* (1975). Other books include *Beyond the Melting Pot* (coauthored with Daniel Patrick Moynihan, 1963), *American Judaism* (1956), *Ethnicity: Theory and Practice* (1975), *Ethnic Dilemmas* (1985), *The New Immigrants: A Challenge to American Society* (1988), and *We Are All Multiculturalists Now* (1997).

Emma Goldman (1869–1940), anarchist and radical activist who came to represent to many Americans the potential danger of unlimited immi-gration from eastern and southern Europe. Born in Kovno, Lithuania, to Jewish parents, she emigrated to the United States in 1885 and soon became active in anarchist politics, founding and editing the principal an-archist journal, *Mother Earth* (1906–17). Active in many kinds of reform, including campaigns for better conditions in American slums, she never-theless was suspect to the U.S. government. In 1917 she was imprisoned for opposing military registration, and two years later, she was deported to the Soviet Union. After her return in 1924, she continued to support anarchist causes, including their interests in the Spanish Civil War (1936–39). Her published works include *Anarchism and Other Essays* (1910), *My Disillusionment in Russia* (1923), and *Living My Life* (1931).

Samuel Gompers (1850–1924), labor union leader who represented for many Americans the potential for responsible assimilation among im-migrant workers. Born in London to working-class Jews of Dutch de-scent, Gompers immigrated to the United States in 1863 and was soon apprenticed as a cigarmaker. He was elected president of a local cigar makers' union in New York City during the depression of the 1870s and remained committed to labor organization for the rest of his life. He was elected first president of the American Federation of Labor in 1886 and served almost continuously in that position (1886–94, 1896–1924) until his death. His organizational techniques favored skilled workers, and he tended to oppose high rates of immigration, fearing they would drive down the standard of living for workers.

Immigration

Madison Grant (1865–1937), naturalist and author who wrote one of the most influential anti-immigrant works in American history, reflecting the xenophobia of many Americans in the second decade of the 20th century. Born into a wealthy family, Grant was educated at Yale and Columbia and opened a law practice. He devoted most of his time, however, to hunting and high society. As an authority on North American wildlife, he was on the committee selected to establish the New York Zoological Society and long served as its secretary (1895–1924). Though not trained as an expert on race or ethnicity, in 1916 he published *The Passing of the Great Race*, which argued that the Nordic race, "domineering, individualistic, self-reliant and jealous of their personal freedom," was clearly superior to other races. Opposing a policy of open immigration, he warned that "if the Melting Pot is allowed to boil without control . . . the type of native American of Colonial descent will become as extinct as the Athenian of the age of Pericles, and the Viking of the days of Rollo."

Oscar Handlin (1915–), historian who was one of the most influential scholars of immigration, both in terms of his own writings and that of his students. Born in Brooklyn, New York, to immigrant Ukrainian Jews, he was attracted early to history and received his Ph.D. from Harvard in 1940 and began teaching there the previous year (1939–86). His most famous book, *The Uprooted* (1951), won the Pulitzer Prize in 1952. By the 1960s, scholars focusing on the process of assimilation had already dismantled many of Handlin's conclusions, which stressed the alienation of immigrants, though his work served as an important stimulus for further research. Among his other works are *Commonwealth* (1947), *Boston's Immigrants, 1790–1865* (1941), *Adventure in Freedom: 300 Years of Jewish Life in America* (1954), *Race and Nationality in American Life* (1957), *The Newcomers—Negroes and Puerto Ricans in a Changing Metropolis* (1959), and *The Dimensions of Liberty* (1961), *Liberty in America* (1986), and *Truth in History* (1998). One of his students, Stephan A. Thernstrom, edited *The Harvard Encyclopedia of American Ethnic Groups* (1980), for which Handlin served as consulting editor.

Samuel Ichiye Hayakawa (S. I. Hayakawa) (1906–92), U.S. senator from California who was best known for his movement to make English the official language of the United States. Born in Vancouver, British Columbia, to Japanese immigrant parents, Samuel Ichiye Hayakawa immigrated to the United States to attend the University of Wisconsin. After several teaching positions in English and semantics, in 1955 he became a naturalized U.S. citizen and a faculty member at San Francisco State College, eventually rising to become its president in 1968. Hayakawa was elected to the U.S. Senate as a Republican in 1976. Arguing that "bilingualism for the individual is fine, but not for a country," Hayakawa introduced the English Language Amendment in support of a common official language.

Biographical Listing

He served as honorary chairman of the organization U.S. English until his death and was special adviser to the Secretary of State for East Asian and Pacific Affairs from 1983 to 1990. His best-known book on semantics is *Language in Thought and Action* (1949, 5th edition: 1991).

Lewis Wickes Hine (1874–1940), photographer who visually chronicled the immigrant experience from Ellis Island to immigrants' work and life in urban America. Born in Oshkosh, Wisconsin, he studied sociology in Chicago and New York and spent much of the first decade of the 20th century photographing immigrant life in New York City. Between 1908 and 1915, he became a pioneering photojournalist, clandestinely producing photographic evidence of child labor practices. At the end of World War I, he began to photograph refugees for the American Red Cross. During the 1930s, much of his work focused on the effects of the Great Depression.

Dolores Fernández Huerta (1930–), migrant labor activist best known for her work in founding and organizing agricultural laborers in California. Born in Dawson, New Mexico, Huerta became involved in the Latino Community Service Organization in 1955 after moving to Stockton, California. She was instrumental in lobbying for the end of what she called the "captive labor" system of the Bracero Program (1962). In 1962 she joined Cesar Chavez in organizing the National Farm Workers Association (later the United Farm Workers). She remained active in labor politics into the 1990s.

John Joseph Hughes (1797–1864), Roman Catholic archbishop of New York and a passionate exponent of Irish assimilation in America. Immigrating from County Tyrone in northern Ireland in 1817, Hughes worked vigorously to combat anti-Catholic prejudice against Irish immigrants who began to arrive in large numbers during the 1840s and 1850s. Concerned about the Protestant influence in schools, Hughes played a large part in establishing a Catholic system of education. He promoted organizations such as the Irish Emigrant Society, the Emigrant Savings Bank, and the Ancient Order of Hibernians, arguing that naturalized citizens should assimilate to become patriotic Americans. Nevertheless his efforts to provide cradle-to-grave services within the Catholic Church tended to preserve Irish group identity. He was perhaps most influential in heightening the role of the Irish clergy in the Roman Catholic Church in the United States.

Thomas Jefferson (1743–1826), third president of the United States (1801–09), who was deeply concerned about immigration and did as much as anyone to foster it by doubling the size of the United States with the purchase of the Louisiana territory from France in 1803. Jefferson began to write on immigration as early as 1774, publishing a pamphlet entitled *A Summary View of the Rights of British America*, in which he argued for the right of one to leave his country for another. According to Jefferson, his ancestors "possessed a right which nature has given to all men, of departing from the country in which chance, not choice, has placed them, of going in quest of new habitations, and of there establishing new societies." Many of Jefferson's ideas from the Declaration of Independence influenced immigration law generally. In public office in both the Commonwealth of Virginia and the federal government of the United States, Jefferson was ambivalent about immigration. From a theoretical point of view, he believed in the right of migration, though practically he was concerned about an influx of non-Anglo settlers.

Mary Harris Jones (Mother Jones) (1830–1930), socialist, labor activist, and one of the staunchest defenders of immigrant laborers. Born in County Cork, Ireland, her family migrated to Toronto, Canada, in 1838. She immigrated to the United States in 1859. Her husband and four young children died of yellow fever in 1867, leading her back into the workforce as a seamstress. It was during this period that she developed an interest in the working classes. "Often while sewing for the lords and barons," she observed, "I would look out of the plate glass windows and see the poor, shivering wretches, jobless and hungry, walking alongside the frozen lake front. . . . The contrast of their condition with that of the tropical comfort of the people for whom I sewed was painful to me. My employers seemed neither to notice nor to care." In 1871 she lost all her belongings in the great Chicago fire. Soon after she began attending meetings of the Knights of Labor and in 1877 first assisted strikers in Pittsburgh. In 1890 she began working as an organizer for the United Mine Workers. Throughout the remainder of her life, she was involved with many labor movements, including the Pullman strike of 1894, the West Viriginia coal strikes of 1912–13, and the Colorado miners' strike of 1913–14. She helped found the Social Democratic Party (1898) and the Industrial Workers of the World (1905). Well into her 90s, "Mother Jones," as she came to be known, was still actively supporting strikes and organizing workers.

Denis Kearney (1847–1907), labor organizer and the public face of the anti-Chinese campaign that flourished in the American West during the 1870s. Born in County Cork, Ireland, Kearney came to San Francisco as a seaman in 1868. He quit the sea in 1872, developing a hauling business, and he soon became involved with the Draymen and Teamster's Union. Speaking on behalf of the "intelligent American laborer" trying to make it during the depression of 1873–77, Kearney began to work with the Workingmen's Party to rid California of Chinese labor "as soon as possible, and by all the means in our power." Successful in promoting a new state constitution in which Chinese would be excluded, the Workingmen were nevertheless defeated by U.S. constitutional protections embodied in the Fourteenth Amendment. Kearney's agitation had raised the consciousness of the nation, however, leading to passage of the Chinese Exclusion Act of 1882, the first American legislation aimed at a specific immigrant group.

Edward M. Kennedy (Ted Kennedy) (1932–), U.S. senator and one of the most influential members of Congress regarding immigration legislation in the period after 1960. Born into a Massachusetts political dynasty that included a U.S. president (John F. Kennedy) and U.S. attorney general (Robert F. Kennedy), Edward had plenty of help from his older brothers. First taking his seat in January 1963, just 11 months before his oldest brother was assassinated, Kennedy made it part of his mission to complete the work of the president, speaking vigorously in favor of the Civil Rights Bill and the Hart-Celler Immigration Bill. Ted Kennedy became floor manager of the latter bill, successfully seeing the complicated measure through the Senate. It formed the basis for the Immigration and Naturalization Act of 1965, which ended national quotas. Because the new measure did not include specific provisions for refugees, Kennedy continued to press the matter as chair of the Subcommittee on Refugees. His efforts eventually led to passage of the Indochina Migration and Refugee Assistance Act (1975) and the Refugee Act (1980). The latter measure brought the U.S. definition of "refugee" into conformity with that of the United Nations and created a separate category in the admissions process. Kennedy was also instrumental in gaining passage for the diversity lottery, embodied in the Immigration Reform and Control Act (1986).

John Fitzgerald Kennedy (1917–63), 35th president of the United States (1961–63). After serving in World War II, Kennedy served in the U.S. House of Representatives (1948–54) and U.S. Senate (1954–60), before becoming the first Roman Catholic elected president. His *A Nation of Immigrants* furthered the view that immigrants had entered the mainstream of American life. A staunch anticommunist, Kennedy promoted the Migration and Refugee Assistance Act of 1962 and encouraged abolition of national quotas established in 1924 by sending a new immigration measure to Congress in July 1963. After Kennedy's assassination in November, his views were taken up by his youngest brother, Edward ("Ted"), and were embodied in the Immigration and Nationality Act of 1965.

Fiorello Henry LaGuardia (1888–1947), longtime mayor of New York City who represented the rise of the "New Immigrants" from southern and eastern Europe. Born in Manhattan to an agnostic Italian father and an Austrian Jewish mother, LaGuardia represented New York as a Republican in the U.S. House of Representatives for most of the period between 1917 and 1932. In 1934 he became mayor of New York City, installed by the reformers in a bid to rid the city offices of corruption.

Immigration

LaGuardia was successful in creating a well-administered, modern city, with public housing and a unified system of city transport, becoming one of New York's best-loved mayors. After leaving office in 1945, he served as director general of the United Nations Relief and Rehabilitation Administration from 1946 to 1947.

Emma Lazarus (1849–87), poet and author who gained fame for her poem "The New Colossus," which embodied the liberal vision toward immigrants represented by the new Statue of Liberty. Born in New York City to a family of Sephardic Jews, she came to champion Jews and other immigrants in her writing. Her poem "The New Colossus" was contributed to help raise funds for the erection of the new Statue of Liberty, then being prepared as a gift by the French government. With the sonnet's famous last line—"I lift my lamp beside the golden door"—the statue seemed to offer not just liberty to the world but opportunity within America. She also wrote *Admetus and Other Poems* (1871), *Songs of a Semite* (1882), and *By the Waters of Babylon* (1887).

Henry Cabot Lodge (1850–1924), politician and historian who was a principal proponent of a literacy test to limit the number of immigrants coming into the United States. Born into a distinguished Boston family, Lodge edited the influential *North American Review* and lectured at Harvard (1876–79). During the 1880s, he wrote a number of well-received histories and served in the Massachusetts State House. In 1886 he was elected to the U.S. House of Representatives and in 1893 to the U.S. Senate, where he served until his death. During the 1890s, he became concerned about what he considered to be the moral degradation of many "new immigrants." For more than a quarter of a century, Lodge promoted the literacy test as the best and simplest way to keep undesirable immigrants out of the country. The xenophobia caused by World War I finally enabled the Literacy Test to be passed in 1917, over President Woodrow Wilson's veto. In leading opposition to U.S. entry into the League of Nations in 1919, Lodge was concerned that immigrant exclusion might become unenforceable and that the diversity of immigrant interests would lead to division within the country.

Patrick Anthony McCarran (1876–1954), longtime Democratic senator from Nevada who was one of the staunchest anticommunists of the post–World War II era and who was best known for coauthoring the restrictive McCarran-Walter Act. Born in Reno, Nevada, McCarran served as Nevada chief justice (1917–18), chairman of the Nevada State Board of Parole Commissioners (1913–18), and chairman of the Nevada State Board of Bar Examiners (1919–32). After two unsuccessful runs at the U.S. Senate in 1916 and 1926, he was finally elected in 1932 and served there until his death. After World War II, he became chairman of the Senate Internal Security Subcommittee, looking into the question of

126

potential communist threats to the United States. In 1950 he helped secure passage of the McCarran Internal Security Act, which authorized the president to detain or deport people who might pose a threat to national security. He joined fellow Democrat Francis Walter in proposing the McCarran-Walter Act (Immigration and Nationality Act, 1952), a measure that codified U.S. immigration law, maintained national and racial quotas, and generally made it easier to detain and deport suspected communists. President Harry Truman vetoed the measure—according to McCarran, "one of the most un-American acts" he had witnessed—but the veto was overridden, and the bill became law on June 27, 1952.

Samuel Finley Breese Morse (1791–1872), artist and inventor best remembered for inventing the Morse Code; also one of the leading anti-Irish, anti-Catholic activists of the period between 1830 and 1860. Born in Charlestown, Massachusetts, and educated at Yale University, he traveled widely in Europe in 1829–32 in order to develop his artistic skills. He also was an early student of photography and became a founder and president of the National Academy of Design (1826–45, 1861–62). Morse assured his financial position by securing a government contract to build a telegraph line between Baltimore and Washington, D.C., in 1843. During his earlier visit to Rome, Morse became suspicious of papal authority and wrote a series of articles that were collected and published as *A Foreign Conspiracy against the Liberties of the United States* (1834), in which he denounced Catholic proselytizing in the United States. In the following year, he published *Imminent Dangers to the Free Institutions of the United States through Foreign Immigration and Present State of the Naturalization Laws*, in which he expressed particular concern about the "naturalized *foreigner*" who professed to "become an American" but "talks (for example) of Ireland as 'his home,' as 'his beloved country,' resents anything said against the Irish as said against him, glories in being Irish," and generally forgets his "new obligations as an American." During the Civil War, Morse moderated his views.

Daniel Patrick Moynihan (1927–2003), senator and author who became a leading expert on immigration issues during the second half of the 20th century. Born in Tulsa, Oklahoma, Moynihan earned his Ph.D. from Tufts University and received a law degree from the Fletcher School of Law and Diplomacy. Although a Democrat, he often differed from the left wing of his party and eventually served in the John F. Kennedy, Lyndon Johnson, Richard Nixon, and Gerald Ford administrations. He became director of the Joint Center for Urban Studies at Harvard University and the Massachusetts Institute of Technology, writing widely about the problems of the urban poor, which led President Nixon to offer him a staff position as urban affairs adviser. Moynihan also taught at Harvard University (1971–73). After ambassadorships to India (1973–75)

Immigration

and the United Nations (1975–76), he was elected to the U.S. Senate in 1976, where he served until his retirement in 2000. His most influential book was *Beyond the Melting Pot* (1963), a study of American ethnicity that he coauthored with Nathan Glazer in 1963. In it he argued that urban life fostered many channels for maintaining ethnic identity, even when original language and customs were lost. Other works include *The Negro Family: The Case for National Action* (*The Moynihan Report*, 1965), *Family and Nation* (1986), *Came the Revolution* (1988), *On the Law of Nations* (1990), and *Secrecy* (1998).

Thomas Nast (1840–1902), journalist and illustrator who provided a potent visual image of urban ethnic politics and culture during the last half of the 19th century. Born in Landau, Germany, he immigrated to the United States with his mother in 1846. After studying at the National Academy of Design, he worked for *Frank Leslies Illustrated Newspaper*, the *New York Illustrated News*, the *Illustrated London News*, and most consistently for *Harper's Weekly* (1859–1860 and 1862–1886). His political cartoons were generally sympathetic toward immigrants and hostile toward slavery, though he was concerned about the potential Catholic threat in public education. Among the most notable images he created or popularized were the Democratic donkey, the Republican elephant, a classic depiction of Santa Claus, John Bull, and the Tammany Hall Tiger.

A. Mitchell Palmer (1872–1936), lawyer and politician who became famous for his zealous opposition to communists and immigrants during his tenure as U.S. attorney general. Born in Moosehead, Pennsylvania, he practiced law in Stroudsburg before serving three terms as a Democrat in the U.S. House of Representatives (1909–15). Failing in a bid for the Senate, he declined Woodrow Wilson's offer to become secretary of war (because of his pacifist beliefs), instead serving as Alien Property Custodian (1917–19) and U.S. attorney general (1919–21). As attorney general, he contended with a strong wave of xenophobia known as the Red Scare. On top of general fears of socialism as a result of World War I and the Bolshevik Revolution in Russia, an extensive bombing campaign in May and June of 1919 created considerable panic. In response Palmer authorized an ongoing watch list of socialists and radicals, looked the other way when violence was used against them, and launched a series of raids from November 1919 to January 1920 that netted more than 10,000, most of whom were deported under provisions of the new Immigration Act of 1917. With the decline in violence after 1920, fears of a socialist revolution subsided, and Palmer's political influence began to wane.

William Penn (1644–1718), colonizer, politician, and one of the most influential figures supporting early immigration of non-British groups to the American colonies. Born into an aristocratic family in London, Penn converted to Quakerism in the 1660s and traveled extensively throughout

Britain and Europe to promote his new faith. Enjoying the support of kings Charles II and James II, Penn became deeply involved in plans to settle the American colonies, first becoming a proprietor of the West Jersey colony in the 1670s, and then gaining a charter for the settlement of a new colony to be named Pennsylvania (1681). His "holy experiment" was designed to provide religious toleration for Christian dissenters of all kinds, including Quakers. As a result, Pennsylvania soon became the most ethnically diverse colony in America. By the end of the 18th century, Penn boasted that the people of Pennsylvania were "a collection of divers nations in Europe," including "French, Dutch, Germans, Swedes, Danes, Finns, Scotch, Irish, and English." By 1790 almost two-thirds of Pennsylvania's population was non-English. Penn advertised widely in Europe, publishing *A Brief Account of the Province of Pennsylvania* (1681) and *A Further Account of the Province of Pennsylvania and Its Improvements* (1685).

Louis Freeland Post (1849–1928), lawyer and assistant secretary of labor who assisted immigrants wrongly accused in the Red Scare following World War I. Born in rural New Jersey, Post was descended from English immigrants who came to Massachusetts in 1633. Deeply influenced by Thomas Paine's *Age of Reason*, he became a committed reformer in the early days of the reform movement. He was briefly assistant U.S. attorney general for the Southern District of New York (1874–75) before turning to a career in journalism, as writer and editor, most prominently with the penny paper *Truth* and the *Standard*, the weekly paper of the single-tax movement, inspired by economic reformer Henry George. He was appointed by President Woodrow Wilson as assistant secretary of labor in 1913 and was threatened with impeachment for defending immigrants wrongly accused of radicalism during the A. Mitchell Palmer raids of 1919–20. His writings include *The Ethics of Democracy* (1903), *Ethical Principles of Marriage and Divorce* (1906), *What Is the Single Tax* (1926), and *The Basic Facts of Economics* (1927).

Terence Vincent Powderly (1849–1924), labor leader and commissioner-general of immigration. Born to Irish immigrants in Carbondale, Pennsylvania, Powderly first worked as a machinist. He rose quickly in the Knights of Labor after joining the new labor union, becoming head of the organization in 1879. He served as mayor of Scranton, Pennsylvania (1878–84), representing the Greenback-Labor Party. Under Powderly's leadership, the Knights achieved their greatest influence, effectively using strikes to increase their power. Powderly also broadened the appeal of the Knights by lessening much of the secrecy surrounding the organization, and working through Bishop James Gibbons to have the Roman Catholic Church remove sanctions against Roman Catholics who joined labor unions. The rapid growth of the Knights and the lack of a strongly centralized organization led to internal disputes, and to Powderly's

Immigration

resignation in 1893. After campaigning for William Mckinley, Powderly was appointed U.S. Commissioner General of Information (1897–1902) and eventually became head of the Division of Information in the Bureau of Immigration (1907–21). His writings include *Thirty Years of Labour* (1889) and *The Path I Trod* (published posthumously in 1940). Terence Powderly died on June 24, 1924.

Ronald Reagan (1911–2004), 40th president of the United States (1981–89) and the 33rd governor of California (1967–75). Before entering politics, Reagan was a broadcaster and actor, elected president of the Screen Actors Guild in 1947. Reagan's presidency marked a turning point for the Republican Party. In 1980 he defeated incumbent President Jimmy Carter. Though the destruction of communism and the implementation of supply-side economics were the primary goals of his presidency, Reagan's commitment to "free and open markets" led necessarily to questions of immigration. At an Ellis Island ceremony in 1982, he praised immigrants who had the qualities he prized in citizens generally—"a determination that with hard work and freedom, they would live a better life and their children even more so." Reagan appointed the Task Force on Immigration that eventually led to the Immigration Reform and Control Act of 1986, which enhanced border enforcement, established sanctions against employers who knowingly hired illegal workers, and legalized almost 2 million undocumented workers. Reagan also signed the Civil Liberties Act of 1988, which compensated Japanese-American victims of internment during World War II.

Johan Reinert Reiersen (1810–64), colonizer, writer, and publisher who was one of the prime publicists in his native Norway for immigration to the United States. Born in Norway, he attended the University of Oslo before becoming an editor and translator in Denmark and Germany. After returning to Norway, in 1839 he began publication of the liberal newspaper *Christiansandsposten* (Christiansand Post), through which he preached the economic benefits of emigration. In 1843 he traveled to the United States, visiting Norwegian settlements across the north-central states, before finally meeting with Texas president Sam Houston, who encouraged him to establish a Norwegian colony there. Reiersen's *Pathfinder for Norwegian Emigrants to the United North American States and Texas* (1844) dealt with natural conditions in the midwest and Texas, in those regions' agriculture, politics, and economies. Before immigrating with his family and a group of settlers to Texas in 1845, he established the journal *Norge og Amerika* (Norway and America) to publish immigrant letters, personal stories, and articles regarding the value of emigration.

Janet Reno (1938–), attorney general of the United States (1993–2001), who gained notoriety for presiding over the return of young Cuban émigré Elián

Biographical Listing

González to the custody of his father in Cuba. Reno's father was a police officer and an immigrant from Denmark, while her mother became a reporter for the *Miami News*. After graduating from Harvard Law School, she served in a number of county and state legal positions, including state attorney from 1978. Her tenure as U.S. attorney general was controversial for a number of reasons, including her revelation of Parkinson's disease and, more prominently, her handling of the Elián González case. After surviving a boat wreck in which his mother died in November 1999, González lived in Miami with relatives for five months, while a legal battle raged over who should have legal custody of the six year old. Despite the protests of Miami mayor Joseph Carollo and Miami-Dade County mayor Alex Penelas, Reno ordered federal marshals to seize González and reunite him with his father. Despite the opposition, a three-judge panel of the U.S. Court of Appeals upheld Reno's position, leading to the return of González to Cuba in June 2000.

Jacob A. Riis (1849–1914), Danish-American photojournalist who became famous for his crusading representations of the life of the immigrant poor in American cities. Born in Denmark, Riis immigrated to the United States in 1870. He worked first as an itinerant laborer, then as a reporter, before purchasing the *South Brooklyn News*. Riis established his reputation as a police reporter for the *New York Tribune* (1877–90) and *New York Evening Sun* (1890–99). Working in the worst slums of New York City, he saw the horrors of slum life, particularly for children, and used innovative photographic techniques and progressive prose to show the plight of the urban poor. His *How the Other Half Lives: Studies among the Tenements of New York* (1890) remains the classic photographic representation of the great wave of immigration to the United States between 1880 and 1914. His friendship with Theodore Roosevelt, who successively served as New York police commissioner, governor of New York, and president of the United States, led to a variety of progressive reforms. Riis's principal publications are *The Children of the Poor* (1892), *Out of Mulberry Street* (1898), *A Ten Years' War* (1900), and *Children of the Tenements* (1903).

Ole Edvart Rölvaag (1876–1931), author and educator, who became one of the premier chroniclers of the Norwegian immigrant experience in the United States. Rölvaag was born in Norway, immigrating in 1896 to South Dakota, where he worked on a farm for an uncle. After earning a degree at St. Olaf College in Minnesota, he returned for a year of study at the University of Oslo before returning to join the faculty of St. Olaf College, where he taught Norwegian and literature. Having experienced a life of hard work and loss, with the death of two children, he wanted to encourage second- and third-generation Norwegians to maintain their native culture, though he realized that it was impossible to do so. "Again and again," he wrote, second-generation Norwegians "have had impressed on them: all that has grown on American earth is good, but all

Immigration

that can be called foreign is at best suspect." His masterpiece, *Giants in the Earth* (1927), is considered one of the most powerfully written novels about pioneer life in America. He also wrote *Letters from America* (1912), *On Forgotten Paths* (1914), *Pure Gold* (1930), *Their Father's God* (1931), and *The Book of Longing* (1933).

Theodore Roosevelt (1858–1919), 26th president of the United States (1901–09), who was known for his aggressive nationalism abroad and progressive politics at home. Born into a wealthy New York family, Roosevelt nevertheless had to overcome sickness and a serious asthmatic condition. After attending Harvard College, he developed an extraordinarily wide range of interests, most in pursuit of the benefits of the "strenuous life." He served in the New York state assembly (1881–84) and owned a ranch in the Badlands of the Dakota territories (1884–85). During the 1880s and 1890s, he published several significant works of history, including *The Naval War of 1812* (1882) and a four-volume history of the frontier, *The Winning of the West* (1889–96). In the early 1890s, he served on the U.S. Civil Service Commission, then for two years as president of the New York Board of Police Commissioners. During the 1890s, he developed a friendship with pioneering photojournalist Jacob Riis, with whom he cooperated in cleaning up slums and providing a better urban environment for the poor of New York. In 1897 Roosevelt became vice president under William McKinley, then was elevated to the presidency following McKinley's assassination in 1901. Roosevelt's most notable achievement regarding immigration was settlement of a standoff with Japan over the rights of Japanese laborers in the United States. With a rapid influx of Japanese workers, the mayor of San Francisco and the Asiatic Exclusion League pressured the San Francisco school board to pass a measure segregating Japanese students. Not wishing local affairs to undermine his Far Eastern policy, which required a good working relationship with Japan, Roosevelt negotiated three separate but related agreements—collectively known as the Gentlemen's Agreement—between December 1906 and January 1908, addressing both Japanese concerns over the welfare of the immigrants and Californian concerns over the growing numbers of Japanese laborers. More generally, Roosevelt's work as a trust buster and progressive reformer did much to improve the lives of urban workers, many of whom were immigrants. Roosevelt was the fifth cousin of the later President Franklin D. Roosevelt and the uncle of Eleanor Roosevelt.

Carl Schurz (1829–1906), journalist and politician, who was the first German immigrant elected to the U.S. Senate (1860). Born in Germany, Schurz attended the University of Bonn, where he became a revolutionary and assisted in editing the *Bonner Zeitung*. The failure of the Revolution of 1848 led him to flee Germany and live in Switzerland, England, France, and eventually the United States. He supported Abraham Lincoln among

Biographical Listing

German speakers in Lincoln's senatorial campaign of 1858 and was eventually appointed as Lincoln's minister to Spain (1861–62) before resigning his post to serve as a general of volunteers for the Union in the Civil War. He served as Republican senator from Missouri (1869–75), though he quarreled with the Ulysses Grant administration due to questions of fiscal responsibility. After supporting Rutherford B. Hayes for the presidency, in 1876 he was named secretary of the interior. Upon his retirement in 1881, he moved to New York and became editor in chief of the *New York Evening Post* (1881–83) and editorial writer for *Harper's Weekly* (1892–98). He was for a number of years a representative of the Hamburg American Steamship Company, one of the principal transporters of central European immigrants to the United States. Schurz unsuccessfully opposed William Jennings Bryan the Republican presidential nomination in 1896. A strong anti-imperialist, he is remembered for his epithet: "Our country right or wrong. When right, to be kept right; when wrong, to be put right."

Alan K. Simpson (1931–), longtime Republican senator from Wyoming (1979–97) and, for two decades, one of the most influential congressmen in immigration matters. After earning B.S. and J.D. degrees from the University of Wyoming, he served as city attorney for Cody (1959–69) and in the Wyoming House of Representatives (1964–77). After his election to the U.S. Senate in 1978, he coauthored the bills that eventually developed into the Immigration Reform and Control Act (1986), and he played an important role in crafting the Immigration Act of 1990. Liberal in many social areas, Simpson was often at odds with members of the Republican Party, and he was forced out of the position of Republican Senate Whip in 1995.

Upton Beall Sinclair, Jr. (1878–1968), progressive author and socialist who is best remembered for his novel *The Jungle* (1906), a ringing manifesto against the evils of capitalism. Sinclair came from an old and distinguished family that had fallen upon hard times during the Civil War. After attending City College of New York and Columbia, he worked as a joke writer and dime novelist while he pursued more serious literary ambitions. His first novel, *Manassas* (1904), was moderately successful, but it was *The Jungle* that brought him international fame. The novel led to important reforms in the meatpacking industry but did little to rouse the public regarding the plight of urban workers, which was his principal intent. With royalties from the novel, he established a socialist commune (1906–07), where novelist and playwright Sinclair Lewis lived for a brief period. He ran for governor of California twice. During the Great Depression, he earned Democratic Party support for his campaign to end poverty in California, and later gained the party's nomination. Conservatives, though, painted Sinclair as a communist, pointing not only to his long history of socialist views but also to his work with the Soviet Film

Immigration

Industry in the abortive *Que Viva Mexico!* Between 1940 and 1953, he wrote a series of novels revolving around the character Lanny Budd. The third book in the series, *Dragon's Teeth*, won a Pulitzer Prize in 1943.

Alfred Emmanuel Smith (1873–1944), politician who was the first political figure to build a national reputation by appealing to ethnic groups and the first Roman Catholic to run for president. Raised on New York City's Lower East Side, Smith worked for the Tammany Hall political machine and was picked by them to run for the New York state assembly in 1903, where he sat until selected as sheriff of New York City in 1915 and president of the Board of Alderman two years later. He gradually developed a progressive reform program that appealed especially to immigrants, and he won a surprising victory in the gubernatorial election of 1918. While in office, he enhanced workmen's compensation provisions, supported higher teachers' salaries, and fought for state care for the mentally ill. Defeated in the Republican landslide election of 1920, he was reelected governor in 1922, 1924, and 1926. He was nominated as the Democratic presidential candidate on the first ballot in 1928. Though he had little chance to defeat Herbert Hoover in the midst of a booming economy, he did help turn immigrant voters toward the Democratic Party and enable Democrats to carry most large urban areas for the first time.

George Soros (1944–   ), entrepreneur, political activist, and philanthropist who became one of the leading supporters of educational and social programs in countries emerging from decades of communist repression. Born into an assimilated Jewish family in Hungary, he and his family resisted both fascist and communist governments. Escaping to England, he studied at the London School of Economics. After moving to New York in 1956, he made a fortune investing in international markets. As part of his philanthropic work, he created scholarships for students in South Africa, eastern Europe, and the Soviet Union. Through the Open Society Institute, he endowed the Emma Lazarus fund with $50 million. Through it and a network of related philanthropic organizations, he gave more than a billion dollars, mainly for educational programs in central and eastern Europe. In 1992 Soros helped found Central European University, with its primary campus in Budapest. He raised controversy during the 2004 presidential election, speaking often and spending heavily in attempts to defeat incumbent President George W. Bush. Soros wrote a number of books, including *The Bubble of American Supremacy* (2004); *George Soros on Globalization* (2002); *The Alchemy of Finance* (1987); *Opening the Soviet System* (1990); *Underwriting Democracy* (1991); *Soros on Soros: Staying ahead of the Curve* (1995); *The Crisis of Global Capitalism: Open Society Endangered* (1998); and *Open Society: Reforming Global Capitalism* (2000).

Josiah Strong (1847–1916), clergyman and author who was best known for his pioneering work in the Social Gospel movement, which believed that social problems were best solved by the application of Protestant religious principles. Born in Illinois, he became a congregational minister and missionary to Native Americans. He served as general secretary of the Evangelical Alliance for the United States (1886–98), then founded the League for Social Service (1898–1916) and edited its magazine, *The Gospel of the Kingdom*. Strong became nationally famous with the publication of *Our Country: Its Possible Future and Its Present Crisis* (1885). Though written to encourage missionary work in the cities and to put an end to racial conflict, his look at the "perils" facing America—socialism, immigration, intemperance, wealth, Roman Catholicism, and urbanization—suggested the superiority of Protestant Anglo-America and provided support for a growing policy of imperialism in the United States. By the time the revised edition arrived in 1891, the "new immigration" from southern and eastern Europe had become even more prominent, suggesting to many readers, particularly in rural areas, a prescience on his part. According to Strong, and to many Americans who feared massive immigration from Roman Catholic countries, there was "an irreconcilable difference between papal principles and the fundamental principles of our free institutions. . . . Our fundamental ideas of society, therefore, are as radically opposed to Vaticanism as to imperialism, and it is inconsistent with our liberties for Americans to yield allegiance to the Pope as to the Czar."

John Tanton (1934–), anti-immigration activist. His father was a Canadian who migrated during the Great Depression to Detroit, where Tanton was born. Raised in rural Michigan during much of his childhood, he developed a strong sense of environmental responsibility. After earning a medical degree at Michigan State University, during the 1960s and 1970s he practiced ophthalmology and became deeply involved in both the conservation and Zero Population Growth (ZPG) movements. He served as president of ZPG from 1975–77. By the late 1970s, his interests in the environment and population growth "evolved into a crusade against immigration flows into the United States, particularly from Latin American and Caribbean nations." In 1979 he cofounded the Federation for American Immigration Reform (FAIR) and in 1983 the "official English" organization, U.S. English. According to the Tolerance.org project of the Southern Poverty Law Center, clearly hostile to Tanton, the anti-immigration movement was "almost entirely the handiwork of one man, Michigan activist John H. Tanton." From the 1980s, Tanton worked through a number of related organizations, including the Center for Immigration Studies, Federation for American Immigration Reform, NumbersUSA, Pro English, Social Contract Press, U.S. English, and U.S. Inc. Tanton argued that he was not against all immigration but rather was an opponent of massive immigration. "Most Americans oppose mass immigration because mass immigration is not in their interests . . . Americans do not see

135

Immigration

the loss of their jobs or wages to immigrants to be in their interests. They do not see the crowding of their children's schools with large numbers of kids who have language and other difficulties to be in their interests. They do not see rapid cultural and linguistic transformations of their neighborhoods to be in their interests." By the late 1980s, Tanton became more closely associated with supremacist doctrines, losing some support among the general public. His books include *The Immigrant Invasion* (with Wayne Lutton, 1993) and coedited *Immigration and the Social Contract: The Implosion of Western Societies* (1996).

CHAPTER 5

GLOSSARY

The following terms are frequently used in discussion of immigration history and politics. Where terms have specific, technical meanings in current immigration policy, definitions have been taken or closely adapted from the web site of the U.S. Citizenship and Immigration Services (http://uscis.gov/graphics/glossary.htm#A), formerly the U.S. Immigration and Naturalization Service (http://www.ins.usdoj.gov/graphics/glossary.htm). Simplified interpretations sometimes can be found at the Nolo web site (http://www.nolo.com/definition.cfm).

adjustment to immigrant status   A procedure that allows certain aliens admitted to the United States as nonimmigrants to have their status changed to that of permanent resident if they are eligible to receive an immigrant visa and one is immediately available. In such cases, the alien is counted as an immigrant as of the date of adjustment.

agricultural worker   A class of alien type, as defined by the secretary of labor, to describe an alien who comes temporarily to the United States as a nonimmigrant to perform agricultural labor or services.

alien   Any person who is not a citizen or national of the United States; generally referred to as a "foreign national" in Canada.

alien registration receipt card   The official name of the photo identification card given to legal permanent resident noncitizens of the United States; commonly known, both inside and outside the government, as a green card (despite the fact that it is now actually pink). The green card enables the holder to reenter the United States after temporary absences and to work legally in the country.

Amerasian (Vietnamese)   Immigrant category provided for by an act of December 22, 1987, providing for the admission of aliens in Vietnam after January 1, 1962, and before January 1, 1976, whose father was a U.S. citizen.

Amerasian Act   Measure enacted on October 22, 1982, providing for immigration to the United States of certain Amerasian children born in

Immigration

Cambodia, Korea, Laos, Thailand, or Vietnam after December 31, 1950, and before October 22, 1982, that had been fathered by a U.S. citizen.

asylee   An alien in the United States who is unable or unwilling to return to his or her homeland because of persecution or a well-founded fear of persecution based on race, religion, nationality, membership in a particular social group, or political opinion. Asylees are eligible to apply for lawful permanent resident status after one year of continuous residence in the United States.

asylum   Legal status granted to an asylee.

beneficiaries   Aliens on whose behalf a U.S. citizen, legal permanent resident, or employer have filed a petition for said alien to receive immigration benefits from the U.S. Citizenship and Immigration Services.

business nonimmigrant   An alien temporarily in the United States to engage in international commerce on behalf of a foreign company.

cancellation of removal   A discretionary benefit arising from application made during the course of a hearing before an immigration judge, adjusting an alien's status from that of deportable alien to one lawfully admitted for permanent residence.

child   In legal terms, an unmarried person under 21 years of age who is: a child born in wedlock; a stepchild, provided that the child was under 18 years of age at the time that the marriage creating the stepchild relationship occurred; a legitimated child, provided that the child was legitimated while in the legal custody of the legitimating parent; a child born out of wedlock, when a benefit is sought on the basis of the relationship with his or her mother, or to his or her father if the father has or had a bona fide relationship with the child; a child adopted while under 16 years of age who has resided since adoption in the legal custody of the adopting parents for at least two years; or an orphan, under 16 years of age, who has been adopted abroad by a U.S. citizen or has an immediate-relative visa petition submitted in his/her behalf and is coming to the United States for adoption by a U.S. citizen.

conditional resident   Any alien granted permanent resident status on a conditional basis who is required to petition for the removal of the set conditions before the second anniversary of the approval of his or her conditional status.

country of chargeability   The country to which an immigrant is charged under the quotas of the preference system.

country of former allegiance   The previous country of citizenship of a naturalized U.S. citizen.

Cuban/Haitian entrant   Immigrant status leading to permanent residence accorded by the Immigration Control and Reform Act of 1986 to (1) Cubans who entered illegally or were paroled into the United States between April 15, 1980, and October 10, 1980, and (2) Haitians who

Glossary

entered illegally or were paroled into the country before January 1, 1981, who have continuously resided in the United States since before January 1, 1982, and who were known to the INS before that date.

Department of Homeland Security The U.S. government department responsible for coordinating anti-terror activities in the country. Among its many agencies, three deal primarily with immigration issues: U.S. Immigration and Citizenship Services, U.S. Immigration and Customs Enforcement, and U.S. Customs and Border Protection.

Department of Labor The U.S. government agency responsible for approving job-related visas; it determines whether there is adequate American labor to fill positions within U.S. companies.

Department of State The U.S. government agency responsible for embassies and consulates around the world and that generally determines who is eligible for visas and green cards when applications are filed outside the country.

departure under safeguards The departure of an illegal alien from the United States that is observed by a U.S. Immigration and Customs Enforcement official.

deportable alien An alien within the United States who is subject to removal, either because of application fraud or violation of terms of his or her nonimmigrant classification, under provisions of the Immigration and Nationality Act.

deportation The formal removal of an alien from the United States when immigration laws have been violated. Deportation is ordered by an immigration judge without any additional punishment being considered. The Illegal Immigration Reform and Immigrant Responsibility Act of 1996 consolidated deportation and removal procedures, which were previously separate.

derivative citizenship Citizenship conveyed to children through the naturalization of their parents.

diversity Under provisions of the Immigration Act of 1990, a category for redistributing unused visas to aliens from underrepresented countries. Beginning in fiscal year 1995, the permanent diversity quota was established at 55,000 annually. The diversity program is sometimes referred to as the green-card lottery program.

docket control The U.S. Citizenship and Immigration Services mechanism for tracking the status of aliens potentially subject to removal.

employer sanctions Provision of the Immigration Reform and Control Act of 1986 that prohibits employers from hiring aliens known to be in violation of immigration laws. Violators are subject to civil fines for violations and to criminal penalties when a pattern of violations is proven.

exchange visitor An alien temporarily in the United States as part of a State Department–approved program involving teaching, studying, conducting research, consulting, or use of special skills.

139

Immigration

exclusion   Prior to the Illegal Immigration Reform and Immigrant Responsibility Act of 1996, *exclusion* was the formal term for denial of an alien's entry into the United States. The decision to exclude an alien was made by an immigration judge after an exclusion hearing. Since April 1, 1997, the process of adjudicating inadmissibility may take place in either an expedited removal process or in removal proceedings before an immigration judge.

exempt from numerical limit   Those aliens accorded lawful permanent residence who are exempt from the provision of the flexible numerical limit of 675,000 set by the Immigration Act of 1990. Exempt categories include immediate relatives of U.S. citizens, refugees, asylees (limited to 10,000 per year), Amerasians, aliens adjusted under the legalization provisions of the Immigration Reform and Control Act of 1986, and certain parolees from the former Soviet Union and Indochina.

fiscal year   The 12-month period beginning October 1 and ending September 30. Prior to 1831 and from 1843 to 1849, it was the 12-month period ending September 30 of the respective year; from 1832 to 1842 and from 1850 to 1867, the 12-month period ending December 31 of the respective year; and from 1868 to 1976, the 12-month period ending June 30 of the respective year. The transition quarter for 1976 covers the three-month period, July–September 1976.

foreign government official   A nonimmigrant class of admission, covering aliens residing temporarily in the United States as an accredited official of a foreign government, along with their spouses and unmarried minor or dependent children.

foreign state of chargeability   The independent country to which an immigrant entering under the preference system is accredited. No more than 7 percent of the family sponsored and employment-based visas may be issued to native-born residents of any one independent country in a fiscal year. No one dependency of any independent country may receive more than 2 percent of the family sponsored and employment-based visas issued. Since these limits are based on visa issuance rather than entries into the United States, and immigrant visas are valid for six months, there is not total correspondence between these two occurrences. Chargeability is usually determined by country of birth. Exceptions are made to prevent the separation of family members when the limitation for the country of birth has been met.

general naturalization provisions   The basic requirements for naturalization, unless a member of a special class; includes (1) being 18 years of age and a lawful permanent resident with five years of continuous residence in the United States, (2) having been physically present in the country for half that period, and (3) having established good moral character.

geographic area of chargeability   One of five regions—Africa, East Asia, Latin America and the Caribbean, Near East and South Asia, and the

140

Glossary

former Soviet Union and eastern Europe—against which refugees to the United States are charged. Annual consultations between the executive branch and congress determine the ceilings for each region. Beginning in fiscal year 1987, an unallocated reserve was incorporated into the admission ceilings.

green card Informal name given to the alien registration receipt card, the photo identification card given to legal permanent residents of the United States. The green card enables the holder to reenter the United States after temporary absences and to work legally in the country.

hemispheric ceilings Under provisions of the Immigration and Nationality Act of 1965, the highest levels imposed on immigration numbers from each hemisphere between 1968 and 1978. Immigration from the Eastern Hemisphere was set at 170,000, with a per-country limit of 20,000. Immigration from the Western Hemisphere was set at 120,000, without any per-country limit prior to 1977 and a 20,000 per-country limit thereafter. From October 1978, hemispheric ceilings were abolished in favor of a single comprehensive ceiling.

immediate relatives In immigration and legal terms, certain immigrants—including spouses of citizens, unmarried children under 21, and parents of citizens 21 and older—who are exempt from the numerical limitations imposed on immigration to the United States due to familial status with a current legal resident.

Immigration and Naturalization Service (INS) The federal agency in the U.S. Department of Justice that administered and enforced immigration and naturalization laws between 1933 and 2003, when it was abolished. Its various functions were taken over by the Bureau of Citizenship and Immigration Services, the Bureau of Immigration and Customs Enforcement, and the Bureau of Customs and Border Protection, all branches of the Department of Homeland Security.

immigration judge An attorney appointed by the U.S. attorney general to conduct various immigration proceedings.

inadmissible (formerly excludable) The status of an alien seeking admission who does not meet the criteria established for admission, generally because of criminal records, health problems, an inability to provide financial support, or potential subversiveness.

I-94 card A card given to all nonimmigrants entering the United States as evidence that they have entered legally.

international representative A nonimmigrant class of admission under which an alien temporarily resides in the United States as an accredited representative of a foreign government to an international organization; includes spouses and unmarried minor or dependent children.

labor certification Requirement for U.S. employers seeking to employ immigrants whose admittance to the United States is based on job skills.

141

Certification is issued by the secretary of labor and contains attestations by U.S. employers as to the numbers of U.S. workers available to undertake the employment sought by an applicant and the effect of the alien's employment on the wages and working conditions of U.S. workers similarly employed. It is often a first step toward obtaining a green card.

legalized aliens   Under provisions of the Immigration Reform and Control Act of 1986, certain illegal aliens were eligible to apply for temporary resident status, which then could lead to permanent residency. Eligibility required continuous residence in the United States as an illegal alien from January 1, 1982; that one not be excludable; and to have entered the United States either (1) illegally before January 1, 1982, or (2) as a temporary visitor before January 1, 1982, with their authorized stay expiring before that date or with the government's knowledge of their unlawful status before that date.

legitimated   A legal procedure for natural fathers of children born out of wedlock to acknowledge their children. A legitimated child from any country has two legal parents and cannot qualify as an orphan unless (1) only one of the parents is living or (2) both of the parents have abandoned the child.

lottery program   See **diversity.**

migrant   A person who seeks residence in a country other than his or her own.

national   A person owing allegiance to a state.

natives of underrepresented countries   Under the Immigration Amendments of 1988, 10,000 visas were reserved for natives of underrepresented countries in each of the fiscal years 1990 and 1991 (those receiving less than 25 percent of the maximum allowed under the country limitations in fiscal year 1988). See **diversity.**

nativism   An anti-immigrant attitude, based upon the belief that ethnic, religious, or political ideas brought into the country by immigrants will adversely affect the predominant culture.

naturalization   Conferring U.S. citizenship upon a person after birth. Requirements include (1) being at least 18 years of age, (2) having been lawfully admitted to the United States for permanent residence, and (3) having resided in the country continuously for at least five years. Applicants must also demonstrate a certain level of knowledge of U.S. government and history; have the ability to speak, read, and write English; and be of good moral character. A prominent exception is spouses of citizens, who may be naturalized after three years of residence.

nonimmigrant   An alien who seeks temporary entry to the United States. Nonimmigrant classifications include foreign government officials, business travelers, tourists, aliens in transit, students, international representatives, temporary workers, representatives of foreign media, exchange visitors, fiancées of U.S. citizens, intracompany transferees, North Atlantic Treaty Organization (NATO) officials, religious workers, and some others. Most nonimmigrants can be accompanied by spouses and unmarried minor or dependent children.

non-preference category Non-preference visas were available to qualified applicants not entitled to a visa under one of six preference categories until the category was eliminated by the Immigration Act of 1990. Non-preference visas for persons not entitled to the other preferences had not been available since September 1978 because of high demand in the preference categories.

North American Free Trade Agreement (NAFTA) Agreement of 1993, superseding the United States–Canada Free Trade Agreement as of January 1, 1994, but continuing the special, reciprocal trading relationships among the United States, Canada, and Mexico. NAFTA eased temporary admissions restrictions for professionals, intracompany transferees, traders, investors, and others engaged in business activity.

orphan For purposes of immigration, a child may be considered an orphan because of the death or disappearance of, abandonment or desertion by, or separation or loss from both parents. The child of an unwed mother or surviving parent may be considered an orphan if that parent is unable to care for the child properly and has, in writing, irrevocably released the child for emigration and adoption. The child of an unwed mother may be considered an orphan, as long as the mother does not marry (which would result in the child's having a stepfather) and as long as the child's biological father has not legitimated the child. If the father legitimates the child or the mother marries, the mother is no longer considered a sole parent. The child of a surviving parent may also be an orphan if the surviving parent has not married since the death of the other parent (which would result in the child's having a stepfather or stepmother).

Panama Canal Act immigrants A special immigrant category created by an act of September 27, 1979, including (1) certain former employees of the Panama Canal Company or Canal Zone Government, their spouses, and accompanying children and (2) certain former Panamanian nationals who were employees of the U.S. government in the Panama Canal Zone, their spouses, and children. The act provided for admission of a maximum of 15,000 immigrants, at a rate of no more than 5,000 each year.

parolee An alien who appears to be inadmissible but who is allowed into the United States for urgent humanitarian reasons or for reasons of significant public benefit. Parole confers temporary status only. Parolees include: those with documents but when some questions remain; those coming for emergencies not permitting time for ordinary application for documentation, as in the case of firefighters or

Immigration

other emergency workers, or for funerals; those requiring emergency medical care; those who take part in legal proceedings on behalf of the government; and those authorized for certain long-term admissions under special legislation.

per-country limit The maximum number of preference visas that can be issued to citizens of any country in a fiscal year. The limits are calculated each fiscal year depending on the total number of family sponsored and employment-based visas available. Each country is limited to a maximum of 7 percent of the visas, though the combined workings of the preference system and per-country limits keep most countries from reaching the maximum.

permanent resident alien An alien given permanent residence in the United States; also known as a green-card holder. Permanent residents are commonly referred to as immigrants, though under provisions of the Immigration and Nationality Act, some illegal aliens are officially immigrants without being permanent resident aliens. They are commonly known in Canada as "landed immigrants."

port of entry Any location designated by the U.S. government as a point of entry for aliens and U.S. citizens, including all district and files control offices, which become locations of entry for aliens adjusting to immigrant status.

preference system The system utilized to allocate visas to the United States. Between 1981 and 1991, the 270,000 immigrant visas were allocated in six categories: (1) unmarried sons and daughters (over 21 years of age) of U.S. citizens (20 percent); (2) spouses and unmarried sons and daughters of aliens lawfully admitted for permanent residence (26 percent); (3) professionals or persons of exceptional ability in the sciences and arts (10 percent); (4) married sons and daughters of U.S. citizens (10 percent); (5) brothers and sisters of U.S. citizens over 21 years of age (24 percent); and (6) needed skilled or unskilled workers (10 percent). A nonpreference category, historically open to immigrants not entitled to a visa number under one of the six preferences just listed, had no numbers available beginning in September 1978. This system was amended by the Immigration Act of 1990, effective fiscal year 1992 and including nine categories. Family sponsored preferences include (1) unmarried sons and daughters of U.S. citizens; (2) spouses, children, and unmarried sons and daughters of permanent resident aliens; (3) married sons and daughters of U.S. citizens; and (4) brothers and sisters of U.S. citizens. Employment-based preferences include (1) priority workers, including outstanding professors and researchers and multinational executives and managers; (2) professionals with advanced degrees or aliens with exceptional ability; (3) skilled workers, professionals without advanced degrees, and needed unskilled workers; (4) special immigrants; and (5) investors.

Glossary

principal alien   The alien who applies for immigrant status and from whom another alien derives lawful status; usually spouses and minor unmarried children.

refugee   Any person outside his or her country of nationality who is unable or unwilling to return to that country because of persecution or a well-founded fear of persecution based upon race, religion, nationality, membership in a particular social group, or political opinion. Under the Refugee Act of 1980, refugee admission ceilings are established annually by the president in consultation with Congress. Refugees are eligible to adjust to lawful permanent resident status after one year of continuous presence in the United States. This is commonly known in Canada as "convention refugee."

refugee-parolee   A qualified applicant for conditional entry under the seventh preference category, paroled into the United States under the authority of the attorney general between February 1970 and April 1980 because of inadequate numbers of seventh preference visas.

removal   The expulsion of an alien from the United States based on grounds of inadmissibility or deportability; formerly known as deportation. Those removed are not allowed to return to the United States for at least five years.

resettlement   Permanent relocation of refugees in a host country; generally carried out by private voluntary agencies working with the Department of Health and Human Services Office of Refugee Resettlement.

safe haven   Temporary refuge given to migrants who have fled their countries of origin to seek protection or relief from persecution or other hardships, until they can return to their countries safely or, if necessary, until they can obtain permanent relief from the conditions they fled.

special agricultural workers (SAW)   Under provisions of the Immigration Reform and Control Act of 1986, aliens who performed labor in perishable agricultural commodities for a specified period of time were admitted as special agricultural workers for temporary, and then permanent, residence. Applicants were required to have worked at least 90 days in each of the three years preceding May 1, 1986, to be eligible. Adjustment to permanent resident status was "essentially automatic."

special immigrants   Certain categories of immigrants exempt from numerical limitations by special legislation, including religious workers, foreign doctors, former employees of the U.S. government, and Panama Canal Act Immigrants.

sponsor   Generally, a petitioner to the U.S. government on behalf of a prospective immigrant. Sponsors are usually prospective employers or close relatives who are citizens or permanent residents.

stateless   Having no nationality.

stowaway   An alien coming to the United States surreptitiously on an airplane or vessel without legal status of admission. Such an alien is subject

145

Immigration

to denial of formal admission and return to the point of embarkation by the transportation carrier.

temporary protected status (TPS)   Status established by the attorney general for allowing a group of persons temporary refuge in the United States, initially for periods of six to 18 months, though extensions may be granted.

temporary resident   See *nonimmigrant.*

temporary worker   An alien temporarily residing in the United States for specifically designated purposes of work, including health-care workers, agricultural workers, athletes and performers, and others performing work for which U.S. citizens are not available. Nonimmigrant temporary worker classes of admission are:

1. **H-1A:** registered nurses (valid from October 1, 1990, through September 30, 1995)
2. **H-1B:** workers with "specialty occupations" admitted on the basis of professional education, skills, and/or equivalent experience
3. **H-1C:** registered nurses to work in areas with a shortage of health professionals under the Nursing Relief for Disadvantaged Areas Act of 1999
4. **H-2A:** temporary agricultural workers coming to the United States to perform agricultural services or labor of a temporary or seasonal nature when authorized workers are unavailable in the United States
5. **H-2B:** temporary nonagricultural workers coming to the United States to perform temporary services or labor if unemployed persons capable of performing the service or labor cannot be found in the United States
6. **H-3:** aliens coming temporarily to the United States as trainees, other than to receive graduate medical education or training
7. **O-1, O-2, O-3:** temporary workers with extraordinary ability or achievement in the sciences, arts, education, business, or athletics; those entering solely for the purpose of accompanying and assisting such workers; and their spouses and children
8. **P-1, P-2, P-3, P-4:** athletes and entertainers at an internationally recognized level of performance; artists and entertainers under a reciprocal exchange program; artists and entertainers under a program that is "culturally unique"; and their spouses and children
9. **Q-1, Q-2, Q-3:** participants in international cultural exchange programs; participants in the Irish Peace Process Cultural and Training Program; and spouses and children of Irish Peace Process participants
10. **R-1, R-2:** temporary workers to perform work in religious occupations and their spouses and children

Glossary

treaty trader or investor A nonimmigrant class of admission, allowing an alien manager or investor, along with spouse and unmarried minor children, to enter the United States under provisions of a treaty of commerce and navigation between the United States and another country.

U.S. Citizenship and Immigration Services (USCIS) The U.S. government agency that oversees immigration benefits, including asylum, work programs, and citizenship. Prior to 2003, these benefits were handled by the Immigration and Naturalization Service.

U.S. Customs and Border Protection (CBP) The U.S. government agency responsible for U.S. border enforcement at land borders, airports, and seaports. Prior to 2003, these responsibilities were handled by the Immigration and Naturalization Service.

U.S. Immigration and Customs Enforcement (ICE) The U.S. government agency responsible for enforcing immigration laws within the U.S. borders. Prior to 2003, these responsibilities were handled by the Immigration and Naturalization Service.

U.S. Border Patrol The uniformed agency responsible for controlling illegal entry along U.S. land borders and at airports and seaports. During most of the 20th century, it operated under the Immigration and Naturalization Service, but in 2003 was transferred to U.S. Immigration and Customs Enforcement, an agency of the Department of Homeland Security.

U.S. Border Patrol sector One of 21 geographic areas of the United States covered by the activities of the U.S. Border Patrol.

visa Permission granted to aliens to apply for entry into the United States, usually represented by a stamp placed in a passport. Principal visa classifications include: F, student; B, visitor; H, temporary worker.

visa waiver program Program provided by the Immigration Reform and Control Act of 1986 allowing business and tourist travelers of selected countries temporary entry to the United States for a period of up to 90 days without obtaining nonimmigrant visas.

voluntary departure The departure of an alien from the United States without an order of removal, conceding removability but allowing for reapplication of admission at a port of entry at any time.

withdrawal An arriving alien's voluntary retraction of an application for admission to the United States in lieu of a removal hearing before an immigration judge.

PART II

GUIDE TO FURTHER RESEARCH

CHAPTER 6

HOW TO RESEARCH IMMIGRATION ISSUES

Immigration is one of the most complex topics in American history. It is also one of the most important. It may in fact provide a plausible framework for understanding the entirety of U.S. history. The implications of introducing a new people group to a prairie, village, town, or country have been dramatic and continue to be so. The Appalachian Mountains were transformed by Scots-Irish, the upper midwest by Scandinavians and Germans, Boston by Irish, and Miami by Cubans. Immigration has changed the way Americans think and do business and the way they entertain and interact with the world. Immigration changed the immigrants too, and the countries they came from, as thousands of separated relatives have eloquently testified in letters, diaries, and memoirs. Though Americans will never know precisely how many immigrants touched the shores of the United States, they can clearly see the impact of their presence. Americans know, too, that new waves of immigrants will reshape the face of U.S. society and redefine the structure of its economy.

Unlike other controversial contemporary issues such as privacy rights on the Internet or embryonic stem-cell research, the debate over immigration is deeply rooted in the very origins of the United States. To understand immigration, one must know something about who the immigrants were (ethnic or national identity), why they left their homelands (push factors), why they chose to come to America (pull factors), and how they fared in America (assimilation). But this is only one side of the story. One must also know the nature of the country that received the immigrants. Who were the Americans of 1607, of 1850, of 2005? How many of them were immigrants themselves, and did it make a difference in the reception of those seeking a new home? What roles did immigrants play in the economic and cultural life of the nation? Finally, to comprehend fully the scope of the immigration issue today, one must appreciate the evolving interdependence of the peoples of the world. It is impossible to understand immigrant migration without a fair knowledge of international relations, and it is impossible to appreciate

151

the nation's response without some understanding of the domestic implications of new settlers.

To be a knowledgeable student of immigration then, one must combine the insights of the historian, the political scientist, the sociologist, the economist, and the United Nations diplomat with a good citizen's sense of human justice and state welfare. When a particular aspect of immigration to research has been decided upon, it is important to remember that there will likely be challenges peculiar to this field as research proceeds.

RESEARCH CHALLENGES

QUANTIFICATION

Quantifying the extent of immigration is in itself an enormous challenge. Prior to 1850, it was scarcely attempted, but since that time, the process has become more complex, varied, and thorough. For the period following World War II, numbers and assessments provided by the Immigration and Naturalization Service (INS), the Citizenship and Immigration Service, and the U.S. Census Bureau provide a reasonably accurate picture of the broad landscape of immigration and of its relation to the ethnic composition of American society. One should not seek for more precision than the numbers will bear, however. In every large-scale reporting of immigration figures, it is understood, and usually explicitly stated, that reported numbers are approximate. In the Immigration and Naturalization Service table on "Immigration by Region and Selected Country of Last Residence for Fiscal Years 1820–2002," for instance, there are 25 qualifications indicated in footnotes, in addition to a general note on data limitations. The farther back in time, generally speaking, the less precise the number.

The U.S. census, from which ethnic profiles for cities, states, and the nation are derived, is compiled using unscientific methods of self-identification. As a result, one person might identify as a part of every ethnic group in his ancestry, while another might only list a predominant ancestry group. Respondents may even report family traditions or hearsay, without actual knowledge of ancestry. Thus, for some groups such as Germans and Poles, numbers may be overreported in the sense that there is no strong sense of ethnic identity for most of those reporting. In the case of nationals from many Central and South American countries, numbers are underreported, as a large percentage of their populations are unauthorized and therefore subject to official proceedings should their ethnic origin become known. Also, ethnic identification is confused across time by marriages between members of ethnic groups and the variation of group cohesion from one ethnic group to another.

Even if one could determine an exact overall number of immigrants, it would be impossible to determine which ethnic groups they represented, mainly because of changing geopolitical boundaries. Polish immigrants, for instance, were included in numbers for Germany, Austria-Hungary, and Russia/Soviet Union between 1899 and 1919. Data for the Austro-Hungarian Empire, comprised of more than a dozen ethnic groups, were not recorded until 1861, and thereafter the various ethnic groups were not delineated. Thus it is impossible to know with any precision how many Czechs or Hungarians entered the United States at that time. Prior to 1934, Filipinos were considered U.S. nationals and thus were not subject to either immigration restrictions or registration that would enable exact numbers to be determined. Immigrants from British India in the 19th and early 20th centuries were often classed as "Hindu," though most were in fact Muslim.

THE NATURE OF OFFICIAL RECORDS

Because immigration was largely unrestricted until the late 19th century, few official records were kept. When they were kept, people recorded what was then perceived to be important, with information not always consistent with contemporary interests. The earliest immigration records were simply ship manifests, varying widely in terms of information. The British government, for instance, theoretically registered the name, age, and occupation of all emigrants from December 1773 to March 1776. Newspaper accounts and individual ship registers, however, suggest a 15–30 percent underregistration. In the United States, information from 1820 to 1867 represented alien passengers arriving at seaports; thereafter official numbers sometimes represented all arrivals or sometimes only those admitted for permanent residence. There was no attempt to fully document land arrivals until 1908. Even when related information is available, it often is not comparable. Prior to 1906, for instance, data were collected on the country from which the alien emigrated; from 1906 to 1979 and 1984 to 1998, country of last permanent residence; and from 1980 to 1983, country of birth.

THE VARIETY OF IMMIGRANT TYPES

It is not enough to know how many immigrants came into the United States in a given year; one also needs to know who they were, what they believed, and what they brought with them in both goods and ideas. In some cases, culture groups seem to be the relevant category for study; in other cases, country of origin more clearly defines the nature of the migration; while in others a family or individual context is most relevant. Jews, for instance, were usually counted as immigrants from the state of their birth or last residence, along with non-Jewish immigrants from the same country. Any estimates involved in sorting the subgroups from the total—Russian Jews from other Russian immigrants, for instance—must take into account the differences between those who actually practiced Judaism, nonobservant Jews, and radicalized Jews who specifically rejected religion as a basis for social organization. In some cases, the cohesion of an immigrant group such as the Doukhobors or the Mennonites proved more powerful than cultural ties to their home countries, thus leading to a virtually clean break with the source country. On the other hand, immigrants from Mexico frequently immigrate in order to maintain their families economically at home, remitting billions of American dollars each year.

THE RELATIONSHIP BETWEEN LEGAL AND ILLEGAL IMMIGRATION

Illegal immigration by its very nature goes uncounted. In the important report on "Immigrants at Mid-Decade: A Snapshot of America's Foreign-Born Population in 2005" available online at (http://www.cis.org/articles/2005/back1405release.html), it was estimated that nearly half of post-2000 immigrants to the United States were illegal. While observing the factors that lead researchers to estimate with some confidence the number of illegal immigrants, author Stephen A. Camarota concedes that "there is no definitive means of determining whether a respondent in the survey is an illegal alien . . . the actual size of this population is almost certainly larger" than even the most accurate surveys will suggest. In the case of most countries or immigrant groups, this does not greatly alter the overall immigration numbers or affect the general government response.

In some cases, however, such as illegal immigration of Mexicans to the United States, the flow is so great and the impact so substantial as to require a separate study based on unofficial sources, projections, and secondary figures. Because illegal immigrants are largely unskilled and without health-care insurance, their presence in states such as California, Texas, and New York must be accounted for in order to make some of the most basic policy decisions. As international migration becomes more common and terrorism a greater threat, the study of illegal immigration will become increasingly important to a comprehensive understanding of the nature and process of immigration. In monitoring almost 2,000 miles of the U.S.-Mexican border in the early 21st century, for instance, aliens from more than 60 countries were apprehended, including from countries not in Central or South America.

THE COMPLEXITY OF IMMIGRATION POLICY AND PROCESS

Multiple agencies are responsible for varying aspects of the immigration process and sometimes work at cross-purposes. For instance, newly arriving aliens are granted visas by the U.S. Department of State, while aliens already temporarily in the United States and eligible to become adjusted to legal permanent resident status are granted immigrant status by the Citizenship and Immigration Service. Cooperative Extension Service Agents—usually hired by the state but often with county and federal funding—assist agricultural workers without requiring knowledge of their status, while Border Patrol agents are required to determine legality and to enforce immigration provisions.

Even within the context of a single agency such as the Border Patrol, policy varies depending upon the country of origin. Thus a Mexican immigrant will be treated differently than one from Guatemala. Also, some migrants may reside permanently in a country without being required to adjust to permanent resident status and thus are not officially counted as immigrants. Parolees, rufugees, and asylees generally fall into this category. These numbers are generally small but can fluctuate dramatically in times of international crisis or war.

THE LEVEL OF INVESTIGATION

The history of every ethnic group can be examined from every level—from the individual to the homestead, village, town, city, state, area, or nation. The results will not be the same from level to level. Establishment of an economically successful Korean community in Oklahoma City does not always suggest a comparable success in Portland, Maine, or in the nation as a whole. The group experience may have as much to do with general circumstances and opportunities as with ethnicity. And in every case, the achievements and experience of individuals may have more to do with unique personalities and characteristics than with their ethnic group identity.

CHANGES ACROSS TIME

Immigration researchers should be sensitive to changes across time, in relation to the perception of American citizens, social status and cultural contributions of immigrants, and the self-perception of immigrants. Attitudes toward particular immigrant groups have changed in the past, and they will certainly change in the future. In fact they are constantly in the process of change. Whereas the Chinese were the first ethnic group to be formally excluded from entry into the United States, for instance, they are among the most welcome today. It is important to remember that what appears to be a dramatic shift of opinion was gradually and constantly evolving between 1882, when the Chinese Exclusion Act was passed, to the present time. There were a host of specific reasons for changed attitudes, and as America's attitude and policy evolved, so, too, did Chinese perceptions of their "American" identity. Likewise, the economic and political characteristics of Cubans as an immigrant group changed significantly between the 1950s and the 1990s, leading to divisions within the Cuban community itself. A grasp of the scope and nature of such historical processes is important in understanding the contemporary debate over immigration.

RESEARCH RESOURCES

Research resources are frequently categorized as "print" or "online," though these distinctions have become increasingly blurred during the past five years. Generally, traditional academic research is still published in books and refereed journals, though these are often available in full-text format in online databases. It is also becoming increasingly common for government and research organizations, advocacy groups, and think tanks both to publish research reports and statistical data and to simultaneously post the same information online, sometimes in extended versions. Online resources usually provide the best starting point for research. For most historical research projects focusing on the period prior to 1980, these may quickly take one to more substantial research in the print media. For questions relating to the policy debate over immigration, or to the issue of immigrant lives, one is more likely to find a much greater percentage of the resources needed online.

ONLINE RESOURCES

There is no longer an academic stigma to utilizing the Internet; it is, in many cases, the single most important tool available to a researcher. It has also become the federal government's principal means of disseminating information to the public. (See, for instance, Barbara Salazar Torreon, "Immigration: A Guide to Internet Sources," Congressional Research Service Report for Congress, September 9, 2004, which promises that "this report will be updated periodically as new information becomes available and to ensure the currency of the Web Addresses," http://hutchison.senate.gov/RS20936.pdf. It is more necessary now than ever, however, to understand the nature of sources. Online there are few editorial processes that screen information. Every individual or group who takes an interest in immigration may post their views. Their data may or may not be accurate; their assessments will almost certainly have been developed and compiled with some particular view toward the subject. For the sake of accuracy, then, it is necessary to identify the variety of online resources available. For the sake of efficiency, understanding how to navigate the almost unlimited access to information through the World Wide Web is essential. In few cases will online research alone provide the basis for extended studies of immigration. The resources available online are, however, immense, and will inform virtually every good research project.

The Internet is today so widely available through user-friendly softwares that one need hardly understand how it works in order to make good use of it. Knowledge of a few basic concepts will, however, be helpful. The Internet is a global digital infrastructure that connects computers worldwide in an "internetwork" (a network of networks, or Internet), using common protocols and languages. The most common and fastest-growing part of the Internet is the World Wide Web, a uniform method of accessing and retrieving information on the Internet by way of the hypertext transfer protocol (http). On the Internet, information is provided to computers through a software "server." Information is not actually found "on" the Internet but rather "through" the Internet, which enables the user to access files on another computer. Most people log on to the Internet using a computer program on their computer—known as a "browser"—which enables users to make use of text, graphic, and audiovisual links on the World Wide Web. The most common browsers are Netscape Navigator, Microsoft Internet Explorer, Firefox, and Safari.

Web Directories and Search Engines

Once the user has gained access to the Internet, the next stop is usually to visit a web directory (or web index) or a search engine. Web directories are constructed by people who evaluate web sites and organize material in a hierarchical fashion. Some of the most popular web directories include About. com (http://www.about.com), Infomine (http://infomine.ucr.edu), Librarians Index to the Internet (http://lii.org), and Yahoo! (http://www.yahoo. com). They are best used for general searches rather than specialized research, though they will usually lead to more specialized sites. They do filter much of the nonsense from the search results, but they do not contain full-text documents, and the very process of evaluation will often exclude partisan or eccentric information of considerable use in researching a controversial topic such as immigration.

For many researchers, the listed topics and subtopics are so general in nature that they are often of less use than search engines in doing research. Search Engines are built by computer robot programs ("spiders"), with pages ranked using predetermined computer algorithms. They have the advantage of containing full-text pages, but the materials are largely unfiltered, which puts a premium on the researcher's own skill in evaluating web sites. As search engines have become more sophisticated, organizing and rating listed sites, they are often a better first stop than a web directory. Yahoo! itself, for instance, now has browsing capabilities comparable to the most popular search engines such as Alta Vista (http://www.altavista.com),

Immigration

Google (http://www.google.com), HotBot (http://www.hotbot.com), and WebCrawler (http://www.webcrawler.com).

At the same time, most search engines also have large subject catalogs, providing some of the features formerly found only on web directories. Metasearch sites such as (http://www.ask.com [formerly AskJeeves]), Dogpile (http://www.dogpile.com), and Metacrawler (http://www.metacrawler.com) process key words through multiple search engines and can therefore combine some of the strengths of each site. The downside of metasearch sites is that there is some duplication and a real chance that the result of a search will be one of combined weaknesses.

The best method for using search engines is to learn the searching strategies for each one and find the engine that best suits one's needs. Generally, a simple key-word approach will yield good results. For more sophisticated searches, however, most well-equipped libraries have online tutorials explaining the strategies. One of the best can be found through the University of California, Berkeley, "Finding Information on the Internet: A Tutorial" (http://www.lib.berkeley.edu/TeachingLib/Guides/Internet/FindInfo.html).

Finally, there is much information in databases that is not displayed either by web directories or search engines—what is sometimes called the "invisible web." At present the most important databases related to immigration are accessible through web directories and search engines, but the invisible web may well become more significant in research as technologies evolve. The most authoritative recent information can be found at Robert J. Lackie's "Those Dark Hiding Places: The Invisible Web Revealed" (http://library.rider.edu/scholarly/rlackie/Invisible/Inv_Web.html).

Government Web Sites

The U.S. government routinely collects, analyzes, and publishes data on immigration. Almost all private research into the broader issues surrounding immigration depends on the raw statistics provided by the federal government. The most comprehensive statistics are provided by the Office of Immigration Statistics (OIS, http://uscis.gov/graphics/shared/statistics), within the Office of Policy, Planning and International Affairs of the Department of Homeland Security (DHS), which is responsible for developing, analyzing, and disseminating statistical information needed to assess the effects of immigration in the United States.

The most extensive publication by the OIS is the annual *Yearbook of Immigration Statistics.* The yearbook, available online in PDF format, includes text, tables, and charts about immigrants, temporary visitors (nonimmigrants), parolees, refugees, asylees, and those naturalized or apprehended. Information includes statistical data, discussion of statistical programs, and analysis. Detailed tables, which can be accessed in Excel format, include:

How to Research Immigration Issues

- "Immigrants Admitted by Gender, Age, Marital Status, and Occupation: Fiscal Year 2004"
- "Immigrants Admitted by Major Class of Admission and Selected Demographic Characteristics: Fiscal Year 2004"
- "Immigrants Admitted by Region and Country of Birth: Fiscal Years 1989–2004"
- "Immigrants Admitted by Selected Class of Admission and Region and Country of Birth: Fiscal Year 2004"
- Immigrants Admitted by Selected Class of Admission and Region and Country of Last Permanent Residence: Fiscal Year 2004"
- "Immigrants Admitted by State of Intended Residence: Fiscal Years 1988–2004"
- "Immigrants Admitted by Type and Class of Admission: Fiscal Year 2004"
- "Immigrants Admitted by Type and Selected Class of Admission: Fiscal Years 1986–2004"
- "Immigrants-Orphans Adopted by U.S. Citizens by Gender, Age, and Region and Country of Birth: Fiscal Year 2004"
- "Immigration by Region and Selected Country of Last Residence: Fiscal Years 1820–2004"
- "Immigration to the United States: Fiscal Years 1820–2004"

The most recent yearbook available, for 2003 statistics (published in September 2004), was 220 pages. Earlier yearbooks, reports, and related data are archived as far back as 1994. The Office of Immigration Statistics maintains an e-mail list used to announce new publications and enhancements to its web site (contact immigrationstatistics@dhs.gov.)

The OIS also regularly publishes fact sheets (such as Kelly Jefferys, "Characteristics of Employment Based Legal Permanent Residents, 2004" and "Characteristics of Family-Sponsored Legal Permanent Residents, 2004," both published in October 2005); working papers (such as John Simanski, "Mapping Trends in U.S. Legal Immigration, 1980–2003," September 2005); detailed country and area demographic profiles of legal permanent residents and naturalized citizens; annual general and flow reports; annual population estimates; and monthly and fiscal year-end statistical reports.

OIS statistics and analysis are complemented by the work of the U.S. Census Bureau (http://www.census.gov), which provides important social data on the entire population of the United States, including economic conditions, housing, education, demographics, ethnic origins, and language use, mainly through the Decennial Census and the Current Population Survey.

159

Immigration

The value of the Decennial Census has been proven across time, especially in dealing with broad immigration trends. The Current Population Survey is even more accurate. Even though it is based upon a much smaller sample of the population, sample households all receive an interview by a Census Bureau employee. Census data do not target immigrants but do include the category "foreign-born," which enables the researcher to identify all those who were not U.S. citizens at birth, including naturalized U.S. citizens, lawful permanent residents (immigrants), temporary migrants (such as students), humanitarian migrants (such as refugees), and persons illegally present in the United States. Foreign-born population data are collected annually in the March Current Population Survey for the nation and in the American Community Survey for the nation as well as for states and large counties and cities. The U.S. Census Bureau also estimates net international migration for the nation, states, and counties, based in part on data collected in censuses and surveys. Projections of the U.S. population are also made using assumptions about net international migration.

Most government agencies publish statistical data that reflects in some way the immigrant experience in the Untied States. The U.S. Department of Commerce, for instance, publishes data on the number of foreign tourists visiting the country; the U.S. Department of Labor reports on the certification of aliens who come to the United States; the U.S. Department of Justice administers and interprets federal immigration laws and regulations through the Executive Office of Immigration Review; and the U.S. Department of State issues visas to foreign visitors coming to the country and administers programs for refugees and exchange visitors. For more detailed contact information, see the various agency listings in chapter 8.

If a researcher is seeking statistics but is unsure of the agency that might be responsible for them, it might be useful to start with a visit to FedStats (http://www.fedstats.gov), a portal to the full range of official statistics published by more than 100 federal agencies. Information is searchable, based on more than 400 topics. There are also links to summaries of the major statistical programs, including agriculture, education, energy, environment, health, income, labor, national accounts, safety, and transportation. If the name of an agency is known, there is a browser for access to statistics, as well as links to specific documents and key contact information. FedStats also provides up-to-date press releases on new statistics being released by federal agencies.

Organizations Web Sites

Almost all organizations devoted to understanding immigration issues now have web sites, and many of them include extensive publications. Some, such as the Immigration History Research Center at the University of Minnesota, Public Agenda, and the Brookings Institution, are principally informational, providing resources, statistics and studies in a relatively unbiased manner. Most serious broad studies are in some way based upon figures provided through the OIS, U.S. Census Bureau, and other government agencies, though many valuable studies are based on case studies or research generated at local levels. While many organizations study immigration from a more or less neutral position, seeking to understand the historical or contemporary process and what its results have been, most have been created with a particular point of view regarding immigration. The Center for Immigration Studies is an example of a nonpartisan, independent, research institute, solidly academic in its methods but "animated by a pro-immigrant, low-immigration vision which seeks fewer immigrants but a warmer welcome for those admitted."

An organization such as the New York Immigrant Coalition is specifically organized to link the efforts of more than 150 pro-immigrant organizations. As a result, they help in securing the cooperation of groups such as the American-Arab Anti-Discrimination Committee, Arab-American Family Support Center, Asian-American Legal Defense and Education Fund, Association of the Bar of the City of New York, Coney Island Avenue Project, Council of Peoples Organization, Council on American-Islamic Relations, Islamic Circle of North America, Legal Aid Society, and Lutheran Family and Community Services in opposition to what they perceive to be legislation or attitudes hostile toward immigrants. In 2004, for instance, they worked with their member groups to prepare a "Special Registration Statistical Report" regarding the November 2002 requirement that males from 24 Muslim countries and North Korea register with the federal government. Clearly written to undermine the credibility of the government program, their research is valuable in providing a statistical study of 346 persons seen in legal clinics relative to the law. For descriptions and contact information on specific organizations, see chapter 8.

General Immigration Sites

The most important ongoing web sites regarding immigration research are maintained by government, educational and research, and advocacy and aid organizations. With the evolution of the Internet, however, a variety of advertising and educational sites not linked to specific organizations do provide useful information.

H-Migration (http://www.h-net.org/~migrate) is a site dedicated to "enhancing scholarly communication about the global history of migration and the acculturation of immigrants and their descendants into their new society." Its principal benefit is a weblog dedicated to the exchange of information regarding any aspect of immigration. This site is especially useful in researching new or obscure topics. A limited number of related book reviews are also included.

Immigration

There are a number of sites such as American Immigration Resources on the Internet (http://www.wave.net/upg/immigration/resource.html), the Immigration Index (http://www.immigrationindex.org), and the Immigration Portal (http://www.ilw.com) that provide a mix of advertised services and general information aimed at the immigrant community. These sites, often linked to client services, can be useful in locating recent information on legislation and events affecting immigrants.

See also the U.S. Commission on Immigration Reform (http://www.utexas.edu/lbj/uscir), authorized by Section 141 of the Immigration Act of 1990 to review and evaluate the implementations and impacts of U.S. immigration policy and to report its findings to Congress. The commission expired on December 31, 1997, but its extensive findings are still available through this web site.

Media Web Sites

Any research into the contemporary debate over immigration issues and policy should include a thorough search of the web sites and archives of broadcast and cable networks, news services, newspapers, and news magazines. Not only do they cover the news on a regular basis, but they also provide a wide range of timely and thoughtful commentaries and editorials on the news. In order to get a variety of viewpoints on controversial issues, it is especially important to consult alternative as well as mainstream media sites.

Wire services supply basic news reporting to thousands of media outlets and individuals around the world. The most important are:

- Associated Press (AP) wire, http://www.ap.org (the site includes links to affiliated newspapers across the United States)
- Reuters, http://today.reuters.com/news

Network and cable television web sites not only include an extensive collection of archived materials but also frequently provide video links to on-air resources.

- American Broadcasting Company News, http://abcnews.go.com
- British Broadcasting Corporation (BBC), http://www.bbc.com (especially good for international coverage of controversial events)
- Cable News Network (CNN), http://www.cnn.com
- Fox News Network (FN), http://www.foxnews.com
- National Broadcasting Company News, http://www.msnbc.com

National and international news magazines generally provide more careful analysis of issues than is provided in the daily broadcast or print media:

162

- *The Economist,* http://www.economist.com
- *Newsweek,* http://www.msnbc.msn.com/id/3032542/site/newsweek
- *Time,* http://www.time.com
- *U.S. News and World Report,* http://www.usnews.com/usnews

Newspapers frequently use wire services to provide material for national and international stories. Those catering to national and international readerships, such as the *New York Times* and the *Wall Street Journal,* will conduct their own investigations, and virtually all newspapers will report directly on stories involving their city and region.

- *Los Angeles Times,* http://www.latimes.com
- *New York Times,* http://www.nytimes.com
- *The Times,* http://www.timesonline.co.uk
- *Wall Street Journal,* http://www.wsj.com
- *Washington Post,* http://www.washingtonpost.com

Key alternative sites include:

- *Gotham Gazette,* http://www.gothamgazette.com, publisher of a daily selection of articles from the immigrant presses of New York City; it includes links to more than 50 ethnic newspapers.
- *New California Media* (NCM), http://news.ncmonline.com, a nationwide association of more than 700 ethnic media organizations, founded in 1996 to provide a voice for alternative media viewpoints and to foster intercultural dialogue.

For a list of U.S. city newspapers, go to http://www.newspapers.com. For a more comprehensive portal to a variety of newspapers from around the world, go to http://dir.yahoo.com/News_and_Media/Newspapers/Web_Directories.

BIBLIOGRAPHIC RESOURCES

Despite the usefulness of online resources, most academic discourse related to immigration and immigration history is still reported in monographs and articles published in hard copy. Some of these also may be available on the Internet, but most are not.

Library Catalogs

Usually found online, library catalogs provide access to the holdings of specific libraries. The Library of Congress (http://catalog.loc.gov) provides

Immigration

extensive search capabilities to the largest library in the United States. WorldCat (http://www.oclc.org/worldcat/default.htm) is the world's largest bibliographic database, created by merging the catalogs of thousands of OCLC member libraries. Built and maintained collectively by librarians, WorldCat will direct the researcher to the vast majority of books, pamphlets, and other monographic publications on immigration-related topics. WorldCat is available through many libraries as a part of their FirstSearch subscription. As useful as it is, however, WorldCat often will not include obscure or privately printed resources, such as materials produced by smaller or historic ethnic-related organizations.

Bibliographies, Indexes, and Periodical Databases

Bibliographies, indexes, and periodical databases are usually accessed through the particular library in which one is doing research.

There is no up-to-date bibliography specifically devoted to immigration issues, though reasonably extensive annotated listings can be found in Elliot Robert Barkan, *A Nation of Peoples: A Sourcebook on America's Multicultural Heritage* (Westport, Conn.: Greenwood Press, 1999). For specific immigrant groups and historical topics, see John Powell, *Encyclopedia of North American Immigration* (New York: Facts On File, 2005). For a good general bibliography by a master scholar of immigration, see Rudolph J. Vecoli, *A Selected Bibliography on American Immigration and Ethnicity*, revised edition. (Minneapolis: Immigration History Research Center, University of Minnesota, 2001), a source likely to be updated in the future. Dated, but still useful, are Francisco Cordasco and David Nelson Alloway, *American Ethnic Groups, the European Heritage: A Bibliography of Doctoral Dissertations Completed at American Universities* (Metuchen, N.J.: Scarecrow Press, 1981), and Francisco Cordasco, ed., *A Bibliography of American Immigration History* (Fairfield, N.J.: Augustus M. Kelley, 1979).

Most of the indexes and periodical databases are now maintained by publishing houses in electronic format, regularly updated, and made available to libraries by subscription. Library users are then generally able to print abstracts or full-text articles. Most databases will be available at any research library, and many will be found at good public libraries or other educational libraries. Almost all have extensive search capabilities that allow the researcher to identify and mark useful material, either to be searched for in hard copy or downloaded as a full-text article. Some, like IngentaConnect, make full-text articles available for purchase to anyone with access to the Internet. Among the most useful indexes and periodical databases are:

- **Academic Search Elite:** Provides full text for more than 1,850 journals covering the social sciences, humanities, general sciences, multicultural studies, and education.

164

- **Academic Search Premier:** Provides full text for nearly 4,000 scholarly publications covering academic areas of study including social sciences, humanities, education, computer sciences, engineering, language and linguistics, arts and literature, medical sciences, and ethnic studies.

- **Alternative Press Index (and API Archives, FirstSearch):** Provides access to a wide range of non-mainstream voices regarding social issues, from 1969 to present, including material from more than 700 sources.

- **Alt-Press Watch (ProQuest):** Provides full-text access to more than 130 alternative newspapers, magazines, and journals since 1995.

- **American Humanities Index:** A collection of bibliographic references to more than 1,000 literary, scholarly, and creative journals published in the United States and Canada, including citation information for articles, essays, and reviews, as well as original creative works including, poems, fiction, photographs, paintings, and illustrations.

- **ArticleFirst (FirstSearch):** Includes references to articles, news stories, letters, and other items in business, the humanities, the sciences, the social sciences, medicine, technology, and popular culture, drawn from the tables of content of more than 16,000 publications; provides a list of libraries where journals can be found.

- **Arts and Humanities Search (FirstSearch):** Includes records from 1980 to present from more than 1,100 sources; indexes the world's leading arts and humanities journals has and selected articles from social science and science journals, as well as bibliographies, editorials, letters, and reviews.

- **Chicano Database:** Mainly covers the post-1967 period, including the Mexican, Puerto Rican, Cuban, and Central American immigrant experience.

- **Dissertation Abstracts (FirstSearch):** Includes all doctoral dissertations completed in the United States from 1861 to the present, as well as some foreign dissertations and masters' theses; updated monthly.

- **ERIC (FirstSearch):** Provides access to the broad range of literature relevant to education issues; drawn from more than 1,000 sources.

- **Ethnic NewsWatch (ProQuest):** Comprehensive full-text database of the newspapers, magazines, and journals of the ethnic and minority, press; covers materials since 1991 drawn from 240 publications; an average of 7,500 new articles added each month.

- **Ethnic Newswatch: A History (ProQuest):** Full-text database covering more than 200 newspapers, magazines, and journals of the ethnic and minority press between 1960 and 1989.

- **Heritage Quest (ProQuest):** Includes page reproductions of U.S. federal census records between 1790 and 1930 and a book collection of more than 8,000 family histories and related source materials.

Immigration

- **Historical Abstracts (FirstSearch):** References articles from more than 2,000 sources published since 1954 and includes citations of reviews and dissertations on world history (except United States and Canada) from 1450 to the present.
- **IngentaConnect:** Useful in providing bibliographic information and abstracts to 19 million articles from 29,500 publications; most articles are available for purchase in full text.
- **Sociological Abstracts (FirstSearch):** Indexes articles concerning sociology, anthropology, criminology, law, social psychology, urban studies, race relations, demography, and education drawn from more than 1,600 sources, many of which frequently involve reference to immigration issues.

Journals and Newsletters

Many immigrant groups have published newspapers or journals, some of which lasted for only a brief period. The most comprehensive collection can be found at the Immigration History Research Center at the University of Minnesota (see "IHRC Periodicals," http://www.ihrc.umn.edu/research/periodicals/index.htm). Some useful contemporary academic journals and newsletters are:

- *Asian and Pacific Migration Journal:* Reports on Asian and Pacific migration from a multidisciplinary perspective.
- *Citizenship Studies:* Interdisciplinary coverage of issues related to citizenship, human rights, and political integration.
- *Ethnic and Racial Studies:* Includes studies of race, ethnicity, and nationalism drawn from a wide range of academic disciplines, including sociology, political science, history, anthropology, and economics.
- *Ethnicities:* Reports on ethnicity, nationalism, and related issues, mainly from sociological and political perspectives.
- *Ethnohistory:* Contains scholarly articles and review essays including documentary materials and ethnographic and archaeological data.
- *Forced Migration Review:* Journal of the Refugee Studies Centre, Queen Elizabeth House, University of Oxford; it seeks to foster best practices in refugee policy development.
- *Georgetown Immigration Law Journal:* Scholarly journal including articles, case reviews, and workshop reports related to immigration law.
- *Identities: Global Studies in Culture and Power:* Multidisciplinary journal dealing with national and international manifestations of racial, ethnic, and national identities.

How to Research Immigration Issues

- *Immigrants Action Alert:* Produced by the American Immigration Lawyer's Association to keep immigrants regularly informed about news and legislation affecting their status and specific ways of becoming involved.

- *Immigrants and Minorities:* Journal dealing with the internation history of immigration, particularly as it relates to conceptions of race.

- *Immigration and Ethnic History Newsletter:* Includes articles on historiography and pedagogy related to immigration and has news of conferences, exhibitions, libraries, and research.

- *Immigration Law Today:* Published by the American Immigration Lawyer's Association, it provides current information on immigration law, advocacy, and policy development; articles are written by practicing attorneys and other experts in the field.

- *International Journal of Refugee Law:* Reports on the causes, displacements, and policies related to international migrations, with particular attention to the condition of women and children.

- *International Migration:* A policy-oriented journal covering all aspects of international migration; published by the IGO International Migration organization.

- *International Migration Review:* Published by the NGO Center for Migration Studies, it incorporates the International Sociological Association's International Newsletter on Migration; it is the premier journal of international migration studies.

- *Ìrìnkèrindò: A Journal of African Migration:* Includes original essays, reprints, critical commentaries, and interviews with African immigrants; designed to "document the relevance of African immigration to the world's social, political and economic systems as well as its historical effects on culture."

- *Journal of American Ethnic History:* Published by the Immigration and Ethnic History Society, it includes articles on adjustment and assimilation, group relations, mobility, politics, culture, group identity, or other topics that illuminate the North American immigrant and ethnic/racial experience.

- *Journal of Ethnic and Migration Studies:* Formerly *New Community* (1971–97), deals with migration issues at a global level, focusing on advanced industrial countries.

- *Journal of International Migration and Integration:* Multidisciplinary bilingual (English and French) scholarly journal presenting original research, theoretical examinations, and policy formulations, with the goal of "strengthening policy and highlighting best practices in the settlement of migrants."

Immigration

- *Journal of Refugee Studies:* Multidisciplinary journal promoting theoretical developments and innovative methodological approaches to the study of refugee issues.

- *Migration: A European Journal of International Migration and Ethnic Relations:* Published by the European Research Forum on Migration and Ethnic Relations, it focuses on the work of European social scientists in migration studies.

- *Migration Letters:* Broad, multidisciplinary journal that publishes short accounts of current research dealing with internal, international, and forced migration.

- *Migration News:* Important newsletter published by the University of California–Davis that covers immigration and integration developments each quarter; online version is twice as long as the print copy.

- *Migration Themes—A Journal for Migration and Ethnic Studies:* Published by the Institute for Migration and Ethnic Studies in Zagreb, Croatia, it covers a wide range of migration topics, mostly from an eastern European perspective.

- *Population and Development Review:* Drawing from the disciplines of economics, sociology, political science, and anthropology, the journal explores the interrelationships between population and socioeconomic development and provides a forum for discussion of related issues of public policy.

- *Refugee Reports:* An important newsletter published by the Immigration and Refugee Services of America, generally covering a specific legislative or area issue related to refugees; one issue each year focuses on statistical accounts of refugee status.

- *Refugee Survey Quarterly:* Each issue focuses on a different theme related to refugees and related policies; includes documents and conference reports as well as scholarly articles.

- *Restrictionist Watch:* Published by the American Immigration Lawyer's Association to alert members and partners to the activities of "well-organized and well-funded" immigration restrictionists who "fight any and all positive immigration initiatives."

- *Revue Européenne des Migrations Internationales:* An important journal in international migration, published in French.

- *Rural Migration News:* Important newsletter published by the University of California–Davis that covers news related to immigrant farm workers each quarter; online version is twice as long as the print copy.

- *Social Science Quarterly:* This journal of the Southwestern Social Sciences Association publishes articles in all the social sciences; special issue of 2006 focuses on ethnicity.

- *Wadabagei: A Journal of the Caribbean and Its Diaspora:* An inter-disciplinary journal published by the Caribbean Diaspora Press, Inc., and the Caribbean Research Center, part of the City University of New York. It focuses on the acculturation of Caribbean immigrants in North America.
- *World Refugee Survey:* Published by the U.S. Committee for Refugees and Immigrants, it reports on conditions for refugees and internally displaced persons in 120 countries.

Bookstore Catalogs

Although no substitute for comprehensive searches in library catalogs or important bibliographies, indexes, and periodical databases, a search through online bookstore catalogs such as Amazon (http://www.amazon.com), and Barnes & Noble (http://www.barnesandnoble.com) may be a necessary last step, particularly for recent subjects. Thanks to Internet marketing capabilities and opportunities, online bookstore catalogs will almost always have information on newly published—or soon to be published—books well before even the most frequently updated databases. Catalog web pages will often include links to table of contents, indexes, and sample materials from each work.

IMMIGRATION LAW AND LEGAL RESEARCH

Three factors combine to make information on immigration and the law widely available in the United States. First, the wide access to computers makes it advantageous for anyone seeking to communicate information to put it online. Second, the high value placed on freedom of information encourages the government to make legal information widely available. And third, private lawyers and related companies stand to profit by advertising their services online. Together these factors have led to most primary legal decisions and notices being available online.

Finding and Tracking Legislation

The U.S. Congress has unlimited constitutional authority (plenary power) to legislate in matters regarding immigration. As a result, the most important legal research related to immigration concerns legislation and its regulation. The Supreme Court has been reluctant to interfere with immigration legislation, with most decisions relating to statutory interpretation. For a full description of the nature of immigration law, and the relative powers of the three branches of government, see the introduction to chapter 2 of this book and consult David Weissbrodt and Laura Danielson, *Immigration Law and Procedure*, 5th Edition (Thomson West, 2005).

169

Immigration

In U.S. history, there have been four comprehensive immigration laws: Immigration Act of May 26, 1924; Immigration and Nationality Act of June 27, 1952; Immigration and Nationality Act Amendments of October 3, 1965; and Immigration Act of November 29, 1990 (see chapter 2 for more detailed information). The most important current laws relating to immigration are found in the U.S. Code Title 8, containing laws relating to "Aliens and Nationality." A searchable U.S. Code can be found at the Office of the Law Revision Counsel (http://uscode.house.gov/search/criteria.shtml) and at Cornell Legal Information Institute (http://www4.law.cornell.edu/uscode). The U.S. Code does not include executive regulations, federal court decisions, treaties, or laws enacted by state or local governments. Regulations issued by executive branch agencies are available in the Code of Federal Regulations (http://www.access.gpo.gov/nara/cfr/cfr-table-search.html) and in print in the *Federal Register* (http://www.gpoaccess.gov/nara), a legal newspaper published every business day by the National Archives and Records Administration (NARA). The *Federal Register* also contains proposed rules and notices, executive orders, proclamations, and other presidential documents. Immigration legislation can also be tracked through the THOMAS site of the Library of Congress (http://thomas.loc.gov). In some cases, the best starting point for research will be the Meta-Index for U.S. Legal Research (http://gsulaw.gsu.edu/metaindex), which combines links to many of the sites mentioned above with other important legal sites, in sections relating to judicial opinions (Supreme Court and district courts), legislation, federal regulation, and other legal sources.

Researching Court Decisions

In a U.S. Supreme Court, a typical citation will read:

Graham v. Richardson, 403 U.S. 365 (1971)

The first name listed refers to the plaintiff, the second name to the defendant, with this example case being published in volume 403 of the U.S. Supreme Court Reports (http://www.supremecourtus.gov/opinions/boundvolumes.html), beginning on page 365, and with the case having been decided in 1971. The full text for volumes prior to 502 must be searched in hard copy.

The most important government-related site devoted specifically to immigration law is the Virtual Law Library (http://www.usdoj.gov/eoir/vll/libindex.html), part of the Executive Office for Immigration Review, in the Department of Justice. This site includes links to the U.S. Code and groupings of Federal Register publications directly related to immigration.

It also includes up-to-date information on federal and immigration court decisions, decisions of the Board of Immigration Appeals, administrative judgments, and contact information on all immigration courts. Related information provided by the government includes the Office of Administrative Judges Law Library Immigration Collection (http://www.oalj.dol.gov/libina.htm), highlighting employment and labor-related cases; it includes all recent postings from the U.S. Department of Labor (DOL) regarding regulations for Permanent Foreign Labor Certification, as well as summaries of various DOL decisions.

A number of commercial legal databases include extensive information on immigration law; most publish a wide range of aids for potential immigrants and resources for legal professionals seeking to assist immigrants. The most important are LexisNexis (http://www.lexisnexis.com) and WestLaw (http://west.thomson.com/store/product.asp?product%5Fid=Westlaw&catalog%5Fname=wgstore). See also Nolo (http://nolo.com). Legal research web guides for basic immigration law information or for referral services include FindLaw.com, LawCrawler.com, and LawInfo.com. The FindLaw Library is perhaps the best place to start, including a collection of legal articles and documents on the Web and a section devoted to immigration law (http://library.findlaw.com/Immigration.html).

International cases related to refugees can be followed at the Refugee Caselaw Site of the University of Michigan Law School (http://www.refugeecaselaw.org), which provides a searchable database of more than 400 cases involving refugee and asylum law, drawn from the core countries of the United States, United Kingdom, Switzerland, Germany, Canada, Australia, and New Zealand, with cases from additional countries gradually being added. See also Elisa Mason's excellent "Guide to International Refugee Law Resources on the Web" (http://www.llrx.com/features/refugee.htm).

For printed sources in legal research, see "Immigration Law," chapter 7, below.

NATIONAL AND ETHNIC GROUP RESEARCH

An important part of understanding immigration as a movement is an appreciation of factors affecting ethnic or culture groups, in terms of their reasons for migrating to the United States, the migration experience itself, and the results across time once they arrived in the country. Undoubtedly, every immigrant has had his or her own story to tell. Just as clearly, however, members of the same culture group have tended to move together, to develop links with the old country, to cluster together in settlements, to establish ethnic businesses and media outlets, and otherwise to associate themselves with the "old country" for at least a period of time. This is just as true today as it was in the 17th century. As a result, there is real benefit in examining the labor condition of Arab Americans in New York City in the post-9/11 era or the nature of Polish immigration to America after the fall of the Berlin Wall.

The specific experience of an ethnic or culture group can be researched by using a group identifier in the search engines associated with any of the sites above. Web sites associated with organizations listed in chapter 8 can be searched in the same way. The starting point for primary materials should be the Immigration History Research Center (IHRC) at the University of Minnesota (http://www.umn.edu/ihrc).

The following works include a significant emphasis on ethnic groups: John Powell, *Encyclopedia of North American Immigration* (New York: Facts On File, 2005); Elliott Barkan, ed., *A Nation of Peoples* (Westport, Conn.: Greenwood Press, 1999); Robert von Dassanowsky and Jeffrey Lehman, *Gale Encyclopedia of Multicultural America*, 2d ed., 3 vols. (Detroit: Gale Group, 2000); David Levinson and Melvin Ember, eds., *American Immigrant Cultures: Builders of a Nation*, 2 vols. (New York: Macmillan Reference, 1997); and Stephen Thernstrom, ed. *Harvard Encyclopedia of American Ethnic Groups* (Cambridge, Mass.: Belknap Press, Harvard University Press, 1980). All of these books contain useful bibliographies.

CHAPTER 7

ANNOTATED BIBLIOGRAPHY

GENERAL REFERENCE WORKS

BOOKS

Bakken, Gordon Morris, and Alexandra Kindell, eds. *Encyclopedia of Immigration and Migration in the American West*. 2 vols. London: Sage Publications. Systematically covers migration in the west, including European ethnic groups, African Americans, and the movements of Native Americans; includes a section on "Immigration Laws and Policies."

Bankston, Carl L., III, and Danielle Hidalgo, eds. *Immigration in U.S. History*. 2 vols. Pasadena, Calif.: Salem Press, 2006. Edited by two sociologists from Tulane University, this work is principally drawn from other recent Salem Press publications, with updated bibliographies attached.

Bankston, Carl L., III, ed. *Racial and Ethnic Relations in America*. 3 vols. Pasadena, Calif.: Salem Press, 2000. This is a general reference work that primarily discusses legal and political issues related to race and ethnicity, rather than with specific ethnic groups.

Barkan, Elliott, ed. *A Nation of Peoples*. Westport, Conn.: Greenwood Press, 1999. The starting point for up-to-date immigration studies, Barkan presents 27 ethnic studies that provide an excellent historiographic overview and a good annotated bibliography. The well-written articles contain useful annotated bibliographies, including references to leading journals and primary source collections.

Brown, Mary Ellen. *Shapers of the Great Debate on Immigration: A Biographical Dictionary*. Westport, Conn.: Greenwood Press, 1999. This work includes a series of 20 biographical portraits of figures whose arguments, both for and against immigration, helped shape the nature of immigration policy and attitudes.

Buenker, John D., and Lorman A. Ratner, eds. *Multiculturalism in the United States: A Comparative Guide to Acculturation and Ethnicity*. Westport,

173

Conn.: Greenwood Press, 1992. This is a dated but still useful reference, particularly regarding ethnic institutions.

Canter, Laurence A., and Martha S. Siegel. *U.S. Immigration Made Easy*, 11th ed. Berkeley, Calif.: Nolo Press, 2004. This is a good example of a regularly updated legal guide to the process of immigration, explaining the process and showing potential immigrants what is necessary to qualify for visas, green cards, citizenship, and refugee status; includes 44 related government forms.

Ciment, James, ed. *Encyclopedia of American Immigration*. 4 vols. Armonk, N.Y.: Sharpe Reference, 2001. Ciment focuses less than most multivolume reference works on immigrant groups and more on related topics such as demographics, acculturation, economics, cultural presence, and religion. The work also includes more than 200 pages of related primary materials, including laws and treaties, executive orders, court cases, political platforms, government rulings, historical articles, and personal letters. Although coverage is selective, the 1,200 pages of material covers a wide variety of historical, sociological, cultural, and legal topics, including many recent developments.

Cordasco, Francesco. *Dictionary of American Immigration History*. Metuchen, N.J.: Scarecrow Press, 1990. Maddeningly irregular, this reference work covers obscure issues found nowhere else. Still it can be a useful source.

Cordasco, Francesco, and David Nelson Alloway. *American Ethnic Groups, the European Heritage: A Bibliography of Doctoral Dissertations Completed at American Universities*. Metuchen, N.J.: Scarecrow Press, 1981. In this dated but still useful work, Cordasco identifies some obscure research.

Cordasco, Francesco, ed. *A Bibliography of American Immigration History*. Fairfield, N.J.: Augustus M. Kelley, 1979. Cordasco's dated but still useful work provides annotations of older and little-known pamphlets and articles; the further these are removed from contemporary use, the more valuable this resource becomes.

Dassanowsky, Robert von, and Jeffrey Lehman. *Gale Encyclopedia of Multicultural America*. 2nd ed., 3 vols. Detroit: Gale Group, 2000. This is an excellent resource covering 152 separate ethnic groups, including many Native American tribes; focuses on culture and current status.

Foner, Nancy, Rubén G. Rumbaut, Steven J. Gold, eds. *Immigration Research for a New Century: Multidisciplinary Perspectives*. New York: Russell Sage Foundation, 2000. This collection of scholarly articles emanated from a 1998 conference sponsored by the Committee on International Migration of the Social Science Research Council, suggesting a range of new approaches toward exploring immigration studies.

Gibney, Matthew J., and Randall Hansen, eds. *Immigration and Asylum from 1900 to the Present*. 3 vols. Santa Barbara, Calif.: ABC-CLIO, 2005. Gibney presents a superb general reference covering asylum issues; includes good bibliographies and a full volume of significant documents.

Greene, Victor R. *American Immigrant Leaders, 1800–1910: Marginality and Identity.* Baltimore: Johns Hopkins University Press, 1987. Focusing on the leadership of the six major white immigrant groups—Irish, Germans, Norwegians and Swedes, Jews, Poles, and Italians—Greene seeks to identify and delineate common themes across immigrant culture groups.

Haines, David W. *Refugees in America in the 1990s: A Reference Handbook.* Westport, Conn.: Greenwood Press, 1996. Built around a series of articles on 12 specific refugee groups, the scope of the work is broadened by two introductory articles that provide a conceptual framework and five articles that provide useful comparative material, including an article on "Documentary Films about Refugees," by Beatrice Nied Hackett.

Kasinitz, Philip, and Josh DeWind, eds. *The Handbook of International Migration: The American Experience.* New York: Russell Sage Foundation, 1999. Part I examines current theories of international migration, part II deals with how immigrants are affected by their new home, and part III looks at the implications of immigration for American society.

LeMay, Michael C. *U.S. Immigration: A Reference Handbook.* Santa Barbara, Calif.: ABC-CLIO, 2004. Focusing on U.S. immigration policy since 1965, the author provides an overview of the subject with summaries of important legislation, biographies, and court cases, as well as bibliographic listings and organization addresses to facilitate further research. This is an excellent starting point for immigration research.

Levinson, David, and Melvin Ember, eds. *American Immigrant Cultures: Builders of a Nation.* 2 vols. New York: Macmillan Reference, 1997. Covering more than 160 ethnic groups, this is a useful reference book for social and cultural conditions of immigrant groups; bibliographies are sometimes thin and increasingly dated. The books should be consulted for lesser-known groups not covered in depth elsewhere.

Meilaender, Peter C. *Toward a Theory of Immigration.* New York: Palgrave, 2001. Noting a long-term American ambivalence about immigration, the author argues for and against open borders, concluding that nation-states have a right to restrict immigration.

Miller, E. Willard, and Ruby M. Miller. *United States Immigration: A Reference Handbook.* Santa Barbara, Calif.: ABC-CLIO, 1996. This work contains much useful information but is now largely superseded by the 2004 edition by Michael LeMay.

Moody, Suzanna, and Joel Wurl, eds. *The Immigration History Research Center: A Guide to Collections.* Westport, Conn.: Greenwood Press, 1991. This is a necessary guide to the rich archival resources of the Immigration History Research Center, focusing on southern and eastern Europe and the Middle East.

Immigration

Powell, John. *Encyclopedia of North American Immigration.* New York: Facts On File, 2005. This work includes briefer entries than the multivolume sets or the *Harvard Encyclopedia of American Ethnic Groups,* but it contains extensive bibliographies and simultaneous treatment of U.S. and Canadian immigration.

Pozetta, George E. *American Immigration and Ethnicity.* 20 vols. New York: Garland, 1990–91. Pozetta includes reproductions of hundreds of scholarly articles, arranged thematically. For introductory essays on immigration, see the first volume on "Themes in Immigration History."

Rodriguez, Junius P. *The Historical Encyclopedia of World Slavery.* Santa Barbara, Calif.: ABC-CLIO, 1997. Covering the whole range of history, Rodriguez provides background for the African origins of slaves brought to the Americas, as well as other immigrants whose ancestors were held as slaves.

Thernstrom, Stephen, ed. *Harvard Encyclopedia of American Ethnic Groups.* Cambridge, Mass.: Belknap Press, Harvard University Press, 1980. This is the preeminent one-volume reference work on American ethnic groups. It is thorough and analytic, comprising more than a million words, and written by the leading specialists of the day. Though published a quarter of a century ago, the articles remain of the first importance, especially for early immigrant groups and thematic topics, though its usefulness has gradually been eroded by time and changing circumstances. U.S. Bureau of the Census. Historical Statistics of the United States, Colonial Times to 1970. Washington, DC: U.S. Government Printing Office, 1975. This work provides essential data for examining immigration movements.

Vecoli, Rudolph J. *A Selected Bibliography on American Immigration and Ethnicity,* rev. ed. Minneapolis: Immigration History Research Center, University of Minnesota, 2001. This provides a good starting point for research by a preeminent scholar of immigration studies.

ARTICLES

Goldewijk, Kees Klein. "Three Centuries of Global Population Growth: A Spatial Referenced Population Density Database for 1700–2000." *Population and Environment* 26:4 (March 2005): 343–367. This excellent study explores the impact of the colonization of the "New World," updating the "geo-referenced historical population maps" for use in "integrated models of global change."

Moya, Jose C. "A Continent of Immigrants: Postcolonial Shifts in the Western Hemisphere." *Hispanic American Historical Review* 86:1 (February 2006): 1–28. The author suggests that by looking at the "New World" as a single region "populated by arrivals from all the other continents," as is common in Latin America, it will aid in avoiding the host-nation-centered approach that is more common in the United States.

Annotated Bibliography

WEB DOCUMENTS

Costanzo, Joseph M. Cynthia J. Davis, and Nolan Malone. "Guide to International Migration Statistics: The Sources, Collection, and Processing of Foreign-Born Population Data at the U.S. Census Bureau." Available online. URL: http://www.census.gov/population/www/documentation/twps0068/twps0068.html. Updated on August 27, 2004. The authors provide a highly detailed account of the nature and accuracy of the data collection instruments relative to international migration.

Gibson, Campbell J., and Emily Lennon. "Historical Census Statistics on the Foreign-Born Population of the United States: 1850–1990." Available online. URL: http://www.census.gov/population/www/documentation/twps0029/twps0029.html. Updated on January 18, 2001. Gibson and Lennon provide a detailed presentation of tables and analysis updating the U.S. Census Bureau, Historical Statistics of the United States, Colonial Times to 1970 (see above).

Gibson, Campbell J., and Kay Jung. "Historical Census Statistics on Population Totals by Race, 1790 to 1990, and by Hispanic Origin, 1970 to 1990, For the United States, Regions, Divisions, and States." Available online. URL: http://www.census.gov/population/www/documentation/twps0056.html. Updated on September 13, 2002. In the first significant study of racial and Hispanic statistics in more than a quarter century, the authors present and analyze dozens of detailed tables of information.

ATLASES

BOOKS

Allen, James Paul, and Eugene Turner. *We the People: An Atlas of America's Ethnic Diversity.* New York: Simon and Schuster, 1998. Based upon the 1980 U.S. Census, most of the maps are now out of date but still excellent as a historical record of America in the first decade and a half after the open door of 1965; covers 67 ethnic and racial groups.

Gaustad, Edwin Scott, and Philip L. Barlow. *New Historical Atlas of Religion in America.* Oxford: Oxford University Press, 2001. Beginning with the colonial period, this work covers the span of American history, treating major denominations, religions, and unbelief. It includes specific sections on Buddhists; Hindus, Jains, and Sikhs; Muslims and Bahais; and Ethnic Religion after 1800.

Lilley, William, III, Laurence J. DeFranco, and William M. Diefenderfer III. *The State Atlas of Political and Cultural Diversity.* Washington, D.C.: Congressional Quarterly Press, 1997. This work provides a sophisticated analysis of U.S. Census data, showing "precisely how fifteen of the nation's

Immigration

largest and most important racial, ethnic, and ancestral groups . . . are distributed among 6,744 state legislative districts."

Shinagawa, Larry H., and Michel Lang. *Atlas of American Diversity.* Walnut Creek, Calif.: AltaMira Press, 1998. In more than 200 maps and charts, the authors trace residential, occupational, age, and housing patterns of a wide range of ethnic groups; research in the book is based upon U.S. Census and other statistical data.

Tanner, Helen Hornbeck, ed. *The Settling of North America: The Atlas of the Great Migration into North America from the Ice Age to the Present.* New York: Macmillan, 1995. This atlas provides an excellent introduction to the subject, showing a wide range of international, national, regional, and urban distributions, often at the ward or county level. The book contains a good set of accompanying time lines.

WEB DOCUMENTS

"Mapping Census 2000: The Geography of U.S. Diversity." Available online. URL: http://www.census.gov/population/www/cen2000/atlas.html. Updated on October 3, 2003. Contains extensive and detailed social and cultural information on the United States in 2000, broken down by race and ethnicity; based upon self-reported identification.

ECONOMICS OF IMMIGRATION

BOOKS

Bacon, David. *The Children of NAFTA: Labor Wars on the U.S./Mexico Border.* Berkeley: University of California Press, 2004. Based on more than a decade of research in small villages, agricultural fields, and large factories, Bacon suggests the negative results of the new neoliberal economic policy that has led to a growing labor consciousness in Mexico, the United States, and Canada.

Bean, Frank D., and Stephanie Bell-Rose, ed. *Immigration and Opportunity: Race, Ethnicity, and Employment in the United States.* New York: Russell Sage Foundation, 1999. In this collection of articles, mainly by demographers and sociologists, the authors trace the impact of immigration on U.S.-born African Americans.

Bommes, Michael, and Andrew Geddes, eds. *Immigration and Welfare: Challenging the Borders of the Welfare State.* New York: Routledge, 2001. In this work, a panel of experts examines the dynamics of immigrant inclusion and exclusion as they are affected by access to national welfare benefits, emphasizing systemic challenges rather than perceptions of threat or danger.

178

Annotated Bibliography

Borjas, George J. *Friends or Strangers: The Impact of Immigration on the American Economy.* New York: Basic Books, 1990. In this pioneering study from Borjas, an economist, he argues that immigration does not lower native economic opportunities, though he observes that immigrants during the 1980s tended to be less skilled and thus less successful.

———. *Heaven's Door: Immigration Policy and the American Economy.* Princeton: Princeton University Press, 1999. Modifying his earlier approach, Borjas argues that immigration brings both costs and benefits and that the country would be well served to establish a clear skills test for determining who should qualify for entry.

Borjas, George J., ed. *Issues in the Economics of Immigration.* Chicago and London: University of Chicago Press, 2000. Instead of asserting that immigrants either are or are not good for the economy, this team of scholars explores the various ways in which they impact the economy, from education, to welfare, crime, labor markets, and social security.

Camarota, Steven A. *Importing Poverty: Immigration's Impact on the Size and Growth of the Poor Population in the United States.* Washington, D.C.: Center for Immigration Studies, 1999. Written by the director of research at the Center for Immigration Studies, this work examines changes in the demography of poverty in 1979, 1989, and 1997 and explores the impact of immigration on poverty.

Cheng, Lucy, and Edna Bonacich, eds. *Labor Immigration under Capitalism: Asian Workers in the United States before World War II.* Berkeley: University of California Press, 1984. This volume includes essays on the use of Asian labor in a variety of economic situations in the United States and the Hawaiian Islands.

Gamboa, Erasmo. *Mexican Labor and World War II: Braceros in the Pacific Northwest, 1942–1947.* Austin: University of Texas Press, 1990. Gamboa provides a close study of one aspect of the early Bracero Program in the United States.

Guerin-Gonzalez, Camille. *Mexican Workers and the American Dream: Immigration, Repatriation and California Farm Labor, 1900–1939.* New Brunswick, N.J.: Rutgers University Press, 1994. Utilizing archives in both Mexico and the United States, the author examines one of the largest forced repatriations in American history, when some 500,000 Mexican laborers were forced to return to their homeland.

Hammermesh, Daniel S., and Frank D. Bean, eds. *Help or Hindrance?: The Economic Implications of Immigration for African Americans.* New York: Russell Sage Foundation, 1998. Using detailed analysis of African-American labor circumstances, the authors argue that, although employment rates are little changed, immigration has impacted educational and affirmative-action opportunities.

Immigration

Hanson, Gordon H. *Why Does Immigration Divide America? Public Finance and Political Opposition to Open Borders.* Washington, D.C.: Institute for International Economics, 2005. The author, a professor of economics in the Graduate School of International Relations and Pacific Studies and the Department of Economics at the University of California, San Diego, suggests two strategies for making immigration more attractive: to attract individuals likely to pay more in taxes and to "restructure immigrants' rights" to public benefits.

Kretsedemas, Philip, and Ana Aparicio, ed. *Immigrants, Welfare Reform and the Poverty of Policy.* Westport, Conn.: Praeger, 2004. Resulting from an initiative by the W. K. Kellogg Foundation, this series of articles assesses the outcomes of the Welfare Reform Act of 1996 on specific groups in specific locations.

Martin, Philip L. *Promise Unfulfilled: Unions, Immigration, and the Farm Workers.* Ithaca, N.Y.: Cornell University Press, 2003. Martin argues that California's Agricultural Labor Relations Act of 1975 failed to substantially increase wages and improve working conditions primarily because of the increased flow of unauthorized workers.

Ness, Immanuel. *Immigrants, Unions, and the New U.S. Labor Market.* Philadelphia: Temple University Press, 2005. Building on the recent expansion of local worker unions among immigrants in urban areas, Ness suggests a model for future development of organized labor.

Pellow, David Naguib, and Lisa Sun-Hee Park. *The Silicon Valley of Dreams: Environmental Injustice, Immigrant Workers, and the High-Tech Global Economy.* New York: New York University Press, 2002. The authors suggest that immigrants leave a "lighter ecological footprint" than nonimmigrants but bear a disproportionate burden of high-tech pollution.

Portes, Alejandro, ed. *The Economic Sociology of Immigration: The Essays on Networks, Ethnicity and Entrepreneurship.* New York: Russell Sage Foundation, 1995. This work links the theoretical innovations of economic sociology with empirical findings from immigration research, demonstrating that economic success is integrally related to group history.

Shulman, Steven, ed. *The Impact of Immigration on African Americans.* New Brunswick, N.J.: Transaction Publishers, 2004. Arguing that "immigration is not inevitable," the author summarizes contemporary literature on the subject, supporting a more restrictive immigration policy.

Smith, James P., and Barry Edmonston, eds. *The New Americans: Economic, Demographic, and Fiscal Effects of Immigration.* Washington, D.C.: National Academy Press, 1997. In identifying economic gains and losses associated with immigration, contributors explore the influence of immigration on the economy generally, on government budgets, and potentially on the tax-paying demography for the future.

Annotated Bibliography

Trueba, Enrique T. *The New Americans: Immigrants and Transnationals at Work*. Lanham, Md.: Rowman and Littlefield, 2004. Trueba explores the possibilities and potential results of having the poorest of immigrants and transnational workers playing prominent roles in American society.

Waldinger, Roger, and Michael J. Lichter. *How the Other Half Works: Immigration and the Social Organization of Labor*. Berkeley: University of California Press, 2003. Based on interviews with managers and owners of more than 200 Los Angeles workplaces, the authors argue that employers prefer to hire newer immigrants because they have the "right attitude" toward work and that the future of ethnic relations in the country is likely to be one of conflict.

Waldinger, Roger, ed. *Strangers at the Gates: New Immigrants in Urban America*. Berkeley: University of California Press, 2001. In a series of eight articles, leading historians and economists examine the major controversies surrounding immigrant assimilation.

Yoshida, Chisa To, and Alan Woodland. *The Economics of Illegal Immigration*. New York: Palgrave Macmillan, 2005. The authors suggest that traditional methods of border enforcement are problematic as labor shifts in the global marketplace.

ARTICLES

Chiswick, Barry R., Yew Liang Lee, and Paul W. Miller. "A Longitudinal Analysis of Immigrant Occupational Mobility: A Test of the Immigrant Assimilation Hypothesis. *International Migration Review* 39:2 (Summer 2005): 332–353. Using "cross-sectional data" from the United States, Canada, Australia, Israel, and Germany, along with a true longitudinal survey of immigrants in Australia, the authors suggest a pattern of assimilation based upon a variety of factors.

Donato, Katharine M., Michael Aguilera, and Chizuko Wakabayashi. "Immigration Policy and Employment Conditions of US Immigrants from Mexico, Nicaragua, and the Dominican Republic." *International Migration* 43:5 (December 2005): 5–29. Using comparable data for each group, the authors find a broader, negative impact of the Immigration Reform and Control (IRCA) Act of 1986 on Latino migrant wages than was previously thought.

Mora, Marie T., and Alberto Davila. "Mexican Immigrant Self-Employment along the U.S.-Mexico Border: An Analysis of 2000 Census Data." *Social Science Quarterly* 87:1 (March 2006): 91–109. The authors determine that Mexican immigrants in border regions have "significantly higher" self-employment rates than both immigrants in the interior and whites in the border regions, suggesting that "immigration reform that curtails the immigration flow from Mexico might hinder small business formation and economic development on the U.S. side of the Mexican border."

Pries, Ludger. "Determining the Causes and Durability of Transnational Labour Migration between Mexico and the United States: Some Empirical Findings." *International Migration* 42:2 (2004): 3–39. Based upon extensive interviews and other empirical studies of more than 600 migrants moving between Puebla, Mexico, and New York City, the author argues that transnational labor migration is complicated by "the complexity of social and family networks," which might lead to migration strategies extending over several generations.

WEB DOCUMENTS

Camarota, Steven A. "Dropping Out: Immigrant Entry and Native Exit from the Job Market, 2005–2006." Center for Immigration Studies, March 2006. Available online. URL: http://www.cis.org/articles/2006/back206.html. The director of the Center for Immigration Studies uses data from the March 2006 Population Survey of the Census Bureau to challenge the notion that illegal alien laborers are needed in the U. S. economy. Rather, he argues, "that immigration may be adversely impacting less-educated natives."

Martin, Philip. "Labor and Unauthorized U.S. Migration." Available online. URL: http://www.prb.org/Template.cfm?Section=PRB&template=/ContentManagement/ContentDisplay.cfm&ContentID=12567. According to Martin, competing proposals to change the status of illegal immigrants to either guest workers or applicants for legal status "could be laying the groundwork for new waves of migration in the future."

HISTORY OF IMMIGRATION

BOOKS

Bailyn, Bernard. *The Peopling of British North America: An Introduction.* New York: Alfred A. Knopf, 1986. Bailyn provides an insightful, preliminary sketch of a plan to evaluate the origins and destinies of British immigrants to North America, emphasizing the varieties of experience, rather than uniform patterns.

———. *Voyagers to the West: A Passage in the Peopling of America on the Eve of the Revolution.* New York: Alfred A. Knopf, 1986. The first substantial volume in Bailyn's planned work outlined in *The Peopling of British North America, Voyagers to the West* includes a unique, detailed analysis of the circumstances of "every person officially known to have left Britain for America from December 1773 to March 1776."

Annotated Bibliography

Barkan, Elliott R. *And Still They Come: Immigrants and American Society 1920 to the 1990s*. Wheeling, Ill.: Harlan Davidson, 1996. This is the best brief introduction to the period; it includes an excellent bibliographic essay.

Bodner, John. *The Transplanted: A History of Urban Immigrants*. Bloomington: Indiana University Press, 1985. Bodner provides an excellent synthesis of "classic" immigration studies, focusing on the period prior to 1920 and placing immigrant decisions in the context of home cultures.

Daniels, Roger. *Coming to America*. 2nd ed. New York: Harper Perennial, 2002. A good starting point for understanding the parameters of the immigrant experience, Daniels tells the narrative story well without neglecting the most important immigrant groups.

———. *Guarding the Golden Door: American Immigration Policy and Immigrants since 1882*. New York: Hill and Wang, 2004. Utilizing his narrative skills, Daniels tells the story of immigration after 1882, with a nice balance between story and statistics.

Daniels, Roger, and Otis L. Graham. *Debating American Immigration, 1882-Present*. Lanham, Md.: Rowman and Littlefield, 2001. In a highly readable book, two noted historians debate the nature and impact of immigration on the United States as they trace its course.

Dinnerstein, Leonard, and David M. Reimers. *Ethnic Americans: A History of Immigration*. 4th ed. New York: Columbia University Press, 1999. *Ethnic Americans* is a good brief survey of immigration history that combines chronological and thematic approaches. The authors treat the experience more broadly than Daniels's *Coming to America*, but the book also concludes with chapters of synthesis on "Newcomers from South of the Border," "Pilgrim's Progress: Ethnic Mobility in Modern America," "Whither Ethnic America? Assimilation into American Life," and "A New Immigration Debate."

Dinnerstein, Leonard, Roger L. Nichols, and David M. Reimers. *Natives and Strangers: A Multicultural History of Americans*. 4th ed. New York: Oxford University Press, 2003. This is a standard undergraduate text that places the immigrant experience within the larger context of minority experience. Where earlier editions focused on economic development, the fourth edition devotes more space to the immigrant groups themselves.

Foner, Nancy. *From Ellis Island to JFK: New York's Two Great Waves of Immigration*. New Haven, Conn.: Yale University Press, 2002. Explores New York's racial and ethnic history by examining two waves of immigration at the beginning and end of the 20th century. Foner's work won the 2000 Theodore Saloutos Book Award of the Immigration and Ethnic History Society for the best book in American Immigration and Ethnic History.

Foner, Nancy, and George M. Frederickson, eds. *Not Just Black and White: Historical and Contemporary Perspectives on Immigration, Race and Ethnicity in the United States*. New York: Russell Sage, 2004. Originating in a

Immigration

series of workshops sponsored by the Social Science Research Council Committee on International Migration, these 17 articles by sociologists, political scientists, and historians examine the two great waves of recent immigration (1881–1930 and 1965 to present).

Gerber, David A., and Alan M. Kraut, ed. *American Immigration and Ethnicity: A Reader.* New York: Palgrave Macmillan, 2005. This is a useful guide comparing the experiences of European immigrants in the 19th and early 20th centuries and those of Asian, Hispanic, Caribbean, and African immigrants in the late 20th and 21st centuries. More accessible than David Jacobson's *Immigration Reader,* it includes both scholarly essays and primary source documents.

Glazer, Nathan. *Clamor at the Gates: The New American Immigration.* San Francisco: Institute for Contemporary Studies, 1985. The author confronts the central problem of "new immigrants" after 1980 who often wished to maintain their own culture rather than come to "be Americans." Glazer argues for a new and more effective immigration policy, one that would express American values.

Graham, Otis L., Jr. *Unguarded Gates: A History of America's Immigration Crisis.* Lanham, Md.: Rowman and Littlefield, 2006. Focusing on the period between 1880 and 1965, Graham demonstrates that population and policy pressures brought on by immigration are not new.

Handlin, Oscar. *The Uprooted.* 2nd ed. Boston: Little, Brown, 1973. A pioneering account of the "classic" immigration experience prior to 1930, *The Uprooted* was seminal when published in 1951. Tracing the lives of European peasants seeking better lives in the New World, this poetic work served for three decades as the foil for more meticulous historians of immigration.

Higham, John. *Stranger in a Strange Land.* 2nd ed. New Brunswick, N.J.: Rutgers University Press, 1988. Designed to mediate between rival schools of thought and focusing on two periods (1886–96 and World War I), Higham emphasizes the psychology of nationalism, exploring three ideological variants of nativism: anti-Catholicism, anti-radicalism, and racism. This is considered a seminal work in immigration studies.

Jacobson, David, ed. *Immigration Reader: America in a Multidisciplinary Perspective.* Malden, Mass.: Blackwell, 1998. Edited by a sociologist, this work includes 18 readings from the most prominent historians, economists, and sociologists in the field. Jacobson does an excellent job of including a variety of viewpoints regarding his five main sections: history of immigration, immigration and ethnicity, the economy and immigration, comparative perspectives on immigration, and the political debate on immigration.

King, Desmond. *Making Americans: Immigration, Race, and the Origins of the Diverse Democracy.* Cambridge, Mass.: Harvard University Press, 2002.

Annotated Bibliography

King discusses the development of restrictive immigration policy in terms of an American sense of self, and he also provides a careful discussion of the role of eugenics in determining desirable versus undesirable immigrants.

Kraut, Alan. *The Huddled Masses: The Immigrant in American Society, 1880–1921.* 2nd ed. Arlington Heights, Ill.: Harlan Davidson, 2001. This is the best brief introduction to the period and includes a superb bibliographic essay.

Laham, Nicholas. *Ronald Reagan and the Politics of Immigration Reform.* Westport, Conn.: Praeger, 2000. Laham argues that Reagan's failures in immigration policy were due to "a gross lack of accurate and reliable information on immigration." He makes extensive use of materials from the Ronald Reagan Presidential Library.

LeMay, Michael C. *From Open Door to Dutch Door: An Analysis of U.S. Immigration Policy since 1820.* New York: Praeger, 1987. In this historical survey, LeMay distinguishes four phases of immigration policy.

Ngai, Mae M. *Impossible Subjects: Illegal Aliens and the Making of Modern America.* Princeton, N.J.: Princeton University Press, 2005. Tracing the development of the concept of the "illegal alien" between 1924 and 1965, the author argues that "immigration restriction, particularly national-origin and numerical quotas, re-mapped the nation both by creating new categories of racial difference and by emphasizing as never before the nation's contiguous land borders and their patrol." Accepting illegal immigrants into the economy and society without granting them formal status did much to shape the current controversy.

Nugent, Walter. *Crossings: The Great Transatlantic Migrations, 1870–1914.* Bloomington: Indiana University Press, 1992. Nugent approaches the "contours of population change" from the broad perspective of the Atlantic basin. The book includes separate chapters on European "donor" states and American "receiver" states.

Portes, Alejandro, and Rubén G. Rumbaut. *Immigrant America: A Portrait.* 3rd ed. Berkeley: University of California Press, 2006. A readable account by two eminent sociologists, *Immigrant America* offers a thematic interpretation focusing more on the immigrants themselves than the process of immigration. This work provides a good introduction to the variety of sophisticated ways of examining immigration.

Reimers, David M. *Other Immigrants: The Global Origins of the American Peoples.* New York: New York University Press, 2005. A full narrative focusing on the current diversity of the American population, this account by Reimers is rich in statistics and thorough in its treatment of previously marginalized groups.

———. *Still the Golden Door: The Third World Comes to America.* 2nd ed. New York: Columbia University Press, 1992. An excellent survey of the

185

period of immigration after 1965, focusing on the unintended consequences of the Immigration Act of 1965. The second edition includes
extensive discussion of the 1990 Immigration Act, as well as the influx of
eastern European immigrants in the wake of the breakup of the Soviet
bloc. See a fuller expression of his ideas in *Other Immigrants*.

Roediger, David R. *Working toward Whiteness: How America's Immigrants Became White. The Strange Journey from Ellis Island to the Suburbs*. New York:
Basic Books, 2005. Covering the period 1890 to 1945, Roediger demonstrates that although southern and eastern Europeans were discriminated
against, developments in labor, housing, and politics all allowed them to take
on the "mantle of whiteness," while African Americans, Mexican Americans,
and Asian Americans were often precluded from such refashioning.

Sowell, Thomas. *Ethnic America: A History*. New York: Basic Books, 1981.
Sowell begins with a strong statistical base to note essential differences in
the larger ethnic groups in the United States. The book is dated but still
useful.

Takaki, Ronald. *A Different Mirror: A History of Multicultural America*. Boston: Little, Brown, 1993. In keeping with Takaki's trademark style, his
narrative history is full of stories and vignettes that give life to the larger
trends. This book focuses on the larger immigrant groups.

Ueda, Reed. *Postwar Immigrant America: A Social History*. Boston: Bedford
Books, 1994. Ueda emphasizes the important contribution of the large
Asian and Hispanic immigrations to the culture of the United States,
making extensive use of sociological and demographic concepts.

Vecoli, Rudolph J., and Suzanne Sinke, eds. *A Century of European Migrations, 1830–1930*. Urbana: Illinois University Press, 1991. The result of
a symposium held in Wayzata, Minnesota, to mark the centennial of the
Statue of Liberty and the 20th anniversary of the Immigration History
Research Center at the University of Minnesota, the included articles
suggest that the decisions to emigrate were not generally "expressions of
individual will or ambition" but "collective strategies to realize the opti-
mum good for the kinship group."

Wyman, Mark. *Round-Trip to America: The Immigrants Return to Europe,
1880–1930*. Ithaca, N.Y.: Cornell University Press, 1993. A useful
study of an integral and often overlooked aspect of immigration history, this work examines the motives and situations of some 4 million
return immigrants.

Zolberg, Aristide R. *A Nation by Design: Immigration Policy in the Fashion-
ing of America*. Cambridge, Mass.: Harvard University Press, 2006. The
author argues that, contrary to myth, immigration policy in the United
States was frequently manipulated long before the xenophobic period
after World War I. This early engineering went unnoticed, however,
because most of it took place at local and state levels.

Annotated Bibliography

ARTICLES

Gabaccia, Donna R. "Is Everywhere Nowhere? Nomads, Nations, and the Immigrant Paradigm of United States History." *Journal of American History* 86 (December 1999), pp. 1,115–1,134. Drawing upon a decadelong collaborative project covering the global migration of 27 million immigrants from Italy, the author argues for the ongoing significance of "national" categories in the study of immigration.

Gjerde, Jon, "New Growth on Old Vines—The State of the Field: The Social History of Ethnicity and Immigration in the United States." *Journal of American Ethnic History* 18 (Summer 1999): 40–65. Gjerde reexamines the legacy of early scholarly inquiries into the nature of immigration, arguing that the "experience of immigrants varied according to era of migration, motive for migration, and access to citizenship."

Green, Nancy L. "The Politics of Exit: Reversing the Immigration Paradigm." *Journal of Modern History* 77 (June 2005): 263–289. The author argues that the general epistemological shift in the social sciences "from an emphasis on structures to a focus on agency" has not yet brought about an appropriate level of investigation into state attitudes toward the loss of emigrants, who define nations just as do their attitudes toward reception.

Hansen, Marcus Lee. "The History of American Immigration as a Field for Research," *American Historical Review* 32 (1926–27): 500–518. In this seminal work, Hansen suggests the importance of understanding factors that drove emigrants from Europe, rather than focusing solely on the attractive qualities of the United States.

Nackerud, Larry, et al. "The End of the Cuban Contradiction in U.S. Refugee Policy," *International Migration Review* 33:1 (Spring 1999): 176–192. In this important article on the implications of the ending of the cold war on American refugee policy, Nackerud traces the complicated end to the special status afforded Cuban refugees.

WEB DOCUMENTS

Martin, Philip, and Elizabeth Midgley. "Immigration: Shaping and Reshaping America," *Population Bulletin* 58:2 (June 2003). Available online. URL: http://www.prb.org/pdf/58.2ImmigrShapingAmerica.pdf. The authors provide a comprehensive historical overview of the impact of immigration with special reference to demographics, economic effect and migration from Mexico.

"The Migration to North America." Available online. URL: http://www.let. leidenuniv.nl/history/migration/chapter52.html. Updated on December 1, 2003. In this component of the "History of International Migration," there is a concise account of the subject, including a description of the migration movement, causes of migration, consequences of migration, and reactions on migration. The site generally is useful for placing immigration to the United States in the context of larger migration movements.

IMMIGRATION DEBATE AND PUBLIC POLICY: 1990s ONWARD

BOOKS

Barone, Michael. *The New Americans*. New York: Regnery, 2001. A writer for *U.S. News & World Report*, Barone uses comparative case studies of various ethnic groups in American history to demonstrate that future immigrants can be successfully assimilated into society.

Briggs, Vernon M., Jr. *Mass Immigration and the National Interest*. 3rd ed. Armonk, N.Y.: M. E. Sharpe, 2003. In a concise history of immigration policy, the author demonstrates "how the nation's immigration policies consist of a hodge-podge of ineffective, counter productive, and special interest provisions, born from more than forty years of dubious political compromises, rather than serving the national interest." Briggs uses the 2000 census figures to evaluate labor-market trends and to show that mass immigration "constitutes a serious threat to the jobs of American workers."

Brimelow, Peter. *Alien Nation: Common Sense about America's Immigration Disaster*. New York: Random House, 1996. Calling for an end to illegal immigration and a dramatically reduced ceiling for legal immigration, this Forbes senior editor argues that "immigration has consequences" that cannot be ignored.

Buchanan, Patrick J. *The Death of the West: How Dying Populations and Immigrant Invasions Imperil Our Country and Civilization*. New York: Dunne Books, 2001. Buchanan argues that declining birth rates in the West and a continued policy of unchecked immigration will lead to a new world order that is hostile to traditional American values.

———. *State of Emergency: How Illegal Immigration Is Destroying America*. New York: Thomas Dunne Books, 2006. Drawing upon New Mexico governor Bill Richardson's 2005 declaration of a "state of emergency" over the impact of unregulated immigration in his state, Buchanan develops a systematic argument in support of his long-standing opposition to open borders.

Chacon, Justin Akers, and Mike Davis. *No One Is Illegal: Fighting Racism and State Violence on the U.S.-Mexico Border*. Chicago: Haymarket Books, 2006. Writing from a marxist perspective, the authors argue for a pro-immigrant and pro-worker agenda that will help build an international labor movement.

Cornelius, Wayne A., Takeyuki Tsuda, Philip L. Martin, and James E. Hollifield, eds. *Controlling Immigration: A Global Perspective*, 2nd ed. Stanford:

Annotated Bibliography

Stanford University Press, 2004. Published in association with the Center for Comparative Immigration Studies at the University of California, San Diego, these articles compare immigration policies in nine industrialized nations, including the United Sates, in order to discover why these policies so often fail.

Gimpel, James G., and James R. Edwards, Jr. *The Congressional Politics of Immigration Reform*. Boston: Allyn and Bacon, 1999. Whereas most books on the immigration controversy focus on the impact of immigration, this one emphasizes the role of politicians in formulating policy; a good starting point for examining the role of specific politicians in the policy debates of the past 40 years.

Glazer, Nathan. *We Are All Multiculturalists Now*. Cambridge: Harvard University Press, 1997. A thirty-year veteran of the culture question, Glazer here explores the inadequacy of earlier concepts such as the "melting pot," suggesting that they were conceived with European immigrants in mind.

Gozdziak, Elzbieta and Susan F. Martin. *Beyond the Gateway: Immigrants in a Changing America*. Lanham, Md.: Lexington Books, 2005. Gozdziak, director of research at the Institute for the Study of International Migration (ISIM) at Georgetown University, and Martin, executive director of the Institute for the Study of International Migration (ISIM) and Director of the Certificate Program in Refugee and Humanitarian Emergencies at Georgetown University, systematically examine the stress of immigration into areas with no tradition of immigrant acceptance, both on the immigrants and on the receiving communities.

Hayworth, J.D. *Whatever It Takes*. New York: Regnery Publishing, 2006. Conservative congressman J. D. Hayworth makes his case against liberal immigration reform, particularly a guest-worker program that would reward illegal immigrants with access to U.S. jobs and services.

Heranandez, Juan. *The New American Pioneers: Why Are We Afraid of Mexican Immigrants*. Lanham, Md.: Pneuma Life Publishing, 2006. The author, founder of the Center for U.S.-Mexico Studies at the University of Texas at Dallas and former cabinet member for Mexican president Vicente Fox, argues that it is in the best interests of the United States to promote an open immigration policy toward Mexico.

Hing, Bill Ong. *Defining America Through Immigration Policy*. Philadelphia: Temple University Press, 2004. Written by a professor of law and Asian studies at the University of California, Davis, *Defining America* provides a systematic interpretation of the racism and ethnocentrism built in to most U.S. immigration legislation.

Isbister, John. *The Immigration Debate: Remaking America*. Bloomfield, Conn.: Kumarian Press, 1996. Written by the son of Canada's former deputy minister of citizenship and immigration who immigrated to the

189

United States in 1964, this book tries to steer a middle course in the immigration debates, suggesting that immigration figures are historically average and that the influx of risk-takers is good for the United States.

Jacoby, Tamar, ed. *Reinventing the Melting Pot.* New York: Basic Books, 2004. Bringing together many of the most prominent historians, sociologists, and political scientists engaging in the immigration debate today, this work suggests that both extremes miss the mark and that assimilation can still allow for multiculturalism.

Jaynes, Gerald David. *Immigration and Race: New Challenges for American Democracy.* New Haven, Conn.: Yale University Press, 2000. In 10 articles, the impact of immigration on race, ethnicity, and related economies—especially among Latino, Asian, and African-American populations—is explored; the book includes an introductory article on "Immigration and the American Dream."

Joppke, Christian. *Immigration and the Nation-State: The United States, Germany, and Great Britain.* Oxford: Oxford University Press, 1999. Joppke attempts to draw together studies of both sovereignty and citizenship in developing an understanding of immigration as part of a broad spectrum of social change.

Kleinknecht, William. *The New Ethnic Mobs: The Changing Face of Organized Crime in America.* New York: Free Press, 1996. The author discusses the rise of ethnic crime syndicates, particularly since the 1970s, arguing that characteristics within specific culture groups contribute to members of each community filling the vacuum in organized crime when the old families are taken down.

Malkin, Michelle. *Invasion: How America Still Welcomes Terrorists, Criminals and Other Foreign Menaces to Our Shores.* Washington, D.C.: Regnery, 2002. Written in the wake of the terrorist attacks of September 11, 2001, the author identifies a host of persistent problems, including politicization and liberal immigration policies, that will make it difficult for the United States to combat the influx of undesirable aliens.

Millman, Joel. *The Other Americans: How Immigrants Renew Our Country, Our Economy, and Our Values.* New York: Viking, 1997. Using case histories, this former editor at *Forbes* magazine suggests that immigrant families may be the hope of the country, rather than a threat; the book is mostly anecdotal.

Novak, Michael. *Unmeltable Ethnics: Politics and Culture in American Life.* 2nd ed. New Brunswick, N.J.: Transaction, 1996. Beginning life as a collection of articles in the popular press during the late 1960s and early 1970s, this interesting work demonstrates the continuing presence of common issues related to immigration. The author includes in this edition several more recent articles, most notably his "Pluralism: A Humanistic Perspective."

Sheehy, Daniel. *Fighting Immigration Anarchy: American Patriots Battle to Save the Nation.* Bloomington, Ind.: AuthorHouse, 2005. Representative of the extreme restrictionist viewpoint, *Fighting Immigration Anarchy* focuses on the contemporary efforts of six leaders (Glenn Spencer, Terry Anderson, Roy Beck, Barbara Coe, Joe Guzzardi, and Tom Tancredo) to stem the tide of immigration into the United States.

Simon, Rita J., and S. H. Alexander. *The Ambivalent Welcome: Print Media, Public Opinion, and Immigration.* Westport, Conn.: Praeger, 1993. Using the *New York Times* and major magazines of public opinion (including *Atlantic Monthly* and the *Saturday Evening Post*) as a means of exploring attitudes toward immigration after 1880, the authors conclude that public opposition was reflected in the press.

Smith, James P., and Barry Edmonston, eds. *The Immigration Debate: Studies on the Economic, Demographic, and Fiscal Effects of Immigration.* Washington, D.C.: National Academies Press, 1998. Reflecting the work of the Panel on the Demographic and Economic Impacts of Immigration of the National Research Council, this is a book of systematic research with "detailed data and analysis" designed to deepen the scientific parameters of the immigration debate. The book utilizes a number of case studies.

Tancredo, Tom. *Open Borders, Open Wounds: What America Needs to Know about Illegal Immigration.* Fort Lee, N.J. Encounter Books, 2005. Congressman Tom Tancredo, one of America's most vocal critics of an open immigration policy, suggests that in addition to a heavy economic cost, average U.S. citizens, particularly in border regions, are harmed by unregulated immigration.

Tichenor, Daniel J. *Dividing Lines: The Politics of Immigration Control in America.* Princeton, N.J.: Princeton University Press, 2002. Tichenor provides a good survey of the process of immigration policy development, demonstrating that the "immigration debate" has been a staple in American history.

Williamson, Chilton, Jr. *The Immigration Mystique: America's False Conscience.* New York: Basic Books, 1996. Although the author argues that immigration is bad for the economy, he is foremost concerned with the evolution of American culture away from Anglo-Protestant values and is especially vehement in his condemnation of political liberals who would take the United States in the same direction even without the facade of immigrant demand.

ARTICLES

Cornelius, Wayne A. "Death at the Border: Efficacy and Unintended Consequences of U.S. Immigration Control Policy." *Population and Development Review* 27:4 (December 2001): 661–685. Examining long-term effects of enhanced border enforcement policies during the Bill Clinton and George W. Bush administrations after 1993, the author argues that there have been few labor-market effects indicating that the policies are not working. The author suggests that Mexico's labor market and demographics will have more to do with the evolution of illegal immigration.

Durand, Jorge, Douglas S. Massey, and René M. Zenteno. "Mexican Immigration to the United States: Continuities and Changes." *Latin American Research Review* 36:1 (2001): 107–127. A research note based upon data drawn from Mexico's Encuesta Nacional de la Dinámica Demográfica (National survey of demographic dynamics) U.S. Census, and Mexican Migration Project, the article suggests a relatively stable pattern, with most immigrants being males of labor-force age from western Mexican states. The greatest change has been the increased rate of return migration during the 1990s, "reflecting the massive legalization of the late 1980s."

Escobar, Agustín, Philip Martin, Peter Schatzer, and Susan Martin. "Mexico-U.S. Migration: Moving the Agenda Forward." *International Migration* 41:2 (2003): 125–137.

Michaelsen, Scott. "Between Japanese American Internment and the USA PATRIOT Act: The Borderlands and the Permanent State of Racial Exception." *Aztlan* 30:2 (Fall 2005): 87–111. This article argues that the PATRIOT Act must be contextualized with a series of Supreme Court decisions that turned "the U.S. borderlands adjoining Mexico into a permanent racial camp," a place of "legal, racial exceptionalism."

Nezer, Melanie. "The New Antiterrorism Legislation: The Impact on Immigrants." *Refugee Reports* 22, no. 11 (November 2001): 1–8. Nezer, a longtime lawyer and immigrant activist, explores the legislative impact on immigration after 9/11. This work is especially useful in gauging perceptions in the immediate aftermath of the attacks.

Ting, Jan C. "Immigration and National Security." *Orbis* 50:1 (Winter 2006): 41–52. Drawing upon the European example, Ting argues that "the greatest threat to U.S. homeland security comes from illegals who enter the country through its porous border," and he calls upon policy leaders to recognize the obvious flaws in the immigration system and then to demonstrate a will to correct them.

Wells, Miriam J. "The Grassroots Reconfiguration of U.S. Immigration Policy." International Migration Review 38:4 (Winter 2004): 1,308–1,347. Wells argues that "three facets of state structural complexity—its multiple levels, diverse administrative branches, and decentralized agencies"—have made it possible for a wide variety of local impacts on U.S. immigration policy.

WEB DOCUMENTS

Cainkar, Louise. "No Longer Invisible: Arab and Muslim Exclusion after September 11." Middle East Report 224 (Fall 2002). Available online. URL: http://www.merip.org/mer/mer224/224_cainkar.html. Updated in

Annotated Bibliography

Fall 2002. Cainkar traces the history of American ignorance of Arabs in the United States as well as the resulting popular reaction to the September 11 terrorist attacks. The author suggests that one positive effect was a greater awareness of Arab and Muslim issues.

Camarota, Steven A. "Immigrants at Mid-Decade: A Snapshot of America's Foreign-Born Population in 2005." Available online. URL: http://www.cis.org/articles/2005/back1405.html. Updated in December 2005. This extensive report, written by the Director of Research at the Center for Immigration Studies, provides a careful statistical anaylsis of the foreign-born population of the United States, including tables on numbers, percentages in the total population, immigrants by state, source regions, education levels, poverty and employment, health care, and urban distribution.

Jenks. Rosemary. "The USA PATRIOT Act of 2001: A Summary of the Anti-Terrorism Law's Immigration-Related Provisions." Available online. Updated in December 2001. URL: http://www.cis.org/articles/2001/back1501.html. Prepared as a background report for the Center for Immigration Studies, Jenks provides an early profile of the new anti-terror legislation.

Martin, Philip. "The Battle over Unauthorized Immigration to the United States." Population Reference Bureau, April 11, 2006. Available online. URL: http://www.prb.org/Template.cfm?Section=PRB&template=/ContentManagement/ContentDisplay.cfm&ContentID=13735. Martin, a noted demographer and economist, examined the statistical data as the U.S. Congress debated comprehensive immigration reform. He suggested three lessons: that there was little enthusiasm for legalization first, followed by enforcement; that there were fundamental disagreements over how best to deal with illegal immigrants already in the country; and that international free trade agreements produced a natural "hump" in immigration as older industries in countries outside the United States suffered from greater economic pressures.

Massey, Douglas S. "Beyond the Border Buildup: Towards a New Approach to Mexico-U.S. Migration." Available online. URL: http://www.ailf.org/ipc/policy_reports_2005_beyondborder.htm. Updated on September 6, 2005. In the second article in the two-part "Rethinking Immigration" series (see "Five Myths about Immigration"), Massey argues that the best approach to the border issue is to regulate the issue on a binational basis; he specifically suggests that the United States "create a new category of temporary visa that permits the bearer to enter, live, and work in the country without restriction for two years, with an option for renewal once in the lifetime of the migrant."

———. "Five Myths about Immigration: Common Misconceptions Underlying U.S. Border-Enforcement Policy." Available online. URL: http://www.ailf.

193

org/ipc/policy_reports_2005_fivemyths%20previous_version.htm. Updated on August 1, 2005. In the first article in the two-part "Rethinking Immigration" series (see "Beyond the Border Buildup"), an eminent professor of sociology and public affairs at Princeton University argues that most Mexican immigrants would prefer to return to Mexico but that "repressive border-enforcement policies simply make it more difficult" for them to do so.

IMMIGRATION LAW

BOOKS

Adams, Gregory P., ed. *Immigration and Nationality Law Handbook.* 2005–06 ed. New York: American Immigration Lawyers Association, 2005. Annual editions include a wide range of practice-oriented articles written by immigration lawyers, including articles on topics such as removal and relief, asylum and protection, adjustment of status, work authorization, and citizenship and naturalization.

AILA Immigration Regulations: CFR. 2 vols. New York: American Immigration Lawyers Association, 2005. In this authoritative guide, the latest agency regulations are discussed; includes information on Titles 6, 8, 20, 22, 28, and 42.

Aziza, Halina, ed. *AILA's Guide to Technology and Legal Research for the Immigration Lawyer.* 3rd ed. New York: American Immigration Lawyers Association, 2003. Provides a full range of information necessary for working immigrant law practices, including information on general automation, technical terms, and security issues, and a thorough listing of immigration-related web sites.

Browning, Stephanie L., and Randy P. Auerbach, eds. *Immigration and Nationality Act.* 2006 ed. New York: American Immigration Lawyers Association, 2006. Each annual edition includes the most recent laws, amendments, and other regulatory changes to the Immigration and Nationality Act.

Divine, Robert C., and R. Blake Chisam. *Immigration Practice, 2005–2006.* Huntington, N.Y.: Juris Publishing, 2005. Divine, the principal legal adviser to the U.S. Citizenship and Immigration Services Bureau of the Department of Homeland Security, covers all aspects of immigration law, including statutes, regulations, policy memos, agency interpretations, and online resources for immigration law. Originally prepared before Divine took his position with the USCIS, this edition was updated by Chisam, who practices immigration and nationality law.

Federal Immigration Laws and Regulations, 2005. Eagan, Minn.: Thomson West, 2005. This work provides the printed text of Section 8 of the Code of Federal Regulations, including amendments through April 15, 2005.

Annotated Bibliography

Goodwin-Gill, Guy S. I. *The Refugee in International Law*. 2nd ed. Oxford: Clarendon Press, 1996. Among the most authoritative surveys of the question and a good place to start research, this work synthesizes developments in refugee law and policy, though its coverage of events has become dated.

Helewitz, Jeffrey A. *United States Immigration Law*. Upper Saddle River, N.J.: Prentice Hall, 1999. This is a good introduction that includes history and administration of U.S. Immigration Law, various immigrant categories, nonimmigrant categories, questions of admission and removal, and refugee and asylum issues. Forms and case studies are now dated.

Kleinknecht, William. *The New Ethnic Mobs: The Changing Face of Organized Crime in America*. New York: Free Press, 1996. The author discusses the rise of ethnic crime syndicates, particularly since the 1970s, arguing that characteristics within specific culture groups contribute to members of each community filling the vacuum in organized crime when the old families are taken down.

Legomsky, Stephen H. *Immigration and Refugee Law and Policy*. 4th ed. Westbury, N.Y.: West Group, 2004. Legomsky provides an extensive casebook covering the latest developments in questions of immigration law, jurisdiction, legislation, and regulations. Supplements generally published between editions deal with the latest developments.

Proper, Emberson Edward. *Colonial Immigration Laws: A Study of the Regulation of Immigration by the English Colonies in America*. Buffalo, N.Y.: William S. Hein, 2003. Originally published in 1900, this reprint includes chapters such as "Encouragement of Immigration"; "Restriction and Prohibition of Immigration"; "Immigration Laws of the New England Colonies, Middle Colonies, and Southern Colonies"; "Attitude of England toward Immigration"; and "Distribution and Characteristics of Nationalities."

Van Geel, T. R. *Understanding Supreme Court Opinions*. 5th ed. New York: Pearson Longman, 2006. This is a thoroughly updated version of Van Geel's superb introductory text on the subject.

Weissbrodt, David, and Laura Danielson. *Immigration Law and Procedure: In a Nutshell*. Eagan, Minn.: Thomson West, 2005. An excellent introduction to immigration law, this work provides clear summaries with references from text to court cases, the Constitution, the Code of Federal Regulations, and other authoritative documents.

Welch, Michael. *Detained: Immigration Laws and the Expanding I.N.S. Jail Complex*. Philadelphia: Temple University Press, 2002. Approaching the immigration debate from a criminologist's point of view, Welch argues that a "moral panic" led to the restrictive legislation of 1996 and that there has as a result been little interest in the justice of the "warehousing of illegal immigrants."

Immigration

ARTICLES

Chin, Gabriel J. "The Civil Rights Revolution Comes to Immigration Law: A New Look at the Immigration and Nationality Act of 1965." *North Carolina Law Review* 75 (1996): 273–345. Chin examines the application of a heightened sense of civil rights in the immigration legislation of 1965.

Nezer, Melanie. "The New Antiterrorism Legislation: The Impact on Immigrants." *Refugee Reports* 22, no. 11 (November 2001): 1–8. Nezer, a lawyer and immigrant activist, explores the legislative impact of the 9/11 attacks on immigration. This work is especially useful in gauging perceptions in the immediate aftermath of the attacks.

WEB DOCUMENTS

Smith, Marian L. "Race, Nationality, and Reality: INS Administration of Racial Provisions in U.S. Immigration and Nationality Law since 1898." U.S. National Archives and Record Administration, *Prologue Magazine* 34 (Summer 2002). Available online. URL: http://www.archives.gov/publications/prologue/2002/summer/immigration-law-1.html. The senior historian for the U.S. Immigration and Naturalization Service provides a thorough treatment of the racial concept, explaining that part of the historical maze reflects piecemeal attempts to deal administratively with this complex topic.

INTERNATIONAL MIGRATION

BOOKS

Castles, Stephen, and Mark J. Miller. *The Age of Migration: International Population Movements in the Modern World.* 3rd ed. New York: Guilford Press, 2003. The authors provide a thorough, introductory text, arguing that international migration has been a constant factor in human history; focuses on the post-1945 era.

Cohen, Robin, ed. *The Cambridge Survey of World Migration.* Cambridge: Cambridge University Press, 1995. Cohen edits almost 100 essays written by experts in this extensive survey of migration in the modern world. Beginning with the age of European colonialism in the 16th century, scholars cover migration patterns, the flights of refugees, and illegal migration.

Hirschman, Charles, Josh DeWind, and Philip Kasinitz, eds. *The Handbook of International Migration: The American Experience.* New York: Russell Sage Foundation, 1999. The articles included here were first delivered at a conference of the Social Science Research Council in 1996, which had been organized to assess the "state of international migration studies within the United States from an interdisciplinary perspective"; heavily

196

sociological. A second conference was organized in May 2003, with articles being published in *International Migration Review* 38:3 (Fall 2004).

Manning, Patrick. *Migration in World History.* New York: Routledge, 2005. Drawing on examples from a wide range of geographical regions and thematic areas, this book covers the history of migrations from earliest historical evidences through the resurgence of migration in the later 20th century.

Massey, Douglas S., and J. Edward Taylor, eds. *International Migration: Prospects and Policies in a Global Market.* Oxford: Clarendon University Press, 2004. A fulfillment of the work of the North-South Committee of the International Union for the Scientific Study of Population, the editors identify three key themes in international migration: world immigration is increasing, transportation and communication technologies have made migration accessible to ever-increasing numbers, and newly-emerging countries such as China have joined the labor market with important results.

Massey, Douglas S., Joaquín Arango, Graeme Hugo, Ali Kouaouci, Adela Pellegrino, and J. Edward Taylor. *Worlds in Motion: Understanding International Migration at the End of the Millennium.* New ed. Oxford: Clarendon Press, 2005. Organizing their topic to consider the dynamics of a variety of regional labor systems (North American, European, Gulf system, Asia and the Pacific, South America), the authors trace the evolution of migration from land-rich countries of reception toward new trends including migration into the heavily urbanized countries of western Europe, providing a critical analysis of international migration theory.

Toro-Morn, Maura I., and Marixsa Alicea, eds. *Migration and Immigration: A Global View.* Westport, Conn.: Greenwood Press, 2004. Each article in this introductory reference provides an overview of national migration issues and a brief examination of the political, social, and economic ramifications of that policy.

Wang, Gugnwu, ed. *Global History and Migrations.* Boulder, Colo.: Westview Press, 1997. Valuable in approaching global migration from a historical rather than sociological viewpoint, this collection of essays explores the costs and benefits of human mobility; some parts remain excellent as foundational material, but the treatment of some topics has become dated; look for a new edition, if available.

World Migration 2005: Costs and Benefits of International Migration. New York: International Organization for Migration, 2005. Published under the auspices of the United Nations, *World Migration* analyzes the effects of globalization, trade liberalization, economic integration, and the widening gap between rich and poor nations on migration flows.

ARTICLES

Forced Migration Review, special issue, July 2005. Focuses on the effectiveness of the post-2004 tsunami humanitarian response; serves as an example of

the kind of scholarship that deals with unforeseen contemporary circumstances that affect worldwide migration.

Hamilton, Nora, and Norma Stoltz Chincilla. "Central American Migration: A Framework for Analysis." In *Latin American Research Review* 26
(1991): 75–110. In this work, the authors study Central American migration from a broad analytical perspective that takes into account historical and contemporary factors, a wide variety of "economic and political
motivations, and domestic and international structures."

Krissman, Fred. "Sin Coyote Ni Patrón: Why the 'Migrant Network' Fails
to Explain International Migration." *International Migration Review* 39:1
(Spring 2005): 4–44. Argues that the traditional concept of "migrant
networks" cannot explain large-scale international migratory flows.

Portes, Alejandro, and Josh DeWind. "Conceptual and Methodological Developments in the Study of International Migration." *International Migration Review* 38:3 (Fall 2004). Papers originally presented at a conference of
May 2003, jointly sponsored by the Committee on International Migration of the Social Science Research Council, the Center for Migration
and Development at Princeton, and the *International Migration Review.*

Portes, Alejandro, and Josh DeWind. "A Cross-Atlantic Dialogue: The
Progress of Research and Theory in the Study of International Migration." *International Migration Review* 38:3 (Fall 2004): 828–851. This work
reviews the "principal concepts, lines of research, and methodological
problems" identified in Hirschman, et al. *The Handbook of International
Migration* (1999, see above), gauging progress and seeking "novel ideas
and contrasting ways of understanding migration."

Van Kessel, Gerry. "Global Migration and Asylum." *Forced Migration Review*
10 (2001): 10–13. This assessment by the director general of the Refugees
Branch of the Department of Citizenship and Immigration (Canada)
emphasizes the importance of preventing systems abuse in order to help
those truly in need and suggests that "most national systems are ill-
equipped to enforce negative decisions."

REFUGEES AND REFUGEE POLICY

BOOKS

Borjas, George J., and Jeff Crisp, ed. *Poverty, International Migration and
Asylum.* London: Palgrave, 2005. The contributors examine the economic impact of the growth of asylum migration in the international
context.

Carliner, David. *The Rights of Aliens and Refugees: The Basic ACLU Guide to
Alien and Refugee Rights.* Carbondale: Southern Illinois University Press,
1990. Beginning with the premise that constitutional protections are

universal, this book provides a detailed analysis of the post IRCA (1986) landscape, including right to protection, entrance, work, ownership, taxes, military service, and citizenship.

Garcia, Maria Cristina. *Seeking Refuge: Central American Migration to Mexico, the United States, and Canada.* Berkeley: University of California Press, 2006. Garcia provides a detailed history of the policy response toward and reception of more than 2 million Central Americans who fled to Mexico, the United States, and Canada during the political turmoil between 1974 and 1996.

Gibney, Matthew J. *The Ethics and Politics of Asylum: Liberal Democracy and the Response to Refugees.* Cambridge: Cambridge University Press, 2004. Gibney "tests" liberal ethical theory against actual state practice.

Gibney, Matthew J., and Randall Hansen, eds. *Immigration and Asylum from 1900 to the Present.* 3 vols. Santa Barbara, Calif.: ABC-CLIO, 2005. Superb general reference covering asylum issues; includes good bibliographies and a full volume of significant documents.

Haines, David W., ed. *Refugees in America in the 1990s: A Reference Handbook.* Westport, Conn.: Greenwood Press, 1996. Haines, a social anthropologist, provides in this edited collection of articles an overview of how the United States has responded to people seeking political refuge, with organizing emphasis on specific refugee groups, including Afghans, Chinese from Southeast Asia, Cubans, eastern Europeans, Ethiopians and Eritreans, Haitians, Hmong, Iranians, Khmer, Lao, Soviet Jews, and Vietnamese. The authors examine the reasons for and processes involved in migration and resettlement.

Koehn, P. H. *Refugees from Revolution: U.S. Policy and Third World Migration.* Boulder, Colo.: Westview Press, 1991. Based principally upon studies in Washington, D.C., and Los Angeles, this work is valuable principally as a pre-1990s overview of push-and-pull factors affecting refugee policy in the United States.

Loescher, Gil, and John A. Scanlan. *Calculated Kindness: Refugees and America's Half-Open Door: 1945: to the Present.* New York: Free Press, 1986. Consultants to the Select Commission on Immigration and Refugee Policy in 1980, the authors examine America's long-term ambivalence toward refugees, noting that 1980s' policy was becoming "fairer" only in making it more difficult for all refugees to enter. The book includes an extensive bibliography that is especially useful on pamphlets and congressional materials.

Sutter, Valerie O'Connor. *The Indochinese Refugee Dilemma.* Baton Rouge: Louisiana State University Press, 1991. Sutter compares the plight of refugees from Hungary in 1956 to that of refugees from Vietnam, Laos, and Cambodia after 1975, with special attention to the role of the United Nations High Commission for Refugees.

199

Immigration

Waxman, Peter, and Val Colic-Peisker, eds. *Homeland Wanted: Interdisciplinary Perspectives on Refugee Resettlement in the West.* New York: Nova Science Publishers, 2005. This collection of articles includes case studies on Bosnian refugee resettlements in St. Louis and in upstate New York.

Wittke, Carl F. *Refugees of Revolution: The German Forty-Eighters in America.* Philadelphia: University of Pennsylvania Press, 1952. Wittke provides an excellent treatment of one of the earliest refugee groups in America, notable for its attention to the masses as well as the leadership.

World Refugee Survey: An Annual Assessment of Conditions Affecting Refugees, Asylum Seekers and Internally Displaced Persons. Washington, D.C.: U.S. Committee for Refugees, 2002. This essential reference contains recent factual information as well as a series of articles and up-to-date country studies.

Zucker, Norman L., and Naomi Flink Zucker. *Desperate Crossings: Seeking Refuge in America.* Armonk, N.Y.: M. E. Sharpe, 1996. This solid historical account focuses on the combined pressures of a "troika of interests—foreign policy, the costs of resettlement and domestic pressures"—in evaluating American refugee policy from the 1970s; it focuses on Cuba, Haiti, and Central America.

———. *The Guarded Gate: The Reality of American Refugee Policy.* New York: Harcourt Brace Jovanovich, 1987. This work examines the practical effects of the Refugee Act of 1980, explaining how discretionary judgment regarding "distress" creates an unfair system.

ARTICLES

Chimni, B. S. "The Geopolitics of Refugee Studies: A View from the South." *Journal of Refugee Studies* 11:4 (1998): 350–374. Chimni argues that between 1950 and 1989, Western cold-war aims "encouraged a relatively depoliticized discourse" in refugee studies that has from the nineties been abandoned and replaced by a "loss of interest in the refugee."

Donovan, Thomas W. "The American Immigration System: A Structural Change with a Different Emphasis." *International Journal of Refugee Law* 17:3 (2005): 574–592. Donovan argues that with the recent emphasis on protection in the restructuring of the immigration bureaus, there has been a detrimental blurring of the line between immigration and asylum.

Nackerud, Larry, Alytson Springer, Christopher Larrison, and Alicia Isaac. "The End of the Cuban Contradiction in U.S. Refugee Policy." *International Migration Review* 33:1 (Spring 1999): 176–192. The authors evaluate the Balsero Program crisis of 1994 and the implications of resulting policy changes.

WEB DOCUMENTS

"Global Report." Published annually by the United Nations High Commissioner for Refugees. Available online. URL: http://www.unhcr.ch/cgi-bin/texis/vtx/template?page=publ&src=static/gr2004/gr2004toc.htm. Updated in 2004. This annual report provides an overview and systematic survey of refugee concerns worldwide. The report includes regional and country reports; data on persons of concern and gender proportion; color maps; and an appendix on UNHCR standards and indicators.

"New Issues in Refugee Research." United Nations High Commissioner for Refugees, Evaluation and Policy Analysis Unit. Available online. URL: http://www.unhcr.ch/cgi-bin/texis/vtx/doclist?page=research&id=3bbc18ed5. Updated in August 2005. This site provides access to an ongoing series of Working Papers, from May 1999 to present.

"State of the World's Refugees: Fifty Years of Humanitarian Action." United Nations High Commissioner for Refugees. Available online. URL: http://www.unhcr.ch/cgi-bin/texis/vtx/template?page=publ&src=static/sowr2000/toceng.htm. Updated in 2000. This report traces major refugee movements in the post–World War II era, including the Rwandan crisis of the 1990s; includes an excellent bibliography.

"The State of the World's Refugees: A Humanitarian Agenda." United Nations High Commissioner for Refugees. Available online. URL: http://www.unhcr.ch/cgi-bin/texis/vtx/publ?id=3eef1d896. Updated in 1997. This report provides a comprehensive analysis of displacement around the world, with detailed maps and a variety of viewpoints; it is also available in hard copy through Oxford University Press.

SOCIOLOGY OF IMMIGRATION

BOOKS

Foner, Nancy. *In a New Land: A Comparative View of Immigration.* New York: New York University Press, 2005. Foner compares migrants across cities or regions, across nation-states, and across time periods, focusing on issues of race and ethnicity, gender, and transnational connections.

Foner, Nancy, and George M. Frederickson, eds. *Not Just Black and White: Historical and Contemporary Perspectives on Immigration, Race, and Ethnicity in the United States.* New York: Russell Sage Foundation, 2005. A distinguished group of social scientists and historians explore the way immigration has driven social change in the United States. This work includes former U.S. census director Kenneth Prewitt's account of "how racial and ethnic classifications in the census developed over time and how they operate today."

Immigration

Gozdziak, Elzbieta M., and Susan F. Martin, eds. *Beyond the Gateway: Immigrants in a Changing America.* Lanham, Md.: Lexington Books, 2005. Based upon a series of case studies outside the major metropolitan magnets, the editors argue that America has no immigrant policies that "promote social, economic, or civic integration." The book suggests a series of best practices.

Heer, David M. *Immigration in America's Future: Social Science Findings and the Policy Debate.* Boulder, Colo.: Westview Press, 1996. Though dated, Heer's introductory chapters on issues seldom treated, such as "The Values at Stake" and "The Influence of Social Science Findings," remain useful.

Massey, Douglas S., Rafael Alarcón, Jorge Durand, and Humberto González. *Return to Aztlan: The Social Process of International Migration from Western Mexico.* Berkeley: University of California Press, 1987. This is an early model of a fully interdisciplinary study of the process of immigration; it exhaustively explores the experience of four specific Mexican communities.

Noble, Allen G., ed. *To Build in a New Land: Ethnic Landscapes in North America.* Baltimore: Johns Hopkins University Press, 1992. The authors examine the character of North American ethnic groups through an exploration of the landscapes they create.

Pedraza, Silvia, and Rubén G. Rumbaut, eds. *Origins and Destinies: Immigration, Race, and Ethnicity in America.* Belmont, Calif.: Wadsworth, 1996. The editors have created an excellent text, covering a variety of area ethnicities, theoretical concerns, and contemporary issues.

Portes, Alejandro, and Rubén G. Rumbaut. *Legacies: The Story of the Immigrant Second Generation.* Berkeley: University of California Press, 2001. With a solid balance between the personal vignette and the theoretical approach, the authors examine a wide range of factors supporting and hindering the acculturation of second-generation immigrants. For a more systematic examination based upon the same research, see Rumbaut and Portes's *Ethnicities.*

Ramakrishnan, S. Kathick. *Democracy in Immigrant America: Changing Demographics and Political Participation.* Stanford, Calif.: Stanford University Press, 2005. The author explores largely unexamined issues dealing with political acculturation: the relationship between immigrant voting numbers and the population generally; the relationship between traditional models of voting behavior and immigrants; the relationship between immigration adaptation and theoretical knowledge of voter turnout; and a comparison of voting participation and "inequalities in other forms of political participation."

Rumbaut, Rubén G., and Alejandro Portes, ed. *Ethnicities: Children of Immigrants in America.* Berkeley: University of California Press and New York: Russell Sage Foundation, 2001. Based on the Children of Immigrants Longitudinal Study (CILS), which followed more then 5,200 young people from several dozen ethnic groups through their high school years in the 1990s, the editors attempt to "examine systematically the adaptation patterns and trajectories" of the children of immigrants in the Miami/Ft. Lauderdale and San Diego areas.

Suarez-Orozco, Marcelo M., Carola Suarez-Orozco, and Desiree Baolian Qun, eds. *The New Immigration: An Interdisciplinary Reader.* New York and London: Routledge, 2005. A good series of technical articles grouped in three categories: "Conceptual and Theoretical Correlations," "Psychological Aspects of Immigration," and "Immigration, Language, and Education."

Waldinger, Roger, ed. *Strangers at the Gates: New Immigrants in Urban America.* Berkeley: University of California Press, 2001. Identifies new immigrant groups and examines their tendency to cluster in metropolitan areas, especially in Los Angeles, New York City, San Francisco, Miami, and Chicago.

Wong, Janelle. *Democracy's Promise: Immigrants and American Civic Institutions.* Ann Arbor: University of Michigan Press, 2006. Based on a study of Chinese and Mexican immigrants in New York and Los Angeles, the author suggests that their lack of political participation does not result from apathy but to "the inability of American political parties and advocacy organizations to mobilize immigrant voters."

Zuniga, Victor, and Rubén Hernandez-Leon, eds. *New Destinations: Mexican Immigration in the United States.* New York: Russell Sage Foundation, 2005. Contributors to this volume examine several communities where Mexicans have settled, exploring the relationship between the immigrants and community development.

ARTICLES

Conzen, Kathleen Neils, et al. "The Invention of Ethnicity: A Perspective for the U.S.A." *The Journal of American Ethnic History* 12 (Fall 1992): 3–63. Challenging theories of easy assimilation, the authors emphasize ethnicity as a "process of construction . . . which incorporates, adapts, and amplifies preexisting communal solidarities, cultural attributes and historical memories." The article gives greater weight to the active participation of immigrants in defining group identity.

Fujiwara, Lynn H. "Immigrant Rights Are Human Rights: The Reframing of Immigrant Entitlement and Welfare." *Social Problems* 52:1 (February 2005): 79–101. After spending two years in "participatory research in community organizations," the author examines immigrant group counter-rhetorical strategies for reframing the "discourse of the 'immigrant welfare problem.'"

Mohl, Raymond A. "Globalization, Latinization, and the Nuevo New South." *Journal of American Ethnic History* 22:4 (Summer 2003): 31–65. Mohl argues

Immigration

that, while Hispanic workers were generally accepted positively at first, the rapid growth of their numbers is spawning "new forms of nativism" as "Dixie appears to be on the cusp of a long-term process of Latinization.

WEB DOCUMENTS

Camarota, Steven A. "Immigrants at Mid-Decade: A Snapshot of America's Foreign-Born Population in 2005." Center for Immigration Studies, December 2005. Available online. URL: http://www.cis.org/articles/2005/back1405.html. Primarily using the data from the Census Bureau's March 2005 Current Population Survey, the author concludes that more immigrants came to the United States between 2000 and 2005 than any other five-year period, and that "immigrants and their young children (under 18) now account for one-fifth of school age population, one-fourth of those in poverty, and nearly one-third of those without health insurance, creating enormous challenges for the nation's schools, health care system, and physical infrastructure."

WOMEN AND FAMILIES

BOOKS

Alba, Richard D., Douglas S. Massey, and Rubén G. Rumbaut. *The Immigration Experience for Families and Children.* Washington, D.C.: American Sociological Association, 1999. In this brief introduction, the authors highlight 1990s patterns of immigration, with emphasis on the settlement of immigrant families, transition into the educational process, and language use.

Ehrenreich, Barbara, and Arlie Russell Hochschild, eds. *Global Woman: Nannies, Maids, and Sex Workers in the New Economy.* New York: Metropolitan Books, 2003. The editors provide a series of articles on the consequences of globalization on women from underdeveloped countries, focusing on negative aspects that are frequently overlooked in more general studies of global labor movement.

Gabaccia, Donna R. *From the Other Side: Women, Gender and Immigrant Life in the U.S., 1820–1990.* Bloomington: Indiana University Press, 1994. Gabaccia, director of the Immigration History Research Center at the University of Minnesota, focuses on the impact that immigrant women had on the history of the United States.

George, Sheba Mariam. *When Women Come First: Gender and Class in Transnational Migration.* Berkeley: University of California Press, 2005. Focusing on the daily lives of nurses and their families who immigrated from Kerala, India, the author traces the practical difficulties of accul-

204

turation, especially from the perspective of traditional gender concepts transplanted into a different cultural context.

Hondagneu-Sotelo, Pierrette, ed. *Gender and U.S. Immigration: Contemporary Trends.* Berkeley: University of California Press, 2003. This work includes six articles previously published in a special issue of the *American Behavioral Scientist* (January 1999) as well as 11 other articles.

Kelson, Gregory A., and Debra L. DeLaet, eds. *Gender and Immigration.* New York: New York University Press, 1999. The outgrowth of a panel on gender and international migration of the 1996 annual meeting of the International Studies Association in San Diego, the primary goal of *Gender and Immigration* was to provide a "gender-sensitive lens" to the study of international migration. The introduction speaks to the "invisibility of women" in the scholarship of immigration.

Leach, Kristine. *In Search of Common Ground: Nineteenth and Twentieth Century Immigrant Women in America.* San Francisco: Austin and Winfield, 1995. In this study of "human stories," the author focuses on the "commonality of experience" of immigrant women, with emphasis on childrearing and socialization.

Martin, Susan Forbes. *Refugee Women.* 2nd ed. Lanham, Md.: Lexington, 2004. Forbes outlines the situation of refugee women, both in terms of need and potential contributions; designed to encourage discussion and foster specific activities to further aid refugee women.

Weatherford, Doris. *Foreign and Female: Immigrant Women in America, 1840–1930.* Rev. ed. New York: Facts On File, 1995. The included vignettes and anecdotes regarding courting practices, sexual mores, marriage, pregnancy, birth, homes, food, clothing, childrearing, work, separation, desertion, divorce, religion, family relationships, and acculturation are useful as a starting point for further research.

ARTICLES

Dion, Karen K, and Kenneth L. Dion. "Immigrant Perspectives and Adaptations: Gender and Cultural Adaptation in Immigrant Families." *Journal of Social Issues* 57:3 (Fall 2001): 511–522. The authors examine how special conditions associated with immigration may lead to a renegotiation of gender roles within immigrant families, with implications for their "ethnocultural identity."

Gender Issues. Special issue 17:1 (Winter 1999). Includes a variety of relevant articles, including Monica Boyd's "Gender, Refugee Status and Permanent Settlement," Katharine Donato's "A Dynamic View of Mexican Migration to the United States," and Nina Toren's "Women and Immigrants: Strangers in a Strange Land."

Read, Jen'nan Ghazal. "Cultural Influences on Immigrant Women's Labor Force Participation: The Arab-American Case." *International Migration*

Immigration

Review 38:1 (Spring 2004): 52–77. Read argues that Arab immigrant women provide an exception to previous theoretical explanations based on human capital characteristics or family resources, with immigrant employment rates being among the lowest and those of U.S.-born Arab- American women similar to those of U.S.-born white women.

Sana, Mariano, and Douglas S. Massey. "Household Composition, Family Migration, and Community Context: Migrant Remittances in Four Countries." *Social Science Quarterly* 86:2 (June 2005): 509–528. Using logistic regression analyses to survey data gathered by the Mexican Migration Project and the Latin American Migration Project, the authors argue that the "cohesive patriarchal family" in Mexico "ensures the flow of remittances as part of a household strategy for risk diversification."

WEB DOCUMENTS

Beavers, Laura, and Jean D'Amico. "Children in Immigrant Families: U.S. and State-Level Findings from the 2000 Census." Available online. URL: http://www.prb.org/Template.cfm?Section=PRB&template=/ContentManagement/ContentDisplay.cfm&ContentID=12149. Updated in January 2005. Providing general statistics based upon the 2000 census, the authors suggest that children living in immigrant families are more likely to live in married-parent households, in poverty, and in a home not owned by the family, than children born to U.S.-born families.

Zlotnik, Hania. "The Global Dimensions of Female Migration." Available online. URL: http://www.migrationinformation.org/Feature/display.cfm?ID=109. Updated on March 1, 2003. The chief of the Population Estimates and Projections Section of the United Nations Population Division makes use of a new set of statistics released by the United Nations to demonstrate that women have long accounted for a higher percentage of international migrants than has previously been estimated.

MICROFORMS AND CDS

There are a wide range of resources in microform and on CD-ROM available at many of the governmental, advocacy, and research institutions listed in chapter 8; some of these have been commercially published, while others have been filmed for preservation purposes. Sometimes these can be duplicated and are available for purchase. Below is a list of the most useful.

Boehm, Randolph, ed. *Papers of the Select Commission on Immigration and Refugee Policy.* Frederick, Md.: University Publications of America, 1983, 24 microfilm reels. This set includes staff reports on U.S. immigration history, international migration, refugees, legal immigration, temporary workers, and the administration of immigration law; background, briefing, and working papers, meeting agendas, and reports on consultative meetings held with policy makers and interested parties; some official correspondence by the commission; and extensive transcripts and other related documents stemming from nine regional public hearings held between October 1979 and March 1980 on immigration issues.

Documentary Archives: Multicultural America, CD-ROM, Thomson Gale, 1997. This set includes more than 450 documents and 400 images "woven into an information web" that includes 12 thematic essays and includes hyperlinks, timelines, and maps for exploring the immigrant experience of the major immigrant groups to the United States. It is especially beneficial for inclusion of materials in rare book collections, state historical societies, and museums.

Genealogical CD-ROMS in the Archives Library Information Center of the National Archives, Washington, D.C. Includes a wide range of census, military, and immigration records. For the scope and description of 98 CD-ROM resources (as of October 21, 2005), see URL: http://www.archives.gov/research/alic/reference/genealogical-cdroms.html. *Immigrants in America*. Primary Source Microfilm, distributed by Thomson Gale, 250 microfilm reels. Covering the years between 1789 and 1929, *Immigrant in America* documents the first two great waves of immigration prior to the exclusionary legislation of the 1920s. Under the guidance of A. William Hoglund, professor of history at the University of Connecticut and trustee of the Balch Institute for Ethnic Studies, *Immigrant in America* draws sources from several major archives, including the New York Public Library collection, the Balch Institute for Ethnic Studies, and the Immigration History Research Center at the University of Minnesota.

Immigration and Refugee Services of America, 1918–1985, 354 microfilm reels. Primary Source Microfilm (distributed by Thomson Gale). Drawn from the holdings of the Immigration History Research Center at the University of Minnesota, the collection of the Immigration and Refugee Services of America and its predecessor organizations includes extensive correspondence with related service agencies, state and federal government officials, international offices nationwide, and leading public figures as well as "voluminous files on social, cultural, and political issues associated with immigration, race, and ethnicity."

Immigration Records, 1800–1959. National Archives, Washington, D.C. Available online. URL: http://www.archives.gov/genealogy/immigration/passenger-arrival.html#where. This set contains an extensive listing of the variety of sources, including descriptions of each resource and the number and nature of microforms available.

Immigration

Laws Relating to Immigration and Nationality, 1798–1962, and Directories of Courts Having Naturalization Jurisdiction, 1908–1963. National Archives, Washington, D.C. Record Group 287, two microfilm reels. This is an important collection for the close study of immigration law.

Records of the Immigration and Naturalization Service, 1787–1993 (mainly 1882–1957). Available online URL: http//www.archives.gov/research/guide-fed-records/groups/085.html. This is a complete guide to more than 18,000 cubic feet of records stored at 10 different locations, with the bulk of the records being housed in Washington, D.C. Includes extensive history of each kind of resource available within the group.

RefWorld. United Nations High Commissioner for Refugees (UNHCR). Updated semi-annually, this CD-ROM includes a collection of full-text databases, including data on conditions in refugees' countries of origin; national legislation; jurisprudence; international treaties and documents on human rights and refugee law; U.N. General Assembly and Security Council documents; documents emanating from the U.N. Commission on Human Rights and its subcommission; official UNHCR documents; an extensive reference library, including training manuals; refugee statistics; and the library catalog of the UNHCR's Centre for Documentation and Research.

Reports of the Immigrant Commission, 1907–1910. Scholarly Resources. Available online. URL: http://library.stanford.edu/depts/dlp/ebrary/dillingham/body.shtml. This collection reproduces on microfilm 41 volumes of reports by the U.S. Immigration Commission, "analyzing the heavy waves of immigration to America early in this century and their effects on the country"; it was extensively used in crafting the restrictive legislation between 1910 and 1924. It includes assessments of how immigrants affected U.S. industries, cities, and schools; steerage conditions; crime among immigrant groups; immigrant banks; prostitution; and charity groups.

United States Decennial Census Publications, 1790–1980. Primary Source Microfilm, 541 reels. This set brings together U.S. census documents and publications on nearly every important subject, enabling researchers to study social change and urban growth and decline, study immigration and ethnic neighborhoods, find genealogical data, and track other kinds of demographic and economic trends. It is based on the *Catalog of United States Census Publications, 1790–1945;* the *Bureau of the Census Catalog, 1946–1972,* and *Volume IV: North America of the International Population Census Bibliography.* It is organized by year and type of census.

United State Government, 2006 Essential Guide to the ICE—Immigration and Customs Enforcement, Federal Air Marshals, Federal Protective Service, Predator and Cornerstone Initiatives, Smuggling, Detention (CD-ROM). *Progressive Management, 2005.* Combines more than 10,000 pages of public domain U.S. government files and documents relating to Immigration and Customs Enforcement.

Annotated Bibliography

FILM RESOURCES

Film has become one of the most powerful tools in crafting a general impression of the issues, individual and corporate, surrounding immigration. As with other mediums, film should be approached critically with an appreciation of the larger dynamics of the immigration question. One of the best sites providing a wide array of critical and bibliographical resources is "The Movies, Race and Ethnicity," maintained by the Media Resource Center at the University of California, Berkeley. Available online. URL: http://www.lib.berkeley.edu/MRC/EthnicImagesVid.html. The site includes extensive bibliographies for related reference works, magazine and newspaper articles, books, and a broad sampling of videographies of both documentaries and feature films. For online resources, start with the Internet Movie Database (http://www.imdb.com), which includes extensive information on films, actors, producers, and directors from all countries, covering feature films, TV films, documentaries, and shorts.

SELECTED PRINTED WORKS FOR FILM RESEARCH

Books

Barta, Tony, ed. *Screening the Past: Film and the Representation of History.* Westport, Conn.: Praeger, 1998. *Screening the Past* provides a collection of articles, including specialized treatments of Jews, Japanese, and Scots.

Bartov, Omer. The *"Jew" in Cinema: From* the Golem *to* Don't Touch My Holocaust. Bloomington: Indiana University Press, 2005. Written by a master historian of the Second World War, this work deals perceptively with the subject from a rigorous historical perspective.

Berg, Charles Ramirez. *Latino Images in Film: Stereotypes, Subversion, and Resistance.* Austin: University of Texas Press, 2002. Unique in integrally combining Hollywood stereotyping and Latino self-representation, this work discusses how specific actors have subverted popular stereotypes.

Bernstein, Matthew, and Gaylyn Studlar, eds. *Visions of the East: Orientalism in Film.* New Brunswick, N.J.: Rutgers University Press, 1997. The editors present articles on a variety of representations of Asians in films, including those from Disney.

Budd, David H. *Culture Meets Culture in the Movies: An Analysis East, West, North, and South, with Filmographies.* Jefferson, N.C.: McFarland, 2002. Budd explores the adaptability of films in displaying cultural difference; covers mainly popular U.S. and European films.

Garcia, Roger, ed. *Out of the Shadows: Asians in American Cinema.* Milan, Italy: Edizioni Olivares; New York: distributed by Asian CineVision,

209

2001. This collection of articles provides a useful resource in profiling popular Asian actors and filmmakers.

Gevinson, Alan, ed. *American Film Institute Catalog: Within Our Gates: Ethnicity in American Feature Films, 1911–1960.* Berkeley: University of California Press, 1997. This standard reference includes both mainstream and non-Hollywood films, covering production facts and detailed synopses.

Keller, Gary D. *Hispanics and United States Film: An Overview and Handbook.* Tempe, Ariz.: Bilingual Review/Press, 1994. Keller focuses on "brief analyses of Hispanic film roles, players, and film types from the earliest motion pictures" to the early 1990s.

Lee, Robert G. *Orientals: Asian Americans in Popular Culture.* Philadelphia: Temple University Press, 1999. Identifying the "six representations of Asian Americans—the pollutant, the coolie worker, the deviant, the yellow peril, the model minority, and the gook"—Lee explores the origins of each representation.

Miller, Randall M., ed. *Ethnic Images in American Film and Television.* Philadelphia: Balch Institute, 1978. In this series of essays, Miller covers a wide range of both European and non-European ethnic images during an early phase of scholarly investigation.

Rollins, Peter, ed. *The Columbia Companion to American History on Film: How the Movies Have Portrayed the American Past.* New York: Columbia University Press, 2003. Organized thematically, this resource provides an essential starting point for research; includes specialized articles on a variety of ethnic and culture groups.

Shaheen, Jack G. *Reel Bad Arabs: How Hollywood Vilifies a People.* New York: Olive Branch, 2001. In a meticulously researched account based on more than 900 films, Shaheen includes assessments of the best and worst depictions of Arabs in film.

Articles

Ahmed, Akbar S. "Hello, Hollywood: Your Images Affect Muslims Everywhere." *New Perspectives Quarterly* 19:1 (Spring 2002): 73–75. The author suggests the importance of casting Muslims as heroes or main characters as a means of reversing popular stereotypes.

Minh-Ha, T. Pham. "The Asian Invasion (of Multiculturalism) in Hollywood." *Journal of Popular Film and Television* 32:3 (Fall 2004): 121–131. Examining Hollywood films such as *Rush Hour* (1998) and the transnationally produced *Crouching Tiger, Hidden Dragon* (2000), the author explores the contrasting discourse used to represent Asians.

Wall, James M. "Stereotypes In and Out." *Christian Century* 114 (October 15, 1997): 899. Wall argues that stereotypical images of gays, Arab Americans, and Latinos "reveal who does and does not have leverage in Hollywood."

Annotated Bibliography

FILMS INCORPORATING SIGNIFICANT IMMIGRANT THEMES

ABCD (1999). In this film, Krutin Patel presents a common tale of a traditional Indian mother who wishes her children to marry Indian partners, and children who have ideas and interests of their own.

Alamo Bay (1985). Directed by Louis Malle and based upon a true story, *Alamo Bay* explores the tensions between a shrimper and Vietnam War veteran and refugees who have been settled in the Gulf of Mexico port towns and threaten to upset the economic equilibrium of the area.

America, America (1963). Directed by Elia Kazan, this film tells the story of his uncle's journey from the oppressed, Greek-minority community in Turkey to the United States around the turn of the 20th century.

And the Earth Did Not Swallow Him (1994). Director Severo Pérez tells the story of Mexican-American migrant laborers and the perseverance of a young boy to escape poverty and racism through literature.

Better Luck Tomorrow (2002). In this film, director Justin Lin challenges the stereotype of the "perfect" Asian immigrant, exploring subtle ethnic tensions in an American high school.

Between Worlds (1999). This documentary by Shawn Hainsworth follows the lives of Vietnamese Amerasians from their homeland to the Philippines for language study, then to different regions of the United States; highlights procedures under the Orderly Departure Program.

Beyond the Border (2001). Eren Isabel McGinnis and Ari Luis Palos produced this intimate account of four brothers who, over a span of 10 years, migrate from their home in Michoacán, Mexico, to the bluegrass region of Kentucky to work in the horse industry. Filmed in both locations, it presents a balanced view of the costs and benefits of the migration.

The Border (1999). In this six-part PBS series, the history, culture, and current conditions along the U.S.-Mexican border are explored; focuses on stories of everyday life.

Catfish in Black Bean Sauce (2000). Chi Moui Lo here tells the story of Vietnamese orphans adopted by an African-American couple; one of the orphans eventually brings her mother to the United States, leading to a revaluation of identity and family.

A Child of the Ghetto (1910). D. W. Griffith's story of a seamstress, falsely accused, who flees New York's Lower East Side and falls in love with a local farmer. The film views the city as a place of oppression, obliquely suggesting that Jews might benefit by moving out of the ghetto.

La Ciudad (The City, 1998). Filmed by David Riker, working closely with the New York Latino community, this film collectively explores the stories of four illegal Latino immigrants in New York City.

Cohen films (1904–1913). These three films were a series of early comedies (*Cohen's Advertising Scheme*, 1904; *Cohen's Fire Sale*, 1907; *Cohen Saves the Flag*, 1913) based on vaudeville routines and strong Jewish stereotypes; directed by Edwin S. Porter.

Combination Platter (1993). Director Tony Chan tells the story of an illegal Chinese immigrant who attempts to arrange a marriage in order to earn his green card; it won Best Screenplay, at the Sundance Film Festival (1993).

Come See the Paradise (1990). Set during the internment of Japanese Americans during World War II, Alan Parker directs the love story between an Irish-American man and a Japanese-American woman.

Crossing Arizona (2005). A good, balanced documentary covering tensions created on both sides of the Arizona/Sonora border by illegal immigration.

A Day without a Mexican (2004). This is a humorous account of what life in California might be like without one-third of its population. According to director Sergio Arau, the film "was meant as a fable, a warning to be heeded."

DeNadie (2005). This Mexican documentary traces the route and hardships faced by South and Central America immigrants as they leave their homelands for greater opportunity in the north.

Destination America (2005). This is a four-part PBS series organized around themes that have driven people to immigrate throughout history— economic opportunity, religious freedom, and freedom of artistic expression.

Eat a Bowl of Tea (1988). Director Wayne Wang's romance is set in New York's Chinatown during the 1940s, where a young Chinese-American veteran is challenged by his father's cultural expectations.

El Norte (1983). In this film considered a classic of U.S. independent filmmaking, director Gregory Nava follows the trials of a Mayan brother and sister who leave the jungles of Guatemala after their father is killed, only to encounter another "jungle" in Los Angeles.

El Súper (1979). Leon Ichaso and Orlando Jiménez Leal chronicle the life of a Cuban exile who becomes a New York City apartment superintendent, dreaming of his homeland and refusing to make peace with his new surroundings.

The Emigrants (1971). After hard times and the death of their son, a young Swedish couple emigrate to the United States during the 19th century in this film by Jan Troell; their story is continued in *The New Land* (1972).

Everything Is Illuminated (2005). Liv Schreiber traces the journey of enlightenment of a young American Jew who makes a pilgrimage to a small Ukrainian village, where he is befriended by a young man and his grandfather.

Far and Away (1992). Ron Howard presents a romanticized tale of love and the quest for success, from impoverished Ireland to the Oklahoma territory in the 1890s; the film offers much attention to historical detail and stars Tom Cruise and Nicole Kidman.

Focus (2001). Set during World War II, in this film by Neil Slavin a man and his wife are mistaken as Jews and progressively shunned by their Brooklyn community; explores an area of anti-Semitism seldom noted in film.

From the Other Side (2002). Filmmaker Chantal Akerman chronicles life on two sides of the border, as illegal Mexican immigrants wait in Agua Prieta, Sonora, for a chance to cross over to Douglas, Arizona, still relatively untouched by the high-tech border control found along the San Diego corridor.

Funny Girl (1968). William Wyler presents the oft-told story of second-generation Hungarian-Jewish immigrant Fanny Brice (Barbra Streisand), who becomes a star with the Ziegfeld Follies.

Gangs of New York (2002). In this film, director Marin Scorsese presents the reality of interethnic violence in New York City in the wake of the massive Irish immigration of the 1840s and 1850s; stars Leonardo DiCaprio, Daniel Day-Lewis, and Cameron Diaz.

The Gatekeeper (2004). Mexican-American director John Carlos Frey tells the story of a U.S. Border Patrol agent turned vigilante who gets trapped in a Central American drug ring and, in the proces, learns a lesson in humanity.

The Godfather trilogy (1972, 1974, 1990). In Francis Ford Coppola's Oscar-winning all-star dramas tracing the evolution of the Corleone family role in the mafia from the 1920s to the 1980s, many misconceptions about the Italian mafia are fostered, though the experiences of immigrant life are richly portrayed.

God Grew Tired of Us (2006). Winning prizes at the 2006 Sudanese Film Festival, this documentary traces the lives of three Sudanese boys in the United States as they try to recover from the horrors of the brutal Sudanese civil war.

Go for Broke! (1951). In this film, director Robert Pirosh tells the story of the 442nd Regiment—loyal Japanese Americans—and their bigoted lieutenant during World War II.

A Great Wall (1985). In this comedic account of a Chinese native and his U.S. born wife and son as they return to China, director Peter Wang exposes a wide range of distinctive cultural features.

Heaven and Earth (1993). Director Oliver Stone explores the personal legacy of the Vietnam War by examining the marriage of an American soldier and a Vietnamese woman.

Hester Street (1975). Director Joan Micklin Silver explores the tumultuous life of a Russian-Jewish family as they try to adjust to America in the 1890s.

Hollywood Harems (1999). This documentary shows how films from the 1920s to the 1980s reinforced negative stereotypes of Eastern peoples.

Immigration

Hungry Hearts (1922). Based on the 1920 novel by immigrant Anzia Yezierska, *Hungry Hearts* focuses on the trials of an East European family who immigrates to New York City.

I Am Joaquín (Yo Soy Joaquín, 1969). Based on the classic Chicano poem by Rodolpho "Corky" Gonzales, Luis Valdez focuses on the oppression of Mexican-American farm workers.

In America (2002). Director Jim Sheridan recounts the journey of an Irish couple who brings their two daughters to New York City for a fresh start after the death of their son to cancer.

The Immigrant (1917). In Charlie Chaplin's classic comedy, the Little Tramp must transition to American life; the film provides a sympathetic portrayal of the plight of the immigrant.

The Italian (1915). An early silent film, *The Italian* tells the story of ward boss oppression and redemption in the life of an Italian immigrant; it provides a good contemporary visualization of New York's Little Italy.

Japanese War Bride (1952). In this King Vidor film, one finds an early representation of the anti-Japanese resentment in a Californian community as a Korean War veteran brings home a Japanese wife.

The Jazz Singer (1927). Alan Crosland's classic melodramatic account of the son (Al Jolson) of a Jewish cantor who dreams of singing jazz; the film praises the independence to overcome ethnic traditions.

The Journey (1997). The film portrays the struggle of an Indian father who visits his son and American daughter in Pittsburgh, evoking a melancholy awareness of a world where traditions no longer automatically govern behavior.

The Joy Luck Club (1993). Following the death of her mother, a Chinese-American woman learns many family secrets, and thus about her own heritage; it is based on the novel by Amy Tan.

La Bamba (1986). This is a popular Hollywood film of the life of America's first Latino rock-and-roll star, Ritchie Valens; it suggests the ethnic and racial tensions prevalent in the 1950s.

La Boda (The Wedding) (2000). Using a wedding as the focal point, Hannah Weyer chronicles the struggles of the Luis family, Mexican migrant farm workers living in the United States.

Lana's Rain (2003). In this award-wining drama (Milan International Film Festival), director Michael Ojeda explores the dark side of immigrant transition as a young woman and her brother leave Croatia in the wake of Balkan warfare and terror.

Living on Tokyo Time (1987). Steven Okazaki presents the story of a young guitarist who reconnects with his Japanese heritage after marrying a Japanese girl.

Maria Full of Grace (2004). An award-winning film (Sundance, Berlin) about a young Colombian girl whose dead-end life leads her to become a mule for drug smugglers.

214

Annotated Bibliography

Matewan (1987). Directed by John Sayles, *Matewan* tells the story of an attempt to bring nonimmigrant workers, African Americans, and Italians together to form a union in the coal fields of West Virginia in 1920.

Mi Familia (My Family, 1995). Director Gregory Nava presents a three-generation saga of a Mexican family that migrates to California in the 1920s to pursue the American dream, despite opposition and racism.

The Milagro Beanfield War (1988). Directed by Robert Redford, this film suggests the tensions evoked by development and ethnicity in "a magical New Mexican village."

Miller's Crossing (1990). Directed by Joel Coen, this film explores violence in Irish mob life during the 1930s.

Mississippi Masala (1991). In this film, Mira Nair presents an interracial love story between an Indian immigrant and an African-American businessman (Denzel Washington); deals with the shock experienced by both families.

The Molly Maguires (1970). Based upon a true story of exploitation and violence in the Pennsylvania coalfields in the 1870s, Martin Ritt's film provides a sympathetic account of the struggle of Irish-American miners.

Moscow on the Hudson (1984). In this film, Paul Mazursky provides a humorous account of the difficult but rewarding transition of a poor Soviet defector (Robin Williams) who settles in Harlem.

My Big Fat Greek Wedding (2002). This surprise hit film chronicles the culture clash in urban America as a quiet daughter (Nia Verdalus) of a passionately Greek family falls in love with an outsider.

The New Land (1972). Directed by Jan Troell, this Swedish film provides one of the best film treatments of early immigrant life, telling the story of a young Swedish couple living on the Minnesota frontier in the 1850s and their struggles and hardships during the American Indian wars and the Civil War.

Night of Henna (2005). Hassin Zee explores the dilemma faced by a Pakistani girl whose opportunities in the United States are challenged by the prospect of an arranged marriage.

Once upon a Time in America (1984). In this film, director Sergio Leone follows the exploits of groups of New York Jewish gangsters from the 1920s to the 1960s.

Picture Bride (1995). Director Kayo Hata provides a good visual representation of the realities of the picture-bride system, telling the story of a young Japanese woman who comes to Hawaii in 1918 to marry a man she has never met.

The Ring (1952). Director Kurt Neumann's film is an early attempt to dispel the myth of the "lazy Mexican," chronicling the boxing career of a young Mexican American living in Los Angeles.

Roots (1977). In this classic TV miniseries adapted from Alex Haley's work, the story is told of Kunta Kinte's family from the time of his abduction in an African village through the course of American history.

Immigration

Sankofa (1993). Director Haile Gerima presents the story of an African-American model who is mystically transported back to a West Indian plantation, learning of the struggles of her ancestors in the process.

Saving Face (2004). Alice Wu's romantic comedy involves a lesbian Chinese-American doctor who helps her unwed pregnant mother "save face" by finding her a partner.

Scarface (1983). Tracing the violent career of a young Cuban refugee (Al Pacino) who comes to Miami during the Mariel Boatlift, Brian de Palma's classic film suggests both the difficulties in resettlement and the peculiar character of 1980s Cuban immigration.

Sophie's Choice. (1982). Alan J. Pakula chronicles the life and exposes the secrets of a Polish survivor (Meryl Streep) of Auschwitz and her husband.

Spanglish (2004). James Brooks's romantic comedy about a Mexican woman and her young daughter, struggling both with assimilation and the everyday challenges of family life.

The Spectre of Hope (2001). Based upon work in 43 countries in Africa, Asia, eastern Europe, and Latin America, this film provides an impressionistic photographic account of peoples driven from their homes and cultures to the margins of industrialized societies.

Spellbound (2002). An unlikely hit documentary by director Jeffry Blitz, who presents the story of the 1999 National Spelling Bee in which three of the eight finalist were from immigrant families.

Thousand Pieces of Gold (1990). Based on the true story of a young Chinese woman sold by her impoverished father, and learning to survive on the American frontier in the 1880s, *Thousand Pieces of Gold* provides one of the few historical representations of how immigrant women could be treated during this era.

La Tragedia de Macario (2005). Inspired by the story of 19 Mexican immigrants who suffocated to death in a locked trailer in south Texas in 2003, this drama explores the desperation that drove a man and his friend to seek opportunity in the United States.

Troubled Harvest (1990). Examining the lives of women migrant workers from Mexico and Central America as they work in grape, strawberry, and cherry harvests in California and the Pacific Northwest, this documentary is based on interviews with workers. It raises serious questions regarding the use of pesticides, U.S. immigration policy, and family unification.

Uprooted: Refugees of the Global Economy (2001). This documentary tells the story of the disruptions caused by the global economy by tracking three immigrants from Bolivia, Haiti, and the Philippines to the United States. It raises important questions about the relationship between immigration policy and international economics.

West Side Story (1961). This Romeo and Juliet story is set among Anglos and Puerto Ricans in New York's West Side slums.

CHAPTER 8

ORGANIZATIONS AND AGENCIES

This chapter includes names, contact information, and brief descriptions of many of the most important international and national government agencies, academic and other research organizations, and advocacy and aid organizations concerned with immigration issues.

GOVERNMENTAL ORGANIZATIONS AND AGENCIES

Bureau of Population, Refugees, and Migration (PRM)
U.S. Department of State
URL: http://www.state.gov/g/prm
Phone: (202) 647-4000
2201 C Street, NW
Washington, DC 20520
The PRM is the branch of the Department of State primarily responsible for formulating policies on population, refugees, and migration and for administering U.S. refugee assistance and admissions programs. The PRM coordinates U.S. international population policy and promotes its goals through bilateral and multilateral cooperation. It works closely with the U.S. Agency for International Development, which administers U.S. international popula-

tion programs. The bureau also coordinates U.S. international migration policy within the U.S. government and through bilateral and multilateral diplomacy.

Office of Immigration Statistics (OIS)
URL: http://www.uscis.gov/graphics/shared/statistics
E-mail: immigrationstatistics@hgs.gov
Phone: (202) 305-1613
U.S. Department of Homeland Security
425 I Street, NW
Room 4034
Washington, DC 20536
The OIS is the branch of the Department of Homeland Security that gathers information in order to inform the development of im-

217

migration policies and to discover the effects of immigration policies on immigration.

Office of Refugee Resettlement (ORR)
U.S. Department of Health and Human Services
URL: http://www.acf.dhhs.gov/programs/orr
Phone: (202) 401-9246
Fax: (202) 401-5487
Administration for Children and Families
370 L'Enfant Promenade, SW
6th Floor/East
Washington, DC 20447
The ORR is a branch of the Department of Health and Human Services (HHS). Its goals include assisting refugees who come to America in becoming economically self-sufficient. The HHS administers programs such as the Administration for Children and Families, the Health Care Financial Administration, and the Health Care Financial Administration.

United Nations Educational, Scientific and Cultural Organization (UNESCO)
URL: http://www.unesco.org
E-mail: bpiweb@unesco.og
Phone: +33 (0)1 45 68 10 00
Fax: +33 (0)1 45 67 16 90
7, place de Fontenoy
75352 Paris 07 SP
France
Founded on November 16, 1945, as a United Nations agency, its purpose is to work with the mem-

ber states in gathering and sharing ideas related to various ethical issues; in their own words, to "build peace in the minds of men."

United Nations High Commissioner for Refugees (UNHCR)
URL: http://www.unhcr.ch
Phone: +41 22 739 8111
Case Postale 2500
CH – 1211 Genève 2 Dépôt
Switzerland
The United Nations General Assembly established the UNHCR on December 14, 1950, in order to coordinate international action to solve refugee problems and to provide services to refugees. Its primary purpose is to safeguard the rights of refugees.

United Nations Statistics Division
URL: http://www.un.org/Depts/unsd/statdiv.htm
E-mail: statistics@un.org
Fax: (212) 963-4116
Director, Statistics Division
United Nations
New York, NY 10017
The Statistics Division provides a global center for data on international trade, national accounts, energy, industry, environment, transport, and demographic and social statistics gathered from many national and international sources. It promotes international standards of methods, classifications, and definitions used by national agencies; assists member states in improving their statisti-

cal services by giving advice and training; coordinates international statistical programs and activities entrusted to the division by the United Nations Statistical Commission and the Committee for the Coordination of Statistical Activities (CCSA); provides input and secretarial support to the United Nations Statistical Commission and its working group; and promotes modern surveying and mapping techniques as a tool for growth and development.

U.S. Association for United Nations High Commissioner for Refugees (USA for UNHCR)
URL: http://www. usaforunhcr.org
E-mail: infor@usaforunhcr.org
Phone: (202) 296-1115 or
  (800) 770-1100
Fax: (202) 296-1081
1775 K Street, NW
Suite 290
Washington, DC 20006
USA for UNHCR helps educate and raise the consciousness of Americans about refugees and provides a way for Americans to contribute and otherwise become involved in assisting refugees.

U.S. Census Bureau
URL: http://www.census.gov
Phone: (202) 728-6829
Fax: (301) 457-3620
4700 Silver Hill Road
Washington, DC 20233-0001
The U.S. Census Bureau is a branch of the Department of Commerce. Its primary purpose

is to conduct surveys and gather data about the nation's people and economy. The bureau's data are used in tracking immigration and assimilation trends.

U.S. Citizenship and Immigration Services (USCIS)
URL: http://www.uscis.gov
Phone: (800) 375-5283
20 Massachusetts Avenue, NW
Washington, DC 20529
The USCIS is the branch of the Department of Homeland Security responsible for immigration and naturalization. Its functions include adjudication of immigrant visa and naturalization petitions, the processing of asylum and refugee applications, and the performance of service centers.

U.S. Customs and Border Protection (CBP)
URL: http://www.customs.gov
Phone: (202) 354-1000
1300 Pennsylvania Avenue, NW
Washington, DC 20229
The CBP is the branch of Homeland Security dedicated to protecting U.S. borders and ports, with particular emphasis on the prevention of terrorism.

U.S. Department of Homeland Security
URL: http://www.dhs.gov
Phone: (202) 282-8000 or
  (202) 282-8495
Washington, DC 20528
The Department of Homeland Security became fully functional on March 1, 2003. It integrates

all aspects of homeland security, including protection against terrorist attacks, supervision of alien entry and naturalization, and the securing of borders and ports. See, too, its various agencies, including U.S. Citizenship and Immigration Service; U.S. Customs and Border Protection; and the Office of Immigration Statistics.

U.S. Department of Justice
URL: http://www.usdoj.gov
E-mail: askdoj@usdoj.gov
Phone: (202) 514-2000
950 Pennsylvania Avenue, NW
Washington, DC 20530-0001
The Department of Justice is the branch of the federal government responsible for enforcing the law of the United States, for ensuring public safety, for preventing and controlling crime, for punishing those guilty of infringing laws, and for ensuring fair and impartial administration of justice in the country.

U.S. Department of Labor
URL: http://www.oalj.dol.gov/
libina.htm
Phone: (202) 693-7300
Fax: (202) 693-7365
Office of Administrative Law
Judges
800 K Street, NW
Suite 400 N
Washington, DC 20210
The Department of Labor is the branch of the federal government responsible for, among other things, certification and attestation of alien labor applications.

The Office of Administrative Law Judges is a branch of the Department of Labor and presides over labor-related cases. The Law Library of the U.S. Department of Labor contains information concerning alien labor-related cases.

U.S. House Committee on the Judiciary
Subcommittee on Immigration, Border Security, and Claims
URL: http://www.house.gov/judiciary
Phone: (202) 225-5727
B370B Rayburn House Office Building
Washington, DC 20515
This is a subcommittee of the Committee on the Judiciary of the House of Representatives. Some of the committee's jurisdictions include: immigration, naturalization, border security, refugees, treaties, claims against the United States, and other matters as appointed by the chairman.

U.S. Senate Committee on the Judiciary
Subcommittee on Immigration, Border Security, and Citizenship
URL: http://www.senate.gov/~judiciary
Phone: (202) 224-6098
Room SD-224
Dirksen Senate Office Building
Washington, DC 20510
This is a subcommittee of the U.S. Senate Committee on the Judiciary. It has jurisdiction over immigration, citizenship, and refugee

Organizations and Agencies

laws; oversight over departments with relation to the subcommittee; and oversight of international migration and refugee laws and policies and private immigration relief bills.

EDUCATIONAL AND RESEARCH ORGANIZATIONS

Brookings Institution
URL: http://www.brook.edu
Phone: (202) 797-6000
Fax: (202) 797-6004
1775 Massachusetts Avenue, NW
Washington, DC 20036
The Brookings Institution is one of Washington's oldest think tanks, devoted to research, analysis, and public education, with an emphasis in economics, foreign policy, governance, and metropolitan policy.

Cato Institute
URL: http://www.cato.org
Phone: (202) 842-0200
Fax: (202) 842-3490
1000 Massachusetts Avenue, NW
Washington, DC 20001
Cato seeks to encourage traditional American principles of limited government, individual liberty, free markets, and peace in the course of public policy debate. It believes immigration is good for the U.S. economy and favors easing immigration restrictions.

Center for Immigration Research (CIR)
URL: http://www.uh.edu/cir
Phone: (713) 743-3694
Fax: (713) 743-3943
University of Houston
492 Philip G. Hoffman Hall
4800 Calhoun Road
Houston, TX 77204-3474
The Center for Immigration Research is affiliated with the University of Houston. The center studies the consequences of current immigration in order to provide information for international and national policies, institutions, organizations, and policy makers.

Center for Immigration Studies (CIS)
URL: http://www.cis.org
E-mail: center@cis.org
Phone: (202) 466-8185
Fax: (202) 466-8076
1522 K Street, NW
Suite 820
Washington, DC 20005-1202
CIS was founded in 1985 as a think tank devoted to research and policy analysis of the economic, social, demographic, and fiscal impacts of immigration in the United States. The center is pro-immigration but with low immigration ceilings, so that America can provide a warmer welcome to those who are admitted.

221

Immigration

Center for Migration Studies of New York
URL: http://cmsny.org
E-mail: offices@cmsny.org
Phone: (718) 351-8800
Fax: (718) 667-4598
209 Flagg Place
Staten Island, NY 10304-1199
The center studies sociodemographic, historical, economic, political, and legislative aspects of migration and refugee issues. The organization tries to understand and inform the public of the causes and consequences on human migration.

Center for the Study of Race and Ethnicity
URL: http://www.brown.edu/
Departments/Race_Ethnicity
Phone: (401) 863-3080
Fax: (401) 863-7589
Box 1886
Brown University
Providence, RI 02912
Part of Brown University, the center's goals are to develop and coordinate resources for research and teaching concerning racial and ethnic minorities and to assist research on race and ethnicity in American society.

Centre for Refugee Studies (CRS)
URL: http://www.yorku.ca/crs
E-mail: crs@yorku.ca
Phone: (416) 736-5663
Fax: (416) 736-5837
York University
Room 321
York Lanes
4700 Keele Street
Toronto, ON M3J 1P3

Founded in 1988 at York University, the Centre for Refugee Studies is an organized research group that focuses on migration-related studies. It fosters interdisciplinary and collaborative research, and its efforts are focused on five related programs, including gender, refugee law research, development, displacement and repatriation, resettlement, and prevention.

Centre for Research in International Migration and Ethnic Relations (CEIFO)
URL: http://www.ceifo.su.se
E-mail: ceifo.editor@ceifo.su.se
Phone: 08-16 22 64 or
08-16 26 89
Fax: 08 - 15 67 20
Stockholms universitet
SE – 106 91 Stockholm
Sweden
The purpose of CEIFO is to coordinate and develop research in the field of international migration and ethnic relations. Its research covers international migration, ethnicity, nationalism, xenophobia and racism, ethnic relations, immigration policies, and refugee reception models.

Ethnic Studies Library at UC Berkeley
URL: http://www.lib.
berkeley.edu/Collections/Ethnic
E-mail: esl@library.berkeley.edu
Phone: (510) 643-1234 (circulation desk)
Fax: (510) 643-8433
Department of Ethnic Studies

30 Stephens Hall
#2360 Berkeley
University of California
Berkeley, CA 94720-2360
Ethnic Studies is an academic program of the University of California at Berkeley. The library there houses an extensive collection of ethnic materials in African-American, Asian, Chicano, and Native American research and provides updated guidance on research methods in ethnic areas.

Historical Society of
  Pennyslvania
URL: http://www.hsp.org
Phone: (215) 732-6200
Fax: (215) 732-2680
1300 Locust Street
Philadelphia, PA 19107
The society is one of America's largest family history libraries. After merging with the Balch Institute fro Ethnic Studies, the society has grown to be a chief center for the study of ethnic communities and immigration experiences.

History of International
  Migration
URL: http://www.let.leidenuniv.
  nl/history/migration
Phone: +31 (0)71 527 2786
Migration History
Leiden University
P.O. Box 9515
2300 RA Leiden
The Netherlands
The web site for this organization was developed to provide accessible teaching resources regarding international migration. With the support of the Eurydice, the Education Information Network in the European Community, and the Dutch Ministry of Education, a conference met in Leiden in the Netherlands on April 14–16, 1994, leading to creation of this web site, which provides a concise history and documents on various international migrations.

Immigration and Ethnic History
  Society
URL: http://www.iehs.org
Phone: (909) 880-5525
Organized to promote the study of the history of immigration to the United States and Canada from all parts of the world, including studies of the background of emigration in the countries of origin; to promote the study of ethnic groups in the United States, including regional groups, Native Americans, and forced immigrants; and to promote understanding of the processes of acculturation and of conflict.

Immigration History Research
  Center (IHRC)
URL: http://www.umn.edu/ihrc
E-mail: ihrc@umn.edu
Phone: (612) 625-4800
Fax: (612) 626-0018
University of Minnesota
College of Liberal Arts
311 Andersen Library
222-21st Avenue Street
Minneapolis, MN 55455-0439
The IHRC works with various ethnic communities, historical agencies, research specialists, educators,

Immigration

and many others to promote understanding of the immigration process. The center maintains a library and archival collection, conducts research assistance, produces publications, and helps with academic and public programs relating to immigration.

Immigration Policy Center
URL: http://www.ailf.org/ipc
E-mail: info@ailf.org
Phone: (202) 742-5600
Fax: (202) 742-5619
918 F Street, NW
6th Floor
Washington, DC 20004
An initiative of the American Immigration Law Foundation, it provides research and policy analysis on a wide range of issues regarding the contribution and condition of immigrants in the United States.

Institute for Migration and Ethnic Studies (IMES)
URL: http://www.pscw.uva.nl/imes
E-mail: imes@fmg.uva.nl
Phone: 31-20-525-3627
Fax: 31-20-525-3628
University of Amsterdam
O.Z. Achterburgwal 237
1012 DL Amsterdam
The Netherlands
An interdisciplinary institute of the University of Amsterdam, IMES promotes a research program that encourages integration of learning from different perspectives through cooperative efforts in the departments of anthropology, sociology, communication science, political science, social geography, economic geography, econometrics, administrative law, and social and economic history.

International Center for Migration, Ethnicity and Citizenship (ICMEC)
URL: http://www.newschool.edu/icmec
E-mail: icmec@newschool.edu
Phone: (212) 229-5399
Fax: (212) 989-0504
65 Fifth Avenue
Room 227
New York, NY 10003
The center is a part of the New School University in New York. ICMEC conducts research on international migration and refugee flows, the demographic change in and policies of receiving countries, and the implications of these phenomena for contemporary notions of sovereignty and citizenship.

Migration Policy Institute (MPI)
URL: http://www.migrationpolicy.org
E-mail: infor@migrationpolicy.org
Phone: (202) 266-1940
Fax: (202) 266-1900
1400 16th Street, NW
Suite 300
Washington, DC 20036
An independent, nonpartisan, nonprofit think tank that provides studies of migration and refugee policies on all levels of government.

It encourages pragmatic responses to the challenges and opportunities that migration can create for communities around the world. MPI promotes research in migration management, refugee protection and international humanitarian response, North American borders and migration agenda, and immigrant settlement and integration.

PEW Hispanic Center
URL: http://pewhispanic.org
E-mail: info@pewhispanic.org
Phone: (202) 292-3300
Fax: (202) 785-8282
USC Annenberg School for Communication
1919 M Street, NW
Suite 460
Washington, DC 20036
PEW is a nonpartisan organization that seeks to improve understanding of the U.S. Hispanic population and to chronicle Latinos' growing impact on the entire nation. The center does not advocate for or take positions on policy issues.

Public Agenda
URL: http://www.publicagenda.org
Phone: (212) 686-6610
Fax: (212) 889-3461
6 East 39th Street
New York, NY 10016
Public Agenda is a research organization that seeks to bridge the gap between American leaders and the public opinion on a wide variety of issues. Its mission is to help leaders understand the public's viewpoints and help inform citizens about the policy issues in order for them to make an informed decision.

Race and Ethnic Studies Institute (RESI)
URL: http://resi.tamu.edu
Phone: (979) 845-0966 (RESI), (979) 845-0695 (director's phone)
Fax: (979) 845-0696
513 Blocker (J.R.) Building
Texas A&M University
College Station, TX 77843
The Race and Ethnic Studies Institute, officially established in 1991, conducts research pertaining to race, ethnicity, gender, and social class in the areas of education, economics, health, and the environment. It is affiliated with Texas A&M University.

RAND Corporation
URL: http://www.rand.org
Phone: (310) 393-0411
Fax: (310) 393-4818
1776 Main Street
P.O. Box 2138
Santa Monica, CA 90407-2138
RAND Corporation conducts research and analysis on social and economic issues and national security issues in order to help provide effective solutions to improve policy and decision making for the public and private sectors.

Urban Institute
URL: http://www.urban.org
E-mail: paffairs@ui.urban.org

Phone: (202) 833-7200
Fax: (202) 223-3043
2100 M Street, NW
Washington, DC 20037
The Urban Institute was created in response to President Lyndon Johnson's challenge to civic leaders to charter an organization to conduct research and analysis on problems facing American cities in 1968. The institute analyzes policies, evaluates programs, and informs community development on how to improve social, civic, and the economic well-being of cities throughout America and the international community.

ADVOCACY AND AID AGENCIES AND ORGANIZATIONS

America Friends Service Committee
URL: http://www.afsc.org
E-mail: afscinfo@afsc.org
Phone: (215) 241-7000
Fax: (215) 241-7275
1501 Cherry Street
Philadelphia, PA 19102
This organization was created in 1917 to provide pacifist Quakers with a means of assisting refugees of war. The organization lobbies against unfair immigration laws and works for the human rights of immigrants.

American Civil Liberties Union (ACLU)
URL: http://www.aclu.org
Phone: (212) 549-2500
125 Broad Street
18th Floor
New York, NY 10004
The ACLU's mission is to protect the First Amendment, equal protection under the law, due process of the law, and the right to privacy. It publishes reports, position papers, and books that details what freedoms immigrants and refugees have under the U.S. Constitution.

Americans for Immigration Control (AIC)
URL: http://www. immigrationcontrol.com
E-mail: aic@ immigrationcontrol.com
Phone: (540) 468-2023
Fax: (540) 468-2026
P.O. Box 738
Monterey, VA 24465
AIC lobbies Congress and campaigns on the grassroots level to regulate immigration and deter illegal immigration. The organization supports legal reforms that would reduce U.S. immigration, increase funding for border patrol, and create sanctions against employers of illegal immigrants. Also, AIC opposes amnesty for such immigrants.

American Immigration Control Foundation (AICF)
URL: http://www. aicfoundation.com
E-mail: aicfndn@cfw.com
Phone: (540) 468-2022
Fax: (540) 468-2024
P.O. Box 525
Monterey, VA 24465
The foundation's primary goal is development of a workable, anti-immigration policy that would preserve traditional American values.

The American Immigration Law Foundation (AILF)
URL: http://www.ailf.org
E-mail: infor@ailf.org
Phone: (202) 742-5600
Fax: (202) 742-5619
918 F Street, NW
Washington, DC 20004
AILF works to promote a better public education regarding immigration law, to create an awareness of immigration policy and the importance of following established laws, and to promote fairness and due process of the law for immigrants.

American Immigration Lawyers Association (AILA)
URL: http://www.aila.org
E-mail: ilrs@aila.org
Phone: (202) 216-2400
Fax: (202) 783-7853
918 F Street, NW
Washington, DC 20004-1400
Founded in 1946, the AILA is an association of 8,000 attorneys and law professors who work in the field of immigration and na-

tionality law. It is an affiliated organization of the American Bar Association. AILA represents immigrants and businesses that employ immigrants. It also provides its attorneys with further legal education, information, and services.

American Refugee Committee (ARC)
URL: http://www.archq.org
E-mail: archq@archq.org
Phone: (612) 872-7060
Fax: (612) 607-6499
430 Oak Grove Street
Suite 204
Minneapolis, MN 55403
ARC works to help refugees and displaced persons rebuild their lives. They work from the perspective of respect for other cultures and consciously integrate refugees themselves in planning and development programs.

Amnesty International (AI)
URL: http://www.amnesty.org
E-mail: admin-us@aiusa.org
Phone: (212) 807-8400
Fax: (212) 463-9193 or
(212) 627-1451
5 Penn Plaza
14th Floor
New York, NY 10001
Amnesty International is a worldwide movement that works through research and action to promote human rights. It is an international organization with members from more than 150 countries. Amnesty International works to protect the rights espoused in the Universal Declaration of Human Rights.

Immigration

Border Action Network (BAN)
URL: http://www.
borderaction.org
E-mail: BAN@borderaction.org
Phone: (520) 623-4944
Fax: (520) 792-2097
P.O. Box 384
Tucson, AZ 85702
BAN is a grassroots organization that works with Latino and Mexican communities to protect human rights, civil rights, and the Sonoran desert along the Arizona-Mexico border. BAN was formed in 1999 and is located in Tuscan, Douglas, and Nogales, Arizona.

Carrying Capacity Network
URL: http://www.
carryingcapacity.org
E-mail: carryingcapacity@covad.net
Phone: (202) 296-4548
Fax: (202) 296-4609
2000 P Street, NW
Suite 310
Washington, DC 20036
Carrying Capacity Network is a nonprofit advocacy group that promotes population stabilization, immigration reduction, economic sustainability, and resource conservation. It proposes a program that includes a 100,000-person annual limit on immigration.

Catholic Charities USA
URL: http://www.
catholiccharitiesusa.org
Phone: (703) 549-1390
Fax: (703) 549-1656
1731 King Street
Alexandria, VA 22314

Catholic Charities is an organization committed to helping people in need through social service networks, regardless of religion. The members of the organization also help those in need by providing networking opportunities, national advocacy and media efforts, program development, training and technical assistance, and financial support.

Catholic Legal Immigration Network (CLINIC)
URL: http://www.cliniclegal.org
E-mail: national@cliniclegal.org
Phone: (202) 635-2556
McCormick Pavilion
415 Michigan Avenue, NE
Washington, DC 20017
The network's primary duties are to provide legal and nonlegal support services to Catholic charities who help with legal immigration programs. The attorneys of CLINIC serve low-income immigrants, regardless of race, religion, gender, ethnic group, or other distinguishing characteristics.

Center for American Unity
URL: http://www.cfau.org
P.O. Box 910
Warrenton, VA 20188
The center works to preserve the historical unity in America. It tries to answer the national question on whether the United States can survive as a nation-state, the political expression of a distinct American people, in the face of the emerging threats of mass immigration, multiculturalism, multilingualism, and affirmative action. The Cen-

ter of American Unity sponsors the journal *V-Dare*.

Central American Refugee Center (CARECEN)
URL: http://www.icomm. ca/carecen
E-mail: carecen@pb.net
Phone: (516) 489-8330
Fax: (516) 489-8308
91 North Franklin Street
Suite 211
Hempstead, NY 11550
Founded in 1983 as a relief organization for refugees, CARECEN has evolved into a community self-help and advocacy organization for Central Americans. CARECEN is an organization that works to protect the human rights of refugees and immigration community. It also works to build a greater understanding between native-born residents and newcomer communities.

Church World Service (CWS)
URL: http://www. churchworldservices.org
E-mail: info@ churchworldservices.org
Phone: (574) 264-3102, or (800) 297-1516
Fax: (574) 262-0966
28606 Philips Street
P.O. Box 968
Elkhart, IN 46515
CWS works to provide relief, development, and refugee assistance in more than 80 countries. Founded in 1946, the organization consists of more than 36 Protestant, Orthodox, and Anglican denominations within the United States. The organization was created in response to post–WWII needs. CWS works in communities in times of disasters, resettles refugees, promotes fair policies, and provides educational resources.

Cultural Orientation Resource Center
Center for Applied Linguistics
URL: http://www. culturalorientation.net
E-mail: info@cal.org
Phone: (202) 362-0700
Fax: (202) 362-3740
4646 40th Street, NW
Washington, DC 20016-1859
Cultural Orientation Resource Center, formerly known as the Refugee Resource Center, links providers of cultural orientation and domestic resettlement programs, provides information to resettlement caseworkers and basic facts about new refugee groups, and offers cultural orientation activities for trainers overseas and in the United States. The center provides materials to immigrants about housing, community services, transportation, health, employment, and other cultural-related adjustment topics.

December 18
URL: http://www. december18.net
E-mail: info@december26.net
December 18
Postbus 22
B – 9820 Merelbeke
Belgium
On December 18, 1990, the International Convention on the

Immigration

Protection of the Rights of All Migrant Workers and Members of Their Families was approved by the UN General Assembly, providing the philosophical foundation for this online organization formed by Asian migrant organizations. The purpose of December 18 is to promote and protect the rights of migrants with dignity and respect as basic values.

Episcopal Migration Ministries (EMM)
Episcopal Church Center
URL: http://www.ecusa.anglican.org/emm
Phone: (212) 867-8400 or (800) 334-7626
815 Second Avenue
New York, NY 10017
The Episcopal Church reaches out to refugees, displaced persons, and immigrants through EMM by providing resettlement services and places of security and peace. The organization also serves as a means of alerting its membership to the needs of migrants and refugees.

Federation for American Immigration Reform (FAIR)
URL: http://www.fairus.org
Phone: (202) 328-7004
Fax: (202) 387-3447
1666 Connecticut Avenue, NW
Suite 400
Washington, DC 20009
FAIR is composed of 70,000 members who seek to improve border security, stop illegal immigration,

and promote low immigration levels. It believes that the growing flood of immigrants into the United States causes higher unemployment and taxes social services.

Hebrew Immigrant Aid Society (HIAS)
URL: http://www.hias.org
E-mail: info@hias.org
Phone: (212) 967-4100
Fax: (212) 967-4483
333 Seventh Avenue
16th Floor
New York, NY 10001-5004
HIAS is an organization that helps Jews through its mission of rescue, reunion, and resettlement. Established in New York City in 1881 by a Jew who had escaped persecution in Europe, it has assisted more than 4 million Jews in immigrating to Israel, Canada, Latin America, the United States, and other countries. More broadly, it now advocates generally on behalf of refugees and migrants on the international, national, and community level.

Heritage Foundation
URL: http://www.heritage.org
Phone: (202) 546-4400
Fax: (202) 546-8328
214 Massachusetts Avenue, NE
Washington, DC 20002-4999
The Heritage Foundation is a conservative research and educational institute that supports principles of free enterprise, limited government, individual freedom, traditional American values, and a strong national defense. Heritage

230

Foundation also conducts research on immigration policies.

Humane Borders
URL: http://www.humaneborders.org
E-mail: info@humaneborders.org
Phone: (520) 628-7753
740 East Speedway Boulevard
Tucson, AZ 85719
Humane Borders advocates a more humane approach toward immigrants who try to come to America. It establishes water stations along the border and supports the legalization of undocumented workers, the creation of a guest worker program, an increase in the number of visas issued to Mexican nationals, demilitarization of the border, and further economic development in Mexico.

Human Rights First
URL: http://www.humanrightsfirst.org
E-mail: feedback@humanrightsfirst.org
Phone: (212) 845-5200
Fax: (212) 845-5299
333 Seventh Avenue
13th Floor
New York, NY 10001-5004
The organization works to create a secure and humane world by advancing justice, human dignity, and respect for the rule of law. The organization supports those who advocate human rights and basic freedoms on the local level. On the international level, it protects refugees, supports the building of a strong international system of justice and accountability, and monitors the enforcement of human rights laws in the United States and abroad.

Human Rights Watch (HRW)
URL: http://www.hrw.org
E-mail: hrwnyc@hrw.org
Phone: (212) 290-4700
Fax: (212) 736-1300
350 Fifth Avenue
34th Floor
New York, NY 10118-3299
Human Rights Watch is the largest human rights organization in America. It investigates countries and reports on the human rights abuses. It also meets with leaders of countries to create policies that diminish human rights abuses. The organization began in 1978 as Helsinki Watch to monitor human rights in countries of the Soviet bloc. Americas Watch was started in the 1980s to "counter the notion that human rights abuses by one side in the war in Central America were somehow more tolerable than abuses by the other side." The watches of different countries came together under the banner of Human Rights Watch in 1988.

Immigrants' Rights Project (IRP)
American Civil Liberties Union
URL: http://www.aclu.org/immigrants
E-mail: immrights@aclu.org
Phone: (212) 549-2660
Fax: (212) 549-2654
125 Broad Street
New York, NY 10004-2400

Immigration

The Immigrants' Rights Project of the ACLU works to defend the civil and constitutional rights of immigrants through legal and educational means. It was established in 1987 in order to expand the human rights efforts to immigrants. It focuses on unconstitutional restrictions on the right to judicial review, the unfair expedited removal process, new indefinite and mandatory detention rules, and workers' rights.

Immigration Equality
Lesbian and Gay Immigration
  Rights Task Force
URL: http://www.lgirtf.org
Phone: (212) 714-2904
Fax: (212) 714-2973
350 West 31st Street
Suite 505
New York, NY 10001
Immigration Equality is a national grassroots organization that tries to end discrimination in U.S. immigration law. It seeks to reduce the negative impact of that law on the lives of lesbian, gay, bisexual, transgender, and HIV-positive people, and to obtain asylum to the aforementioned who are persecuted in their home country.

InterAction (American Council
  for Voluntary International
  Action)
URL: http://interaction.org
E-mail: ia@interaction.org
Phone: (202) 667-8227
Fax: (202) 667-8236
1717 Massachusetts Avenue, NW
Suite 701
Washington, DC 20036
InterAction works to overcome poverty, exclusion, and suffering by advancing social justice and basic dignity for all. InterAction is a U.S.-based international development and humanitarian organization operating in every developing country.

International Immigrants Foun-
  dation
URL: http://www.10.org
E-mail: info@10.org
Phone: (212) 302-2222
Fax: (212) 221-7206
1435 Broadway
Second Floor
New York, NY 10018-1909
The organization works to help immigrant families develop a better life in America. It also promotes intercultural relations and seeks to change negative perceptions of different races and cultures.

International Organization for
  Migration (IOM)
URL: http://www.iom.int
E-mail: info@iom.int
Phone: +41/22/717 9111
Fax: +41/22/798 6150
17, Route des Morillons
CH-1211 Geneva 19
Switzerland
IOM works with other migration organizations to meet the growing operational challenges, advance understanding of migration issues, encourage social and economic development through migration,

and uphold the human dignity and well-being of migrants.

League of United Latin American Citizens (LULAC)
URL: http://www.lulac.org
E-mail: LNESCNat@aol.com
Phone: (202) 833-6130
Fax: (202) 833-6135
2000 L Street, NW
Suite 610
Washington, DC 20036
LULAC operates to advance the economic condition, educational attainment, political influence, health, and civil rights of the Hispanic population in the United States. It is active in voter registration drives, developing housing units for low-income Hispanics, conducting youth leadership programs, and providing scholarships to Hispanic students.

Lutheran Immigration and Refugee Service (LIRS)
URL: http://www.lirs.org
E-mail: lirs@lirs.org
Phone: (410) 230-2890
Fax: (410) 230-2890
700 Light Street
Baltimore, MD 21230
LIRS is a faith-based organization that works to bring "new hope and new life" to refugees and immigrants through ministries of service and justice. LIRS began in 1918 under the National Lutheran Council to provide aid and support to post–World War I immigrant and refugee resettlements. It began to help Lutherans resettle

but expanded to assist immigrants from a variety of racial, ethnic, and religious backgrounds.

Mexican American Legal Defense Fund (MALDEF)
URL: http://www.maldef.org
Phone: (916) 443-7531
Fax: (916) 443-1541
1107 9th Street
Suite 240
Sacramento, CA 95814
MALDEF's mission is to secure public policies, laws, and programs to safeguard the civil rights of Latinos and to encourage them to participate fully in American society. It accomplishes its mission through employment, education, immigration, political access, language, and public-resource equity issues.

Migrants Rights International (MRI)
URL: http://www.migrantwatch.org
E-mail: migrantwatch@vtx.ch
Phone: +41.22.9177817 or
+41.22.7882873
Fax: +41.22.7882875
c.p. 135, route des Morillons
1211 Geneva
Switzerland
A nongovernmental organization created to protect the human rights of migrants, MRI was founded in Cairo, Egypt, in 1994 during the United Nations International Conference on Population and Development. The membership of the organization is comprised of experts and practitioners who bring

specialized knowledge to promote human rights among migrants.

The Migration Policy Group (MPG)
URL: http://www. migpolgroup.com
E-mail: info@migpolgroup.com
Phone: 32 2 230 59 30
Fax: 32 2 280 09 25
205 Rue Belliard
Box 1
1040 Brussels
Belgium
MPG is committed to policy development on migration and mobility and diversity and antidiscrimination by facilitating the exchange between policy makers, with a view toward innovative and effective responses.

Minuteman Project
URL: http://www. minutemanproject.com
Phone: (949) 222-4266
Fax: (949) 222-6607
P.O. Box 3944
Laguna Hills, CA 92654-3944
The Minuteman Project seeks to raise awareness of the consequences of unregulated illegal immigration, and to peacefully stop illegal border crossings. Their credo is "Americans doing the job Congress won't do."

National Alliance Against Racist and Political Repression (NAARPR)
URL: http://www.naarpr.org
Phone: (312) 939-2750
Fax: (773) 929-2613
Chicago Branch

1325 South Wabash Avenue
Suite 105
Chicago, IL 60605
The NAARPR works to end the death sentence and continuing racism and genocide practiced against African, Latino American, and Third World peoples. NAARPR is a coalition of political, labor, church, civic, student, and community organizations that opposes the many forms of human rights repression in the United States. It seeks to end the harassment and deportation of illegal immigrant workers. The alliance publishes pamphlets and a quarterly newsletter, *The Organizer.*

National Council of La Raza
URL: http://www.nclr.org
E-mail: info@nclr.org
Phone: (202) 785-1670
Fax: (202) 785-1792
1111 19th Street, NW
Suite 1000
Washington, DC 20036
The council exists to reduce poverty and discrimination and improve life opportunities for all Hispanics nationally. Nearly 200 formal affiliates serve 37 states, Puerto Rico, and the District of Columbia. Programmatic efforts focus on civil rights, education, health, housing and community development, employment and training, immigration, and poverty.

National Immigration Forum
URL: http://www. immigrationforum.org

E-mail: info@immigration forum.org
Phone: (202) 347-0040
Fax: (202) 347-0058
50 F Street NW
Suite 300
Washington, DC 20001
The forum works to uphold America's tradition as a nation of immigrants. It advocates public policies that welcome immigrants and refugees and that are fair and supportive of newcomers. The forum was established in 1982 and serves as a link between organizations working on policy issues that affect immigration.

National Immigration Law Center (NILC)
URL: http://www.nilc.org
E-mail: info@nilc.org
Phone: (213) 639-3900
Fax: (213) 639-3911
3435 Wilshire Boulevard
Suite 2850
Los Angeles, CA 90010
The organization is dedicated to protecting and promoting the rights of low-income immigrants and their family members. Created in 1979, NILC has built a reputation for expertise in laws concerning immigrants and refugees and as a source of legal aid to organizations across the country.

National Network for Immigrant and Refugee Rights
URL: http://www.nnirr.org
E-mail: nnirr@nnirr.org
Phone: (510) 465-1984
Fax: (510) 465-7548

310 8th Street
Suite 303
Oakland, CA 94607
An organization composed of different groups that work together to help immigrants and refugees, the National Network serves as a forum to share information and analysis, to educate communities, and to plan actions to help immigrants and refugees. The network involves community, church, labor, and legal groups committed to the cause of equal rights for all immigrants.

New York Association for New Americans
URL: http://www.nyana.org
Phone: (212) 425-2900
17 Battery Place
New York, NY 10004-1102
The NYANA helps immigrants to build a better life for themselves, and to realize the full potential that each immigrant carries. The organization believes that the American economy and culture is strengthened by successful immigrants.

New York Immigration Coalition
URL: http://www.thenyic.org
Phone: (212) 627-2227
Fax: (212) 627-9314
275 Seventh Avenue, 9th Floor
New York, NY 10001
The NYIC is an umbrella policy and advocacy organization organization for approximately 150 groups in New York State that work with immigrants and refugees. The organization analyzes the impact of immigration policy proposals, promotes and protects the rights of immigrants

Immigration

and their family members, improves newcomers access to services, resolves problems with public agencies and mobilizes member groups to respond to emerging issues and needs.

NumbersUSA
URL: http://www.
numbersusa.com
E-mail: info@numbersusa.com
Phone: (703) 816-8820
1601 North Kent Street
Suite 1100
Arlington, VA 22209
NumbersUSA is an organization committed to fighting the threat of overpopulation to the environment, farmland, the community quality of life, schools, wage fairness, and freedom of the U.S. government. The organization advocates a tough policy against illegal immigration and a significant reduction in immigration numbers.

Open Society Institute and the
Soros Foundations Network
URL: http://www.soros.org
Phone: (212) 548-0600
Fax: (202) 548-4600
400 West 59th Street
New York, NY 10019
The Open Society Institute is a private grantmaking foundation that serves as the hub of the Soros Foundation Network. All Soros agencies promote open societies and the establishment of governmental, educational, media, public health, and human rights systems that support such open societies.

Refugee Council USA
URL: http://www.
refugeecouncilusa.org
E-mail: council@
refugeecouncilusa.org
Phone: (202) 541-5402/04
Fax: (202) 722-8737
3211 4th Street, NE
Washington, DC 20017-1194
Refugee Council USA is a coalition of nongovernmental organizations that focus on issues affecting the rights of refugees, asylum seekers, displaced persons, and victims of trafficking and torture in the United States and abroad. It focuses primarily on international standards of refugee rights, promotion of right to asylum, political and financial support for United Nations High Commissioner for Refugees, and solutions to resettlement in the United States.

The Salvation Army World Service Office (SAWSO)
URL: http://www.sawso.org
E-mail: sawso@usn.
salvationarmy. org
Phone: (703) 684-5528
Fax: (703) 684-5536
615 Slaters Lane
P.O. Box 269
Alexandria, VA 22313
SAWSO works to create a safe world in which differences are respected, basic needs are met, and opportunities are afforded to all to learn, work, and worship in freedom. It works with the community to improve the health, economic, and spiritual conditions of the poor throughout the world.

Organizations and Agencies

Southern Baptist Refugee Resettlement Program
URL: http://www.namb.net/ccm
Phone: (770) 410-6000 or (800) 749-7479
Fax: (770) 410-6082
4200 North Point Parkway
Alpharetta, GA 30022-4176
The North American Mission Board of the Southern Baptist Convention partners with World Relief to provide refugee assistance, helping to involve individual Southern Baptist Churches in assisting refugees make a new life in the United States.

Unitarian Universalist Service Committee (UUSC)
URL: http://uusc.org
E-mail: program@uusc.org
Phone: (617) 868-6600 or 1-800-388-3920
Fax: (617) 868-7102
130 Prospect Street
Cambridge, MA 02139
The UUSC promotes human rights and social justice worldwide and affirms the Unitarian Universalist principles of worth, dignity, and human rights for every person. Through advocacy, education, and partnerships with grassroots organizations, UUSC supports policies that empower women, defend the rights of children, and support the struggles of indigenous people and oppressed groups. It also provides financial and technical help to impoverished areas struck with disaster.

United Methodist Committee on Relief (UMCOR)
The United Methodist Church
URL: http://gbgm-umc.org/umcor
E-mail: umcor@gbgm-umc.org
Phone: (212) 870-3816
Fax: (212) 870-3624
General Board of Global Ministries
Room 330
475 Riverside Drive
New York, NY 10115
UMCOR was organized by the United Methodists in 1940 to provide aid to refugees, immigrants, and to countries stricken with poverty and hunger. It is located in nearly 100 countries.

United States Conference of Catholic Bishops/Migration and Refugee Services (USCCB/MRS)
URL: http://www.usccb.org/mrs
E-mail: mrs@usccb.org
Phone: (202) 541-3300
3211 Fourth Street, NE
Washington, DC 20017-1194
The USCCB is an assembly of the hierarchy of the United States and Virgin Islands whose purpose is to promote the greater good that the church offers to all human beings. Its goals are to unify, coordinate, encourage, promote, and carry on Catholic activities; organize religious, charitable, and social welfare work at home and abroad; and to aid in education and care for immigrants.

Immigration

U.S. Committee for Refugees and Immigrants (USCRI)
URL: http://www.refugees.org
Phone: (202) 347-3507
Fax: (202) 347-3418
1717 Massachusetts Avenue, NW
Suite 200
Washington, DC 20036
USCRI's purpose is "to address the needs and rights of persons in forced or voluntary migration worldwide by advancing fair and humane public policy, facilitating and providing direct professional services, and promoting the full participation of migrants in community life." USCRI sponsors a wide range of activities and associated organizations, including the National Center for Refugee and Immigrant Children, which is a partnership between the USCRI and the American Immigration Lawyers Association.

U.S. English
URL: http://www.us-english.org
Phone: (202) 833-0100
Fax: (202) 833-0108
1747 Pennsylvania Avenue, NW
Suite 1100
Washington, DC 20006
Organized in 1983, the goal of U.S. English is to keep the nation unified through a common language. Members believe that legislating English as the official language in the United States will help immigrants succeed.

Wider Church Ministries
United Church of Christ
URL: http://ucc.org
Phone: (866) 822-8224
700 Prospect Avenue
Cleveland, OH 44115
The Wider Church Ministries works to educate its members regarding immigrant and refugee rights, promoting greater tolerance and support.

World Relief
URL: http://www.wr.org
Phone: (800) 535-5433
7 East Baltimore Street
Baltimore, MD 21202
Founded in 1944 as the World Relief Commission, World Relief works with local Evangelical churches to bring relief to suffering people in the name of Christ, sponsoring programs in microenterprise development, refugee care, and immigrant assistance.

PART III

APPENDICES

APPENDIX A

LABOR CERTIFICATION FOR THE PERMANENT EMPLOYMENT OF ALIENS IN THE UNITED STATES; FINAL RULE, DECEMBER 27, 2004

A permanent labor certification issued by the Department of Labor (DOL) allows an employer to hire a foreign worker to work permanently in the United States. In most instances, before the U.S. employer can submit an immigration petition to the Department of Homeland Security's U.S. Citizenship and Immigration Services (USCIS), the employer must obtain an approved labor certification request from the DOL's Employment and Training Administration (ETA). The DOL must certify to the USCIS that there are no qualified U.S. workers able, willing, qualified, and available to accept the job at the prevailing wage for that occupation in the area of intended employment and that employment of the alien will not adversely affect the wages and working conditions of similarly employed U.S. workers. The ETA published a final regulation on December 27, 2004, which required the implementation of a revised permanent labor certification program by March 28, 2005.

DEPARTMENT OF LABOR
Employment and Training Administration
20 CFR Parts 655 and 656

ACTION: Final rule.
Summary: The Department of Labor (DOL) is amending its regulations governing the filing and processing of labor certification applications for the permanent employment of aliens in the United States to implement a new system for filing and processing such applications. The new system requires employers to conduct recruitment before filing their applications. State

Immigration

Workforce Agencies (SWAs) will provide prevailing wage determinations to employers, but will no longer receive or process applications as they do under the current system. Employers will be required to place a job order with the SWA, but the job order will be processed the same as any other job order. Employers will have the option of filing applications electronically, using web-based forms and instructions, or by mail.

Dates: Effective Date: This final rule is effective on March 28, 2005, and applies to labor certification applications for the permanent employment of aliens filed on or after that date.

FOR FURTHER INFORMATION CONTACT: PERM Help Desk, Division of Foreign Labor certification, Employment and Training Administration, 200 Constitution Avenue, NW., Room C-4312, Washington, DC 20210. Telephone (202) 693-3010 (this is not a toll free number). Questions may be sent via e-mail to the following address "PERM.DFLC@dol.gov." We encourage questions to be submitted by e-mail, because the Division of Foreign Labor Certification intends to post responses to frequently asked questions on its Web site (http://www.ows.doleta.gov/foreign/) and e-mail submission of questions will facilitate thorough consideration and response to questions.

SUPPLEMENTARY INFORMATION

I. Introduction

On May 6, 2002, the Department published in the Federal Register a Notice of Proposed Rulemaking (NPRM) to amend its regulations for the certification of permanent employment of immigrant labor in the United States. The NPRM also proposed amending the regulations governing employer wage obligations under the H-1B program. 67 FR 30466 (May 6, 2002). Comments were invited through July 5, 2002.

II. Statutory Standard

Before the Department of Homeland Security (DHS) may approve petition requests and the Department of State (DOS) may issue visas and admit certain immigrant aliens to work permanently in the United States, the Secretary of Labor must certify to the Secretary of State and to the Secretary of Homeland Security:

(a) There are not sufficient United States workers who are able, willing, qualified, and available at the time of the application for a visa and admission into the United States and at the place where the alien is to perform the work; and

(b) The employment of the alien will not adversely affect the wages and working conditions of similarly employed United States workers. 8 U.S.C. 1182(a)(5)(A).

If the Secretary of Labor, through the Employment and Training Administration (ETA), determines there are no able, willing, qualified, and available U.S. workers and employment of the alien will not adversely affect the wages and working conditions of similarly employed U.S. workers, DOL so certifies to the Department of Homeland Security and to the Department of State by issuing a permanent alien labor certification.

If DOL can not make both of the above findings, the application for permanent alien employment certification is denied.

III. CURRENT DEPARTMENT OF LABOR REGULATIONS

DOL has promulgated regulations, at 20 CFR part 656, governing the labor certification process for the permanent employment of immigrant aliens in the United States. Part 656 was promulgated under Section 212(a)(14) of the Immigration and Nationality Act (INA) (now at Section 212(a)(5)(A)). 8 U.S.C. 1182(a)(5)(A).

Part 656 sets forth the responsibilities of employers who desire to employ immigrant aliens permanently in the United States. Part 656 was recently amended through an Interim Final Rule effective on August 20, 2004, which added measures to address a backlog in permanent labor certification applications waiting processing. 69 FR 43716 (July 21, 2004). When this final rule refers to the "current regulation," it refers to the regulation in 20 CFR part 656 as published in April 2004 and amended by 69 FR 43716.

The current process for obtaining a labor certification requires employers to file a permanent labor certification application with the SWA serving the area of intended employment and, after filing, to actively recruit U.S. workers in good faith for a period of at least 30 days for the job openings for which aliens are sought.

Job applicants are either referred directly to the employer or their resumes are sent to the employer. The employer has 45 days to report to either the SWA or an ETA backlog processing center or regional office the lawful job-related reasons for not hiring any referred qualified U.S. worker. If the employer hires a U.S. worker for the job opening, the process stops at that point, unless the employer has more than one opening, in which case the application may continue to be processed. If, however, the employer believes able, willing, and qualified U.S. workers are not available to take the

Immigration

job, the application, together with the documentation of the recruitment results and prevailing wage information, is sent to either an ETA backlog processing center or ETA regional office. There, it is reviewed and a determination made as to whether to issue the labor certification based upon the employer's compliance with applicable labor laws and program regulations. If we determine there are no able, willing, qualified, and available U.S. workers, and the employment of the alien will not adversely affect the wages and working conditions of similarly employed U.S. workers, we so certify to the DHS and the DOS by issuing a permanent labor certification. See 20 CFR part 656 (April 2004) as amended by 69 FR 43716 (July 21, 2004); see also section 212(a)(5)(A) of the INA, as amended.

IV. OVERVIEW OF THE REGULATION

This final rule deletes the current language of 20 CFR part 656 and replaces the part in its entirety with new regulatory text, effective on March 28, 2005. This new regulation will apply to all applications filed on or after the effective date of this final rule. Applications filed before this rule's effective date will continue to be processed and governed by the current regulation, except to the extent an employer seeks to withdraw an existing application and refile it in accordance with the terms of this final rule.

On December 8, 2004, the President signed into law the Consolidated Appropriations Act, 2005. This legislation amends Section 212(p) of the INA, 8 U.S.C. 1182(p), to provide that:

(3) The prevailing wage required to be paid pursuant to (a)(5)(A), (n)(1)(A)(i)(II) and (t)(1)(A)(i)(II) shall be 100 percent of the wage determined pursuant to those sections.

(4) Where the Secretary of Labor uses, or makes available to employers, a governmental survey to determine prevailing wage, such survey shall provide at least 4 levels of wages commensurate with experience, education, and the level of supervision. Where an existing government survey has only 2 levels, 2 intermediate levels may be created by dividing by 3 the difference between the two levels offered, adding the quotient thus obtained to the first level, and subtracting that quotient from the second level.

The 100 percent requirement is consistent with this final rule. The Department will be preparing guidance concerning the implementation of the 4 levels of wages.

The process for obtaining a permanent labor certification has been criticized as being complicated, time consuming, and requiring the expenditure of considerable resources by employers, State Workforce Agencies and the

Appendix A

Federal government. The new system is designed to streamline processing and ensure the most expeditious processing of cases, using the resources available.

The new system requires employers to conduct recruitment before filing their applications. Employers are required to place a job order and two Sunday newspaper advertisements. If the application is for a professional occupation, the employer must conduct three additional steps that the employer chooses from a list of alternative recruitment steps published in the regulation. The employer will not be required to submit any documentation with its application, but will be expected to maintain the supporting documentation specified in the regulations. The employer will be required to provide the supporting documentation in the event its application is selected for audit and as otherwise requested by a Certifying Officer.

This final rule also provides employers with the option to submit their forms either electronically or by mail directly to an ETA application processing center. A number of commenters indicated they wanted the option of filing electronically. Since January 14, 2002, employers have been allowed to submit Labor Condition Applications (LCAs) electronically under the nonimmigrant H-1B program, which has been very successful. Similarly, we expect electronic filing of applications for permanent alien employment certification to be successful and to be used by the overwhelming majority of employers filing applications. Employers will receive more prompt adjudication of their applications than would have been the case under a system that permitted only submission of applications by facsimile transmission or by mail. The new form—Application for Permanent Employment Certification (ETA Form 9089)—has been designed to be completed in a web-based environment and submitted electronically or to be completed by hand and submitted by mail.

Source: "Labor Certification for the Permanent Employment of Aliens." *Federal Register* 69, no. 247 (December 27, 2004): 77325-77327. Available online. URL: http://a257.g.akamaitech.net/7/257/2422/06jun20041800/edocket.access.gpo.gov/2004/04-27653.htm. Updated December 13, 2004.

APPENDIX B

FACT SHEET: SECURING AMERICA THROUGH IMMIGRATION REFORM, NOVEMBER 28, 2005

Ten months after publicly announcing his commitment to a guest worker program, President George W. Bush outlined a comprehensive plan for immigration reform, which includes an end to the practice of "Catch and Release"; acceleration of the removal process; the building of more physical barriers; and implementation of a temporary worker program that would not lead to U.S. citizenship. "The American people should not have to choose between a welcoming society and a lawful society," Bush told border security personnel in Arizona. "We can have both at the same time" (Warren Vieth and Nicole Gaouette, "Bush Links Immigration Crackdown, Worker Plan." Los Angeles Times—Online Edition, November 29, 2005. URL: http://www.latimes.com/news/nationworld/nation/la-na-bush29nov29,0,3853175.story?coll=la-home-nation, accessed November 29, 2005).

For Immediate Release
Office of the Press Secretary
November 28, 2005
Fact Sheet: Securing America Through Immigration Reform
Today's Presidential Action:
Today, President Bush Outlined the Strategy to Enhance America's Homeland Security Through Comprehensive Immigration Reform.
Addressing the Customs and Border Protection agents stationed in southern Arizona, the President discussed the strategy to secure the border, prevent illegal crossings, and strengthen enforcement of immigration laws. The President also proposed to take pressure off the border by creating a Temporary Worker Program that meets the economy's demands while rejecting amnesty for those who break America's laws.

246

Appendix B

• **Securing The Border Is Essential to Securing the Homeland.** Since he took office, the President has increased funding for border security by 60 percent. Border agents have apprehended and sent home more than 4.5 million people coming into the country illegally including about 350,000 with criminal records. The U.S. border must be open to trade and tourism and closed to criminals, drug dealers, and terrorists.

The President Will Work with Congress to Pass and Sign into Law Comprehensive Immigration Reform. Comprehensive immigration reform is a top priority for the Administration. Already, Congress is making great strides and has a chance to move forward on a strategy to enforce immigration laws, secure America, and uphold the Nation's deepest values. The President will continue working with Congress so that he can sign a comprehensive immigration reform bill into law in 2006.

<u>**The President's Strategy for Comprehensive Immigration Reform**</u>

Comprehensive Immigration Reform Begins With Securing The Border. To secure the border, the President is pursuing a three-part plan.

• **First, The U.S. Will Return Every Illegal Entrant Caught Crossing the Southwest Border with no Exceptions.** More than 85 percent of apprehended illegal immigrants are from Mexico, and most are immediately escorted back across the border within 24 hours. To prevent them from trying to cross again, the Federal government is using interior repatriation whereby Mexican illegal entrants are returned to their hometowns, making it more difficult for them to attempt another crossing. This approach is showing great promise. In a West Arizona desert pilot program, nearly 35,000 illegal immigrants were returned to Mexico through interior repatriation, and only about 8 percent turned up trying to cross the border in that sector again. The Administration is working to expand interior repatriation to ensure that when those who violate the country's immigration laws are sent home, they stay home.

   o **The Administration Is Ending The Practice of "Catch And Release."** Because detention facilities lack bed space, most non-Mexican illegal immigrants apprehended are released and directed to return for a court appearance. However, 75 percent fail to show. Last year, only 30,000 of the 160,000 non-Mexicans caught coming across our Southwest border were sent home. Addressing this problem, the President has signed legislation increasing the number of beds in detention facilities by more than 10 percent over the next year. The Federal government is also using "expedited removal"

247

to detain, place into streamlined judicial proceedings, and deport non-Mexican illegal immigrants in an average of 32 days almost three times faster than the usual procedure. Last year, more than 20,000 non-Mexicans caught crossing the border between Laredo and Tucson were deported using expedited removal. The use of expedited removal is now being expanded across the entire Southwest border. When illegal immigrants know they will be caught and sent home, they will be less likely to cross illegally in the first place.

o **The Administration Is Taking Further Steps to Accelerate the Removal Process.** The U.S. is pressing foreign governments to take back their citizens more promptly, while streamlining bureaucracy and increasing the number of flights carrying illegal immigrants home. Testing these steps, "Operation Texas Hold 'Em" along the Rio Grande Valley of the Texas Border recently resulted in Brazilian illegal immigration dropping by 90 percent in the Rio Grande Valley and by 50 percent across the entire border. These efforts are helping change a policy of "catch and release" to a policy of "catch and return."

• **Second, The Administration Will Work With Congress To Reform Immigration Laws.** The President is seeking to eliminate senseless rules that require the government to release illegal immigrants if their home countries do not take them back in a set period of time. Among those the government has been forced to release are murderers, rapists, child molesters, and other violent criminals. The President is also working with Congress to address the cycle of endless litigation that clogs immigration courts, rewards illegal behavior, and delays justice for immigrants with legitimate claims. Lawsuits and red tape must not stand in the way of protecting the American people.

• **Third, The Federal Government Will Act To Stop People From Illegally Crossing The Border In The First Place.** The Administration is increasing manpower, technology, and infrastructure at the Nation's borders, and integrating these resources in innovative ways.

o **Increasing Manpower.** Since 2001, 1,900 Border Patrol agents have been added, and the President has signed legislation allowing the addition of another 1,000 agents in the year ahead. When the hiring is completed, the Border Patrol will have been enlarged by about 3,000 agents from about 9,500 when the President took office to about 12,500 next year. This is an increase of more than 30 percent.

o **Deploying New Technology.** The Administration is giving Border Patrol agents the tools to expand their reach and effectiveness including unmanned aerial vehicles (UAVs) and infrared cameras. In Tucson, agents using UAVs to patrol the border have improved their interception of illegal immigrants and drugs on the border.

Legislation signed by the President is providing $139 million to further upgrade technology and bring a more unified, systematic approach to border enforcement.

o **Constructing Physical Barriers to Entry.** The President has signed legislation providing $70 million to install and improve protective infrastructure across the border. In rural areas, the government is constructing new patrol roads to give agents better access to the border and new vehicle barriers to keep illegal immigrants from driving across. In urban areas, the government is expanding fencing to shut down human smuggling corridors. The Administration recently authorized the completion of a 14-mile barrier near San Diego. Once held up by litigation, this project is vital to helping border agents do their jobs and make those who live near the border more secure.

Comprehensive Immigration Reform Requires Improved Enforcement Of Immigration Laws Within The United States. Catching and deporting illegal immigrants along the border is only part of protecting the American people. Our immigration laws must be enforced throughout America.

• **The Federal Government Is Improving Worksite Enforcement.** The President has signed legislation that more than doubles the resources dedicated to worksite enforcement. The government is placing a special focus on enforcement at critical infrastructure. This year, Operation Rollback the largest worksite enforcement case in American history resulted in the arrest of hundreds of illegal immigrants, criminal convictions against a dozen employers, and a multi-million dollar payment from one of America's largest businesses. Worksite enforcement is critical to the success of immigration reform.

o **To Help Businesses Comply with Immigration Laws, the Government Is Addressing Document Fraud.** Even the most diligent employers find it difficult to spot forged employment documents and verify workers' legal status. So the Administration is expanding the Basic Pilot program enabling businesses to screen the employment eligibility of new hires against Federal records. Since 2001, this program has expanded from only six states to now being available nationwide. The Administration will work with Congress to continue to improve employment verification.

• **The President Has Committed The Resources Necessary To Enforce Immigration Laws.** Since 2001, the Administration has increased funding for interior enforcement by 44 percent; increased the number of immigration and customs investigators by 14 percent; and new funding will allow for an additional 400 immigration enforcement agents and 250 criminal investigators. These skilled officers are getting results. In Arizona alone, 2,300 people have been prosecuted for smuggling drugs, guns, and illegal immigrants across the border. Operation Community Shield has resulted in the arrest of nearly 1,400 illegal immigrant gang members including hundreds of members of violent gangs like "MS-13." Since the creation of the Department of Homeland Security (DHS), agents have apprehended nearly 27,000 illegal immigrant fugitives.

As Part of Comprehensive Immigration Reform, The President Has Proposed the Creation of a New Temporary Worker Program. To match foreign workers with American employers for jobs that no American is willing to take, temporary workers will be able to register for legal status for a fixed time period and then be required to return home. This plan meets the needs of a growing economy, allows honest workers to provide for their families while respecting the law, and relieves pressure on the border. By reducing the flow of illegal immigrants, law enforcement can focus on those who mean this country harm. To improve worksite enforcement, the plan creates tamper-proof I.D. cards for every legal temporary worker.

- **A Temporary Worker Program Would Not Provide Amnesty.** The program does not create an automatic path to citizenship or provide amnesty. The President opposes amnesty because rewarding those who break the law would encourage more illegal entrants and increase pressure on the border. A Temporary Worker Program, by contrast, would promote legal immigration and decrease pressure on the border. The President supports increasing the annual number of green cards, but for the sake of justice and security, the President will not sign an immigration bill that includes amnesty.

By Reforming Immigration Laws, the United States Will Preserve the Promise of America. Immigrants play a vital role in strengthening American democracy. This is a land in which foreigners who respect the laws are welcomed as contributors to American culture not feared as threats. The United States has been strengthened by generations of immigrants who became Americans through patience, hard work, and assimilation. Like generations of immigrants that have come before them, every new citizen has an obligation to learn this Nation's customs and values. At the same time, America will fulfill its obligation to give each citizen a chance to realize the American dream. By enforcing immigration laws, the Federal government is protecting the promise of a tolerant, welcoming America and preserving opportunity for all.

Source: "Fact Sheet: Securing America Through Immigration Reform," Press Release, U.S. White House. Available online. URL: http://www.whitehouse.gov/news/releases/2005/11/20051128-3.html. Updated November 28, 2005.

APPENDIX C

PROPOSED REFUGEE ADMISSIONS REPORT TO THE CONGRESS FOR FISCAL YEAR 2006

Each year the president is required to present his recommendations regarding refugee admissions to Congress for the coming fiscal year (Fiscal Year 2006 runs from October 1, 2005 to September 30, 2006). This proposal provides a good introduction to U.S. refugee policy and the process by which it is implemented. President George W. Bush's proposal for 2006 includes recommendation of a new agency—the Refugee Corps—which will be composed of U.S. Citizenship and Immigration Services (USCIS) officers who will travel to overseas locations in order to facilitate adjudication of refugee applications. For 2006 the overall refugee ceiling remained at 70,000, though the ceiling for refugees from Europe and central Asia (mainly representing countries of the former Soviet Union) was increased from 9,500 to 15,500.

INTRODUCTION

This Proposed Refugee Admissions for Fiscal Year 2006: Report to the Congress is submitted in compliance with Section 207(e) of the Immigration and Nationality Act (INA). The Act requires that before the start of the fiscal year and, to the extent possible, at least two weeks prior to consultations on refugee admissions, members of the Committees on the Judiciary of the Senate and the House of Representatives be provided with the following information:

1. A description of the nature of the refugee situation;
2. A description of the number and allocation of the refugees to be admitted and an analysis of conditions within the countries from which they came;

3. A description of the plans for their movement and resettlement and the estimated cost of their movement and resettlement;
4. An analysis of the anticipated social, economic, and demographic impact of their admission to the United States;
5. A description of the extent to which other countries will admit and assist in the resettlement of such refugees;
6. An analysis of the impact of the participation of the United States in the resettlement of such refugees on the foreign policy interests of the United States; and
7. Such additional information as may be appropriate or requested by such members.

In addition, specific reporting required by section 602(d) of the International Religious Freedom Act of 1998 (Pub. L. 105-292, Oct. 27, 1998, 112 Stat. 2787) (IRFA) on information about religious persecution of refugee populations eligible for consideration for admission to the United States and section 305(b) of the North Korean Human Rights Act of 2004 (Pub. L. 108-333, Oct. 18, 2004, 118 Stat. 1287) on information about specific measures taken to facilitate access to the United States refugee program for individuals who have fled countries of particular concern for violations of religious freedoms, identified pursuant to section 402(b) of the IRFA, is included in this report.

FOREWORD

Each year the President determines that the United States of America should admit refugees of special humanitarian concern for permanent resettlement. Resettlement of refugees is part of a proud American tradition of stepping forward to share responsibility for persons outside our borders—even when there is no legally binding obligation to do so. As has been the case for many years, the United States continues to play a global leadership role and extends resettlement opportunities to more refugees than all other countries combined. For some, we offer urgent protection from immediate persecution. For others in protracted, unresolved situations, we respond by providing a permanent durable solution.

Unlike other immigrants who have relatives or employers to help them adjust to new lives here, many refugees enter the United States without the support of family or friends. They must rely on the American people to support their transition. Experienced nongovernmental agencies contract with the U.S. Government to provide initial support services and place arriving refugees in communities across the country where their chances for successful integration and early self-sufficiency are greatest. Civic leaders from

Appendix C

coast to çoast report that refugee resettlement benefits their communities both culturally and economically.

At the end of 2004, the worldwide refugee population stood at approximately 9.2 million—the lowest level in 25 years. In spite of recent outflows from countries such as Sudan, this represents a reduction of almost three million in just four years. It reflects the continuing and welcome trend toward resolution of several longstanding refugee situations. In 2004, some 300,000 African refugees returned to their home countries, including Sierra Leone, Eritrea, Angola, Rwanda, Burundi, Liberia, Sudan, and parts of Somalia. An even higher level of repatriation in Africa is expected this year. In the Near East/South Asia region over 1.1 million refugees—the vast majority of whom were Afghans and Iraqis—repatriated last year and almost 800,000 are expected to follow them in 2005.

Even in the context of a large-scale repatriation, however, there are always some members of the population who cannot return home. Special security, medical, or other compelling circumstances are often present that preclude the return of individual refugees in safety and dignity. Especially when local integration is not possible, resettlement may be the appropriate solution but must be approached in a manner that does not disrupt the overall repatriation effort. Conducting resettlement processing under such circumstances requires careful planning and coordination among all involved parties. In recent years, as a result of such extra efforts, resettlement has proven to be an appropriate complement to repatriations in West Africa and South Asia. The program has offered resettlement to refugees from some 55 nations who were interviewed in 42 often remote locations this year.

Many refugees are in difficult situations that remain unresolved for many years. Consequently, we will continue to focus our efforts on protracted situations around the globe. Over 100,000 Bhutanese refugees in eastern Nepal remain caught up in a "standoff" as government officials in the region cannot agree on a plan of action. Most of this population has spent almost fifteen years in camps. A similar number of ethnic Burmese in Thailand have endured decades of uncertainty regarding prospects for return to Burma. Some 15,000 Burundi Hutus have resided in camps in Tanzania since 1972 with no prospects for either repatriation or local integration. Through several recent initiatives described in this report, the United States, along with other concerned members of the international community, has resolved to address these and other longstanding humanitarian problems.

During the current fiscal year, the program has consolidated gains and built upon work we have done since September 2001 to adjust the program in light of the complex circumstances of refugee resettlement in the twenty-first century. Security reviews have been completed for most cases that had been on hold since September 11, 2001, allowing many to travel to the United States. Medical issues, which had delayed the admission of a large group of Hmong Lao residing in Wat Tham Krabok in Thailand, were addressed clearing the way for the vast majority to move forward. The flow of Meskhetian Turks from Krasnodar Krai, Russia accelerated. A processing effort for Vietnamese in the Philippines commenced.

In 2005, we continued to work with the United Nations High Commissioner for Refugees (UNHCR) to strengthen the organization's capacity to identify and refer to the United States over 20,000 refugees—either as individual cases or in groups. Department of State funding supported resettlement positions at UNHCR field offices in locations where the organization's personnel resources were insufficient to handle the resettlement workload. It also funded short-term deployments of experienced NGO employees to fill temporary staffing gaps in other locations. The State Department has provided $20 million in this targeted funding during the past seven years and continues to press for additional resettlement positions to be streamlined into UNHCR's core budget to support this important activity.

Also in 2005, the State Department hosted its third regional training workshop for NGO humanitarian assistance workers on how to identify and refer refugees in need of resettlement. The workshop was held in Bangkok for representatives of NGOs working throughout Southeast Asia, and followed workshops held in the past two years in Africa. A targeted response team comprising representatives of USG agencies, international organizations, and NGOs visited Tanzania to assess the resettlement needs of longstanding refugee populations there. Another targeted effort involved the participation of an NGO representative to assist with processing of Meskhetian Turk refugees in the Russian Federation. In the United States, representatives of international and domestic resettlement and human rights organizations met frequently in regional working groups to exchange information on processing developments and caseload identification.

The most important new feature in the program this year is the formation of the Refugee Corps within the Department of Homeland Security. The Refugee Corps will be comprised of a cadre of U.S. Citizenship and Immigration Services (USCIS) officers dedicated to adjudicating applications for refugee status. Refugee Officers will be based in Washington, D.C., but will travel to overseas locations for up to fifty percent of the year. While on international temporary duty assignments, Refugee Officers will conduct interviews of applicants to determine eligibility for resettlement in the United States. While in Washington, officer assignments will support overseas operations, fraud deterrence and security, and training and quality assurance in the refugee program. By establishing such a corps, USCIS will gain increased flexibility to respond to the evolving U.S. Refugee Program. In addition, hiring permanent Refugee Officers will ensure greater consistency and quality of refugee adjudications.

Interest in joining the new corps has been impressive, both from inside and outside the government. From a pool of nearly 800 applicants, 40 individuals have been selected to comprise the first group of Refugee Officers. The Refugee Corps will be headed by a Director at the Senior Executive Service level, as well as managers to oversee the policy and operational aspects of the program. Development of a formalized training program and logistical support initiatives is also currently underway. FY 2006 will be the first full year of a functioning Refugee Corps.

A challenge that the Refugee Corps and the program as a whole will continue to face in FY 2006 is the issue of refugee applicants who have offered material support to a terrorist group or terrorist activity. Legislative changes have substantially broadened the categories of activities that cause an individual to be found ineligible for admission based upon one of the terrorist grounds. This definition will likely have an impact on future processing of various refugee populations, as it already has on the Colombian program.

With these national security concerns in mind, the U.S. Refugee Program remains committed to fulfilling its humanitarian objectives. The Administration proposes in FY 2006 to admit 70,000 refugees to the United States. This reflects the President's continued commitment to this important program. The proposal allocates regionally 60,000 of the 70,000 ceiling based on current identified resettlement needs. The 10,000 unallocated numbers will be utilized in regions where additional needs are identified during the course of the year.

The American people can take justifiable pride in the global leadership role their country plays in providing assistance to and promoting durable solutions for the world's refugees. While the circumstances within which the U.S. program operates may change, the commitment does not. Refugee resettlement in the United States remains a dynamic undertaking that concurrently addresses the needs of large populations as well as the individual case in need of immediate attention. In the coming year, the Administration looks forward to resolving old problems and addressing new challenges. We remain grateful for the support we have received from the Congress and all of our partners in this critically important effort to make a difference in the lives of the world's refugees.

I. OVERVIEW OF U.S. REFUGEE POLICY

At the end of 2004, the estimated refugee population worldwide was 9.2 million, the lowest level in 25 years. While the decrease in the number of refugees is a very positive development, assistance to refugees continues to be an important foreign policy goal of the United States. The United States therefore makes financial contributions to international organizations, as well as to non-governmental organizations, that aid this effort. Under the authority in the Migration and Refugee Assistance Act of 1962, as amended, the United States contributes to the programs of the office of the United Nations High Commissioner for Refugees (UNHCR), the International Committee of the Red Cross (ICRC), the International Organization for Migration (IOM), and other international and non-governmental organizations that provide relief and assistance to refugees. This assistance is targeted to address immediate protection needs of refugees as well as to ensure that basic needs for water, sanitation, food, health care, shelter, and education are met. The United States continues to press for the most effective use of international resources directed to the urgent needs of refugees and internally displaced persons.

During FY 2005, the United States has continued to support major relief and repatriation programs throughout the world. Repatriation to countries including Afghanistan, Angola, Liberia, Burundi, and the Democratic Republic of Congo (DRC) has proceeded on a significant scale during FY 2005. UNHCR-supported repatriation to some locations in Sudan is scheduled to commence in late 2005.

Resettlement to third countries, including the United States, is considered for refugees in urgent need of protection as well as for those for whom other durable solutions are not feasible. In seeking durable solutions for refugees, the United States generally gives priority to the safe voluntary return of refugees to their homelands. This policy, recognized in the Refugee Act of 1980, is also the preference of the international community, including UNHCR. If safe voluntary repatriation is not feasible, other durable solutions are sought, including local integration in countries of asylum or resettlement in third countries. For many refugees, resettlement is the best, or perhaps only, alternative. Recognizing the importance of ensuring UNHCR's capacity to identify and to refer refugees in need of resettlement, the U.S. Government has provided some 20 million dollars during the past seven years to expand the organization's resettlement infrastructure.

For many years, the United States was one of ten countries that worked with UNHCR on a regular basis to provide resettlement opportunities for persons in need of this form of international protection or durable solution. In 2004, UNHCR referred refugees to some 22 countries for resettlement. The majority (90%) was referred to the United States, Canada, and Australia. Smaller numbers of referrals were accepted by New Zealand, Chile, Brazil, and the traditional Western European resettlement countries (Norway, Sweden, Denmark, Finland, the Netherlands, Great Britain, and Ireland). In addition, Belgium, Benin, Burkina Faso, France, Germany, Italy, Pakistan, Spain, and Switzerland each accepted a few individuals. Argentina has committed to developing a small program during 2006. The European Union's official endorsement of refugee resettlement may gen-

Appendix C

erate additional interest in participation of European countries in coming years.

While the overall number of refugees referred by UNHCR and the percentage resettled by various countries fluctuate from year to year, the United States is committed to providing an opportunity for U.S. resettlement to at least 50% of all UNHCR referrals. We would like to see UNHCR make further strategic use of resettlement and expand the number of referrals it makes annually. In calendar year 2004, the United States resettled over 67% of the total number of UNHCR-referred refugees resettled in third countries (see Table IX).

U.S. law allows for the admission of persons of special humanitarian concern to the United States who can establish that they have suffered past persecution or have a well-founded fear of persecution on account of race, religion, nationality, membership in a particular social group, or political opinion. The legal basis of the refugee admissions program is the Refugee Act of 1980, Pub. L. No. 96–212, 201(b), 94 Stat. 103. With some modification, the Act largely adopted the definition of "refugee" in the 1951 United Nations Convention relating to the Status of Refugees, as amended by its 1967 Protocol. The U.S. definition (Section 101(a)(42) of the INA, as amended) is as follows:

The term "refugee" means: (A) any person who is outside any country of such person's nationality or, in the case of a person having no nationality, is outside any country in which such person last habitually resided, and who is unable or unwilling to return to, and is unable or unwilling to avail himself or herself of the protection of that country because of persecution or a well-founded fear of persecution on account of race, religion, nationality, membership in a particular social group, or political opinion, or (B) in such special circumstances as the President after appropriate consultation (as defined in section 207(e) of this Act) may specify, any person who is within the country of such person's nationality or, in the case of a person having no nationality, within the country in which such person is habitually residing, and who is persecuted or who has a well-founded fear of persecution on account of race, religion, nationality, membership in a particular social group, or political opinion.

The term "refugee" does not include any person who ordered, incited, assisted, or otherwise participated in the persecution of any person on account of race, religion, nationality, membership in a particular social group, or political opinion.

For purposes of determinations under this Act, a person who has been forced to abort a pregnancy or to undergo involuntary sterilization, or who has been persecuted for failure or refusal to undergo such a procedure or for other resistance to a coercive population control program, shall be deemed to have been persecuted on account of political opinion, and a person who has a

Immigration

well-founded fear that he or she will be forced to undergo such a procedure or be subject to persecution for such failure, refusal or resistance shall be deemed to have a well-founded fear of persecution on account of political opinion.

The foreign policy interests of the United States have been advanced by our willingness to work with first asylum and resettlement countries to address refugee issues. In some locations, the prompt resettlement of politically sensitive cases has helped defuse regional tensions. During the past few years, U.S. resettlement efforts in Africa, the Middle East, and East Asia have helped energize efforts by UNHCR and other countries to ensure that resettlement is accorded those in need and that first asylum is maintained for the larger population.

Refugees resettled in the United States contribute positively to the diversity and enrichment of our country. The U.S. program emphasizes the goal that refugees become economically self-sufficient as quickly as possible. Department of Health and Human Services–funded programs administered by individual states and the District of Columbia provide cash and medical assistance, training programs, employment, and other support services to arriving refugees. A variety of institutional providers perform these services, including the voluntary agencies that provide initial reception and placement services under cooperative agreements with the Department of State.

During its 25-year history, the U.S. Refugee Program has responded to changing refugee needs. Even before the events of September 11, 2001, the end of the Cold War had dramatically altered the context in which the U.S. refugee admissions program operates worldwide. Having shifted its focus away from large groups concentrated in a few locations, primarily refugees from Vietnam, the Former Soviet Union, and the former Yugoslavia, the program now offers resettlement to refugees of some 55 nationalities scattered around the world, interviewed this year in 42 often remote locations. Overseas processing efforts face numerous challenges. Security conditions for American personnel in refugee camps, the inadequacy of medical facilities required to conduct thorough medical screenings, and concern about program integrity— including fraud and corruption—are some of the issues facing the program.

The U.S. Refugee Program also continues to strive to achieve a balance between humanitarian commitments and national security concerns. Cases involving material support to a terrorist group or terrorist activity highlight the challenge of striking this balance. Legislative changes made in recent years have substantially broadened the categories of activities that would render an individual ineligible for admission under one of the terrorist grounds of inadmissibility. Under these provisions, an individual who provides money, food, shelter, or other assistance to an organization which engages in terrorist activities is inadmissible to the United States, even when the individual was compelled or coerced to provide such support under duress. This "material support" ground has already slowed Colombian processing considerably and other populations may be affected as well. The Departments of State and Homeland Security have been working closely in recent months to examine possible approaches to utilizing the discretionary non-applicability clause in this inadmissibility ground.

We have continued to address the issue of quality medical screening in numerous processing sites and enhanced the physical security arrangements at many others. While taking the necessary steps to improve our capacity to offer resettlement to those for whom it is appropriate, we have aggressively pursued every opportunity to extend the program's accessibility to those in greatest need. There have been many partners in this effort. For example, following our successful resettlement program for Lao Hmong in Thailand last year, we have obtained the agreement of the Royal Thai Government to commence processing of Burmese refugees in one of the camps along its border with Myanmar. We have engaged our voluntary agency and international organization partners in a successful joint "Targeted Response Team" (TRT) mission to Tanzania, which we expect will result in referral of a large group of Burundian refugees in that country. We have enlisted voluntary agency support in an additional TRT to assist with complicated cross-reference processing of the Meskhetian Turk population in Krasnodar Krai in the Russian Federation. In addition, we expanded our pilot non-governmental organization (NGO) referral initiative by providing training to NGO representatives working on refugee assistance projects in East Asia.

Domestically, the Department of State has worked with agencies participating in the Reception and Placement (R&P) program as refugee arrivals have increased to ensure that they were able to provide services according to established standards of care. Far fewer arriving refugees now have close family members living in the United States who are available to provide support and facilitate the integration process. When combined with the significant linguistic diversity, wide-ranging educational/employment histories of the refugee population and the persistent shortage of available affordable housing particularly in urban areas, resettlement agencies have had to adjust their practices to meet the increasing needs of refugees in the program.

II. REFUGEE ADMISSIONS PROGRAM FOR FY 2006
A. Proposed Ceilings

In addition to the proposed ceilings, the President specifies that special circumstances exist so that, for the purpose of admission under the limits established above and pursuant to section 101(a)(42)(B) of the INA, certain persons, if they otherwise qualify for admission, may be considered as refugees of special humanitarian concern to the United States although they

Immigration

TABLE I
REFUGEE ADMISSIONS IN FY 2004 AND FY 2005, PROPOSED CEILINGS FOR FY 2006

Region	FY 2004 Actual Arrivals	FY 2005 Original Ceiling	FY 2005 Revised Ceiling	FY 2005 Projected Arrivals	Proposed FY 2006 Ceiling
Africa	29,125	20,000	20,000	18,500	20,000
East Asia	8,079	13,000	13,000	12,000	15,000
Europe and Central Asia	9,254	9,500	*15,500	14,250	15,000
Latin America/Caribbean	3,556	5,000	*7,000	6,500	5,000
Near East/South Asia	2,854	2,500	*3,500	2,750	5,000
Unallocated Reserve		20,000	*11,000	0	**10,000
Total	52,868	70,000	70,000	54,000	70,000

*-A total of 9,000 numbers from the Unallocated Reserve was allocated as follows during the fourth quarter of FY 2005: 6,000 to Europe/Central Asia; 2,000 to Latin America/Caribbean; and 1,000 to the Near East/South Asia, as arrivals from each of these regions will exceed the original ceilings.
**-The 10,000 unallocated numbers for FY 2006 are funded under the President's FY06 budget request and will be used as needed only upon notification to Congress.

are within their countries of nationality or, in the case of persons having no nationality, within the country in which such persons are habitually residing. The FY 2006 proposal recommends continuing such in-country processing for specified groups in Cuba, Vietnam, and the countries of the Former Soviet Union as well as for extraordinary individual protection cases for whom resettlement is requested by a U.S. ambassador in any location in the world, with the understanding that significant public benefit parole will continue to be the solution to most such cases and that individuals will only be referred to the U.S. Refugee Program following concurrence by USCIS.

B. Admissions Procedures

Eligibility Criteria

Applicants for refugee admission to the United States must meet the following criteria:

• Meet the definition of "refugee" contained in the U.S. Immigration and Nationality Act;

• Be among those refugees determined by the President to be of special humanitarian concern to the United States;

Appendix C

- Subject to certain statutory exceptions and waivers, be otherwise admissible under the INA; and
- Not be firmly resettled in any foreign country.

While applicants who meet the above criteria may be admitted to the United States as refugees in the discretion of DHS, there is no entitlement to U.S. resettlement for these applicants. The admissions program is the legal mechanism for processing refugees who are among those classes of persons of particular interest to the United States. Applicants who fall within the priorities established for the relevant nationality or region are presented to USCIS for determination of eligibility for refugee status under Section 207 of the INA.

Worldwide Priority System for FY 2006

The worldwide processing priority system sets guidelines for the orderly management and processing of refugee applications for admission to the United States within the established annual regional ceilings. These processing priorities are distinct from the issues of whether an applicant is legally admissible to the United States or meets the statutory "refugee" definition. Just as an applicant who may qualify as an admissible "refugee" has no affirmative entitlement to resettlement in the United States, assignment of a person to a particular processing priority only permits access to apply to the admissions program and does not entitle that person to admission to the United States.

Priority 1: Individual Referrals

Priority 1 is reserved for individuals with compelling protection needs or those for whom no other durable solution exists who are identified and referred to the program by UNHCR, a U.S. Embassy, or a non-governmental organization (NGO). This processing priority is available to persons of any nationality.

Priority 2: Group Referrals

Priority 2 is used for groups of special humanitarian concern to the United States designated for resettlement processing. It includes specific groups (within certain nationalities, clans, or ethnic groups) identified by the Department of State in consultation with USCIS, non-governmental organizations (NGOs), UNHCR, and other experts. Some Priority 2 groups are processed in their country of origin.

In-country processing programs included in Priority 2:

Former Soviet Union

This Priority 2 designation applies to Jews, Evangelical Christians, and Ukrainian Catholic and Orthodox religious activists identified in the Lautenberg

261

Amendment, Pub. L. No. 101–167, 599D, 103 Stat. 1261 (1989), as amended ("Lautenberg Amendment"), with close family in the United States.

Cuba

Included in this Priority 2 program are human rights activists, members of persecuted religious minorities, former political prisoners, forced-labor conscripts (1965–68), persons deprived of their professional credentials or subjected to other disproportionately harsh or discriminatory treatment resulting from their perceived or actual political or religious beliefs or activities, and persons who have experienced or fear harm because of their relationship—family or social—to someone who falls under one of the preceding categories.

Vietnam

This Priority 2 designation includes persons eligible under the former Orderly Departure Program (ODP) and Resettlement Opportunity for Vietnamese Returnees (ROVR) programs. It will be expanded during FY 2006 to permit consideration of individuals who, due to no fault of their own, were unable to access the ODP program prior to its cut off date. It also includes Amerasian immigrants, whose numbers are counted in the refugee ceiling.

Groups of Humanitarian Concern outside the country of origin included in Priority 2:

The admissions program will process several Priority 2 groups outside their country of origin and will continue to develop new Priority 2 groups during FY 2006, including Burmese in Tham Hin Refugee Camp in Thailand, Iranian religious minorities, primarily in Austria, and Meskhetian Turks in Krasnodar Krai, Russia. Additional populations under active consideration for group designation in FY 2006 include Burundians in Tanzania and Bhutanese in Nepal.

Priority 3: Family Reunification Cases

In FY 2005, we continued to see improvements in integrity and efficiency in processing family reunification cases. Building on that progress, the P-3 program will continue its incremental expansion and during FY 2006 will be open to the largest number of eligible nationalities since 1999. The administration will continue to pursue refinements in program policy and procedures in order to consider further expansion over the course of the year.

In FY 2006, eligibility for a refugee interview is extended to nationals of certain countries who are the spouses, unmarried children under 21, or parents of persons admitted to the United States as refugees or granted asylum, or persons who are lawful permanent residents or U.S. citizens and were initially admitted to the United States as refugees or granted asylum. Eligible nationalities are developed following review of UNHCR's annual assessment of refugees in need of resettlement and ongoing repatriation programs and opportunities. Eligible nationalities for FY 2006 are listed below.

Afghanistan	Ethiopia
Burma	Haiti
Burundi	Iran
Colombia	Iraq
Congo (Brazzaville)	Ivory Coast
Cuba	Liberia
Democratic People's	Rwanda
Republic of Korea	Somalia
(DPRK)	Sudan
Democratic Republic of	Togo
Congo (DRC)	Uzbekistan
Eritrea	

Eligibility for interview will be established on the basis of an Affidavit of Relationship filed by the relative in the United States and reviewed by USCIS. All Priority 3 applicants must be located outside their countries of nationality or habitual residence and be able to establish a refugee claim independently. Anchor relatives in the United States may also file an I-730 Refugee/Asylee Relative Petition with USCIS to reunite derivative family members. Beneficiaries of an I-730 petition may be located in their country of origin and need not establish a refugee claim. Given these factors, the I-730, or "follow-to-join" process may often be considered the preferred method of reuniting spouses and unmarried children.

DHS/USCIS REFUGEE ADJUDICATIONS

Section 207(c) of the INA grants the Secretary of the Department of Homeland Security (DHS) authority to admit, at his discretion, any refugee who is not firmly resettled in a third country, who is determined to be of special humanitarian concern, and who is admissible to the United States as an immigrant. The authority to determine eligibility for refugee status has been delegated to U.S. Citizenship and Immigration Services (USCIS). During FY 2005, USCIS created a new organizational design to restructure its Office of Refugee Affairs with the establishment of the Refugee Corps. The Refugee Corps will be staffed by USCIS officers dedicated to adjudicating applications for refugee status. The Refugee Corps will provide USCIS with additional resources, as well as increased flexibility, to respond to an increasingly diversified refugee admissions program. USCIS relies on Department of State missions overseas to assess the security environment at proposed circuit ride locations prior to committing to circuit ride travel.

Immigration

The Eligibility Determination

In order to be approved as a refugee, an applicant must establish that he or she has suffered past persecution or has a well-founded fear of future persecution on account of race, religion, nationality, membership in a particular social group, or political opinion, as specified in Section 101(a)(42) of the INA. A USCIS officer conducts a face-to-face interview of each applicant. The interview is non-adversarial and is designed to elicit information about the applicant's claim for refugee status. The officer asks questions about the reasons for the applicant's departure from the country of nationality and problems or fears the applicant may have had or will have if returned to the country of nationality. In the in-country processing programs, the officer's questions focus on problems the applicant has had or fears having if he or she remains in his/her country of nationality. Background information concerning conditions in the country of nationality is considered, and the applicant's credibility and claim are assessed.

Under U.S. law, a person who has ordered, incited, assisted or otherwise participated in persecution on account of race, religion, nationality, membership in a particular social group, or political opinion is not a refugee. Likewise, an applicant who has been "firmly resettled" in a third country may not be admitted under INA 207. Applicants are also subject to various statutory grounds of inadmissibility, including criminal, security, and public health grounds, some of which may be waived.

Actions on Admission

Fingerprints of arriving refugees are taken at the port of entry if they were not taken prior to travel. Refugees are authorized for employment upon admission. After one year, a refugee is eligible to apply for adjustment of status to lawful permanent resident. Five years after admission, a refugee who has been granted lawful permanent resident status is eligible to apply for citizenship.

PROCESSING ACTIVITIES OF THE DEPARTMENT OF STATE
Overseas Processing Services

In most processing locations, the Bureau of Population, Refugees, and Migration (PRM) in the Department of State engages an NGO, IOM, or U.S. Embassy contractors to manage an Overseas Processing Entity (OPE) to assist in the processing of refugees for admission to the United States. All of the OPEs pre-screen applicants to preliminarily determine if they qualify for one of the applicable processing priorities and to prepare cases for USCIS adjudication. The OPEs assist applicants with completing documentary requirements and schedule USCIS refugee interviews as appropriate. If an

264

applicant is approved for resettlement, OPE staff guide the refugee through post-adjudication steps, including obtaining medical screening exams and attending cultural orientation programs. The OPE obtains sponsorship assurances, and, once appropriate security clearances are obtained, refers the case to IOM for transportation to the United States.

In FY 2005, NGOs worked under OPE contracts with PRM at locations in Austria, Kenya (covering East Africa) and Ghana (covering West Africa). International organizations (IOM and the International Catholic Migration Commission [ICMC]) support refugee processing activities in Egypt, Russia, Pakistan, and Turkey. U.S. Government contractors provide processing services in Cuba, Thailand, and Vietnam. Expanded resettlement plans in East Asia will result in the conversion of the contractor-operated OPE in Thailand to a full-scale regional OPE. In addition, PRM will solicit proposals for a regional OPE in Kathmandu. PRM will also host a workshop early in FY 2006 to provide refugee coordinators and processing staffs from overseas OPEs enhanced training on the role of the OPE, case screening and preparation, processing procedures, interagency coordination, anti-fraud measures, and handling refugee cases in a professional, unbiased, and culturally sensitive manner.

Cultural Orientation

The Department of State strives to ensure that refugees who are accepted for admission to the United States are prepared for the significant life changes they will experience through resettlement by providing cultural orientation programs prior to departure for the United States. It is critical that refugees arrive with a realistic view of what their new lives will be like, what services are available to them, and what their responsibilities will be. Every refugee family receives *Welcome to the United States*, a resettlement guidebook developed with input from refugee resettlement workers, resettled refugees, and state government officials. *Welcome to the United States* is produced in ten languages: English, French, Spanish, Russian, Serbo-Croatian, Arabic, Somali, Vietnamese, Amharic, and Farsi. Through this book, refugees have access to accurate information about initial resettlement before they arrive. The material in *Welcome to the United States* is also provided in some locations in video format. In addition, the Department of State enters into cooperative agreements for one- to three-day pre-departure orientation classes for eligible refugees at sites throughout the world.

Transportation

The Department of State makes available funds for the transportation of refugees resettled in the United States through a program administered by IOM. The cost of transportation is provided to refugees in the form of a loan. Beneficiaries are responsible for repaying these costs over time, beginning six months after their arrival.

Reception and Placement (R&P)

PRM maintains cooperative agreements with ten organizations, including nine private voluntary agencies and one state government agency, to provide initial resettlement services to arriving refugees. The R&P agencies agree to provide initial reception and core services (including housing, furnishings, clothing, food, and medical referrals) to arriving refugees. These services are now provided according to standards of care developed jointly by the NGO community and U.S. Government agencies in FY 2001, and implemented in FY 2002. The ten organizations maintain a nationwide network of over 375 affiliated offices to provide services.

The R&P agreement obligates the participating agencies to provide the following services, using R&P funds supplemented by cash and in-kind contributions from private and other sources:

- Sponsorship;
- Pre-arrival resettlement planning, including placement;
- Reception on arrival;
- Basic needs support (including housing, furnishings, food, clothing) for at least 30 days;
- Community orientation;
- Referrals to health, employment, and other services as needed; and
- Case management and tracking for 90–180 days, depending upon availability of anchor relatives.

Source: Available online. URL: http://www.state.gov/g/prm/refadm/rls/rpts/52366.htm. Updated September 2005.

APPENDIX D

ORGANIZATION OF THE DEPARTMENT OF HOMELAND SECURITY

The Department of Homeland Security (DHS) was established by the Homeland Security Act (2002), in response to the terrorist attacks of September 11, 2001. The rapid attempt to bring multiple agencies and programs into a single integrated department, however, has not been easy, and there were a number of structural changes following passage of the act.

For the first major DHS Reorganization Plan of November 2002, see URL: http://www.dhs.gov/interweb/assetlibrary/reorganization_plan.pdf.

The DHS became fully operational on March 1, 2003. On July 13, 2005, Homeland Security Secretary Michael Chertoff announced a new six-point agenda that would, if fully implemented, lead to substantial reorganization in the department's policies, operations, and structures in order to "maximize mission performance." The proposed end state organizational structure can be viewed at URL: http://www.dhs.gov/interweb/assetlibrary/ DHSOrgChart.htm, though even this is likely to change before organization stability is achieved. For a description of the departmental subcomponents and agencies that are likely to be part of any final structure, see URL: http:// www.dhs.gov/dhspublic/interapp/editorial/editorial_0515.xml.

The fundamental operational organization in 2005 can be seen in the organizational chart on the following page.

Immigration

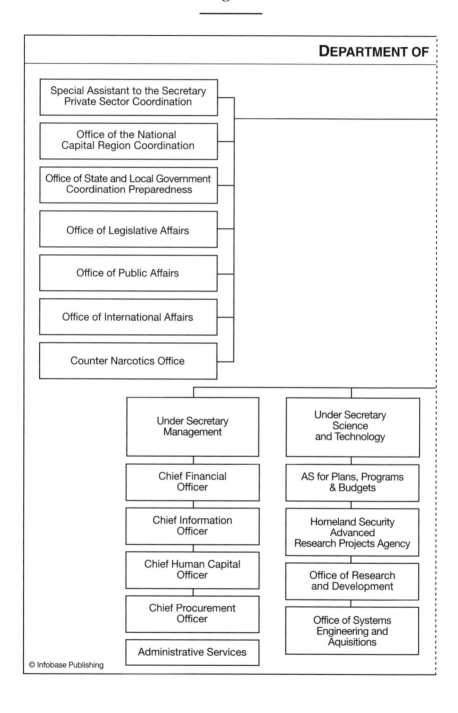

DEPARTMENT OF

Special Assistant to the Secretary
Private Sector Coordination

Office of the National
Capital Region Coordination

Office of State and Local Government
Coordination Preparedness

Office of Legislative Affairs

Office of Public Affairs

Office of International Affairs

Counter Narcotics Office

Under Secretary
Management

Under Secretary
Science
and Technology

Chief Financial
Officer

AS for Plans, Programs
& Budgets

Chief Information
Officer

Homeland Security
Advanced
Research Projects Agency

Chief Human Capital
Officer

Office of Research
and Development

Chief Procurement
Officer

Office of Systems
Engineering and
Aquisitions

Administrative Services

© Infobase Publishing

Appendix D

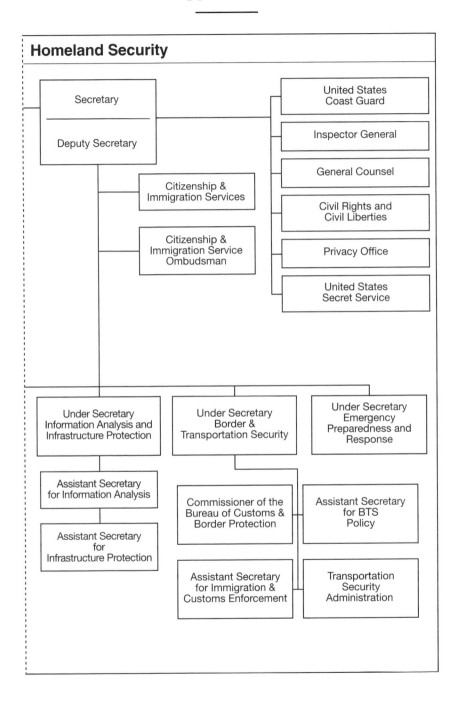

Homeland Security

- Secretary
- Deputy Secretary
  - Citizenship & Immigration Services
  - Citizenship & Immigration Service Ombudsman
  - United States Coast Guard
  - Inspector General
  - General Counsel
  - Civil Rights and Civil Liberties
  - Privacy Office
  - United States Secret Service
- Under Secretary Information Analysis and Infrastructure Protection
  - Assistant Secretary for Information Analysis
  - Assistant Secretary for Infrastructure Protection
- Under Secretary Border & Transportation Security
  - Commissioner of the Bureau of Customs & Border Protection
  - Assistant Secretary for BTS Policy
  - Assistant Secretary for Immigration & Customs Enforcement
  - Transportation Security Administration
- Under Secretary Emergency Preparedness and Response

APPENDIX E

MAPS AND GRAPHS

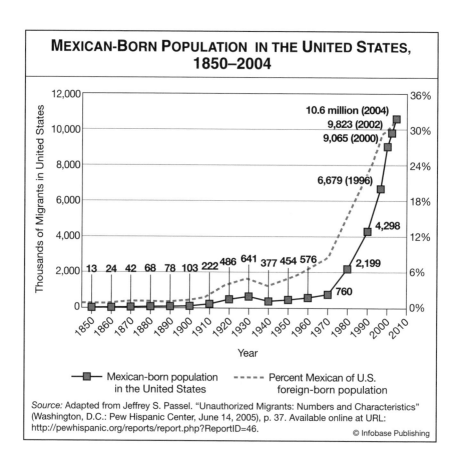

MEXICAN-BORN POPULATION IN THE UNITED STATES, 1850–2004

Source: Adapted from Jeffrey S. Passel. "Unauthorized Migrants: Numbers and Characteristics" (Washington, D.C.: Pew Hispanic Center, June 14, 2005), p. 37. Available online at URL: http://pewhispanic.org/reports/report.php?ReportID=46.

© Infobase Publishing

Appendix E

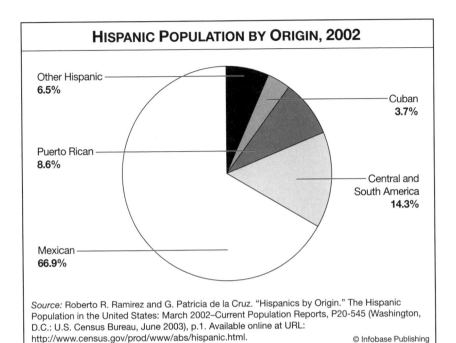

HISPANIC POPULATION BY ORIGIN, 2002

Other Hispanic 6.5%

Cuban 3.7%

Puerto Rican 8.6%

Central and South America 14.3%

Mexican 66.9%

Source: Roberto R. Ramirez and G. Patricia de la Cruz. "Hispanics by Origin." The Hispanic Population in the United States: March 2002–Current Population Reports, P20-545 (Washington, D.C.: U.S. Census Bureau, June 2003), p.1. Available online at URL: http://www.census.gov/prod/www/abs/hispanic.html.

© Infobase Publishing

Immigration

INDIVIDUAL EARNINGS OF YEAR-ROUND FULL-TIME WORKERS BY NATIVITY AND WORLD REGION OF BIRTH, 2002

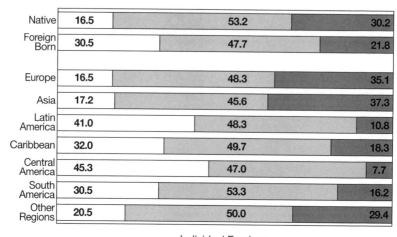

	Less than $20,000	$20,000 to $49,999	$50,000 or more
Native	16.5	53.2	30.2
Foreign Born	30.5	47.7	21.8
Europe	16.5	48.3	35.1
Asia	17.2	45.6	37.3
Latin America	41.0	48.3	10.8
Caribbean	32.0	49.7	18.3
Central America	45.3	47.0	7.7
South America	30.5	53.3	16.2
Other Regions	20.5	50.0	29.4

Individual Earnings

Source: Adapted from Luke J. Larsen. "Foreign Born by World Region of Birth: 2003," *The Foreign-Born Population in the United States: 2003—Current Population Reports,* P20-551 (Washington, D.C.: U.S. Census Bureau, August 2004), p. 6. Available online at URL: http://www.census.gov/prod/www/abs/for-born.html.

© Infobase Publishing

LEADING STATES OF SETTLEMENT FOR UNAUTHORIZED POPULATION, 2002–2004

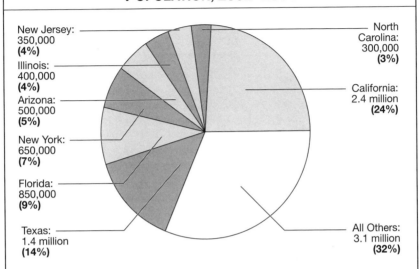

New Jersey: 350,000 (4%)

Illinois: 400,000 (4%)

Arizona: 500,000 (5%)

New York: 650,000 (7%)

Florida: 850,000 (9%)

Texas: 1.4 million (14%)

North Carolina: 300,000 (3%)

California: 2.4 million (24%)

All Others: 3.1 million (32%)

Note: This graph shows estimates of the unauthorized migrant population for states averaged over three current population surveys taken in March 2002–2004.

Source: Adapted from Jeffrey S. Passel. "Unauthorized Migrants: Numbers and Characteristics" (Washington, D.C.: Pew Hispanic Center, June 14, 2005), p. 11. Available online at URL: http://pewhispanic.org/reports/report.php?ReportID=46. © Infobase Publishing

Immigration

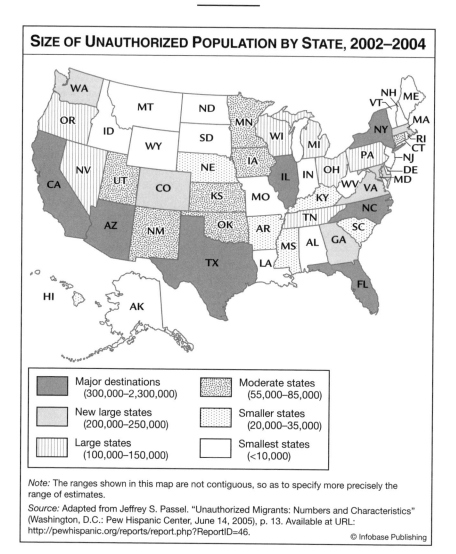

SIZE OF UNAUTHORIZED POPULATION BY STATE, 2002–2004

Legend:

- Major destinations (300,000–2,300,000)
- New large states (200,000–250,000)
- Large states (100,000–150,000)
- Moderate states (55,000–85,000)
- Smaller states (20,000–35,000)
- Smallest states (<10,000)

Note: The ranges shown in this map are not contiguous, so as to specify more precisely the range of estimates.

Source: Adapted from Jeffrey S. Passel. "Unauthorized Migrants: Numbers and Characteristics" (Washington, D.C.: Pew Hispanic Center, June 14, 2005), p. 13. Available at URL: http://pewhispanic.org/reports/report.php?ReportID=46.

© Infobase Publishing

Appendix E

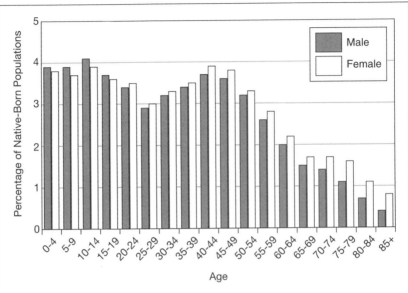

NATIVE POPULATIONS IN THE UNITED STATES BY
AGE AND SEX, 2003

Source: Adapted from Luke J. Larsen. "Foreign Born by World Region of Birth: 2003."
The Foreign-Born Population in the United States: 2003—Current Population Reports, P20-551,
p. 3 (Washington, D.C.: U.S. Census Bureau, August 2004)
http://www.census.gov/prod/www/abs/for-born.html.   © Infobase Publishing

Immigration

FOREIGN-BORN POPULATIONS IN THE UNITED STATES BY AGE AND SEX, 2003

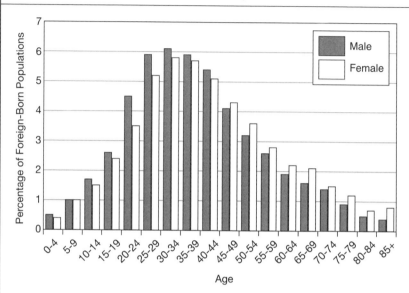

Source: Adapted from Luke J. Larsen. "Foreign Born by World Region of Birth: 2003," *The Foreign-Born Population in the United States: 2003—Current Population Reports,* P20-551, (Washington, D.C.: U.S. Census Bureau, August 2004), p. 3. Available online at URL: http://www.census.gov/prod/www/abs/for-born.html.

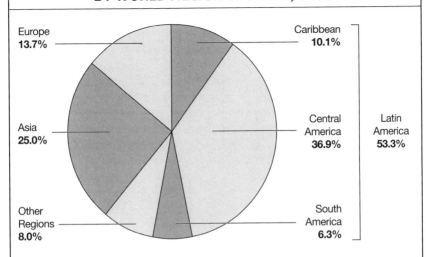

FOREIGN-BORN POPULATION OF THE UNITED STATES BY WORLD REGION OF BIRTH, 2003

Europe 13.7%

Caribbean 10.1%

Asia 25.0%

Central America 36.9%

Latin America 53.3%

Other Regions 8.0%

South America 6.3%

Source: Adapted from Luke J. Larsen. "Foreign Born by World Region of Birth: 2003," *The Foreign-Born Population in the United States: 2003—Current Population Reports,* P20-551, p. 6 (Washington, D.C.: U.S. Census Bureau, August 2004), Available online at URL: http://www.census.gov/prod/www/abs/for-born.html.
© Infobase Publishing

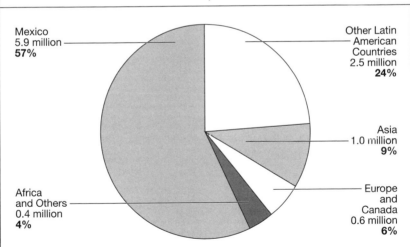

UNAUTHORIZED IMMIGRANTS BY REGION OF BIRTH, MARCH, 2004

Mexico 5.9 million 57%

Other Latin American Countries 2.5 million 24%

Asia 1.0 million 9%

Africa and Others 0.4 million 4%

Europe and Canada 0.6 million 6%

Note: This graph shows estimates of the unauthorized migrant population as of March 2004, subdivided by region of birth.

Source: Adapted from Jeffrey S. Passel. "Unauthorized Migrants: Numbers and Characteristics" (Washington, D.C.: Pew Hispanic Center, June 14, 2005), p. 4. Available online at URL: http://pewhispanic.org/reports/report.php?ReportID=46.
© Infobase Publishing

TOP TEN COUNTRIES OF CITIZENSHIP BY ACTIVE STUDENTS, AS OF DECEMBER 31, 2005

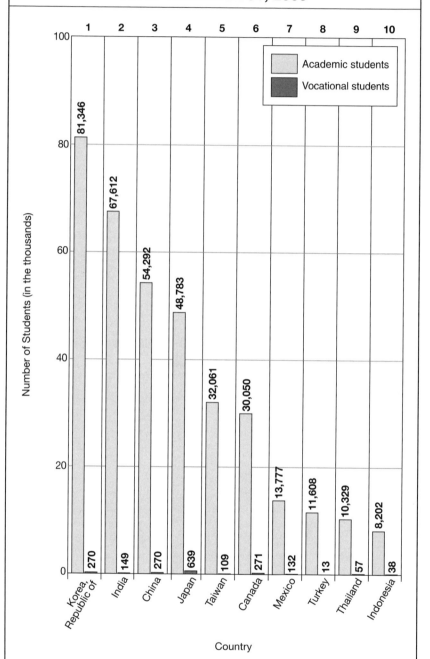

Note: This graph includes academic and vocational visa holders but not exchange students.

Source: U.S. Immigration and Customs Enforcement. "Top 20 Countries of Citizenship by Active Students," December 31, 2005. Available online at URL: http://www.ice.gov/sevis/numbers/student/country_of_citizenship.htm.

Appendix E

TOP TWENTY ACTIVE FOREIGN STUDENT POPULATIONS, AS OF DECEMBER 31, 2005

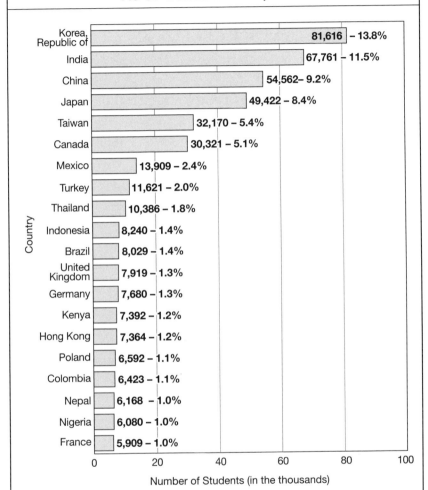

Korea, Republic of: 81,616 – 13.8%
India: 67,761 – 11.5%
China: 54,562 – 9.2%
Japan: 49,422 – 8.4%
Taiwan: 32,170 – 5.4%
Canada: 30,321 – 5.1%
Mexico: 13,909 – 2.4%
Turkey: 11,621 – 2.0%
Thailand: 10,386 – 1.8%
Indonesia: 8,240 – 1.4%
Brazil: 8,029 – 1.4%
United Kingdom: 7,919 – 1.3%
Germany: 7,680 – 1.3%
Kenya: 7,392 – 1.2%
Hong Kong: 7,364 – 1.2%
Poland: 6,592 – 1.1%
Colombia: 6,423 – 1.1%
Nepal: 6,168 – 1.0%
Nigeria: 6,080 – 1.0%
France: 5,909 – 1.0%

Country

Number of Students (in the thousands)

Note: This graph includes academic and vocational visa holders, but not exchange students.
Source: U.S. Immigration and Customs Enforcement. "Top 20 Countries of Citizenship by Active Students," December 31, 2005. Available online at URL: http://www.ice.gov/sevis/numbers/student/country_of_citizenship.htm.   © Infobase Publishing

279

APPENDIX F

U.S. REQUIREMENTS FOR NATURALIZATION

Requirements	Time as Permanent Resident
If you: Have been a Permanent Resident for the past 5 years and have no special circumstances *Note: Over 90% of applicants fall into this category.*	5 years
If you: Are currently married to and living with a U.S. citizen AND Have been married to and living with that same U.S. citizen for the past 3 years AND Your spouse has been a U.S. citizen for the past 3 years	3 years
If you: Are in the U.S. Armed Forces (or will be filing your application within 6 months of an honorable discharge) AND Have served for at least 1 year	You must be a Permanent Resident on the day of your interview
If you: Were in the U.S. Armed Forces for less than 1 year OR If you: Were in the U.S. Armed Forces for 1 year or more, but you were discharged more than 6 months ago	5 years
If you: Performed active duty military service during: • World War I (November 11, 1916-April 6, 1917); • World War II (September 1, 1939-December 31, 1946); • Korea (June 25, 1950-July 1, 1955); • Vietnam (February 28, 1961-October 15, 1978); • Persian Gulf (August 2, 1990-April 11, 1991); or • On or after September 11, 2001.	You are not required to be a Permanent Resident. *Note: If you did not enlist or reenlist in the United States or its outlying possessions, you must be a Permanent Resident on the day you file your application.*

Appendix F

Continuous Residence	Physical Presence in the United States	Time in District or State
5 years as a Permanent Resident without leaving the United States for trips of 6 months or longer	30 months	3 months
3 years as a Permanent Resident without leaving the United States for trips of 6 months or longer	18 months	3 months
Not required	Not Required	Not Required
5 years as a Permanent Resident without leaving the United States for trips of 6 months or longer Note: If you were out of the country as part of your service, this time out of the country does not break your "continuous residence." It is treated just like time spent in the United States. Not Required	30 months Note: Time in the U.S. Armed Forces counts as time "physically present" in the United States no matter where you were. Not Required	3 months Not Required

(table continues)

Immigration

Requirements	Time as Permanent Resident
If you: Were married to a U.S. citizen who died during a period of honorable active duty service in the U.S. Armed Forces *Note: You must have been married to and living with your U.S. citizen spouse at the time of his/her death.*	You must be a Permanent Resident on the day of your interview.
If you: Are a U.S. national (a non-citizen who owes permanent allegiance to the United States) AND Have become a resident of any State AND Are otherwise qualified for naturalization	You are not required to be a Permanent Resident.

If you:
    Served on a vessel operated by the United States
OR
If you:
    Served on a vessel registered in the United States and owned by U.S. citizens or a U.S. corporation.
	5 years

If you: Are an employee or an individual under contract to the U.S. Government	5 years
If you: Are a person who performs ministerial or priestly functions for a religious denomination or an interdenominational organization with a valid presence in the United States	5 years

Appendix F

Continuous Residence	Physical Presence in the United States	Time in District or State
Not Required	Not Required	Not Required
The same requirements as any other applicant for naturalization, depending on your qualifications. *Note: Any time you resided in American Samoa or Swains Island counts the same as the time you resided within a State of the United States.*	The same requirements as any other applicant for naturalization, depending on your qualifications. *Note: Any time you resided in American Samoa or Swains Island counts the same as the time you resided within a State of the United States.*	3 months or not required, depending on your qualifications.
5 years as a Permanent Resident without leaving the United States for trips of 6 months or longer *Note: If you were out of the ountry while serving on a vessel, this time out of the coutnry does not break your "continuous residence." It is treated just like time spent in the United States.*	30 months *Note: Time served on the vessel counts as time "physically present" in the United States no matter where you were.*	3 months
5 years as a Permanent Resident without leaving the United States for trips of 6 months or longer *Note: An absence from the United States for I year or more will break your "continuous residence." You may keep your "continuous residence" if you have had at least 1 year of unbroken "continuous residence" since becoming a Permanent Resident and you get an approved N-470 before you have been out of the United States for 1 year.*	30 months *Note: Time spent in this type of employment counts as time "physically present" in the United States no matter where you are as long as you get an approved N-470 before you have been out of the United States for 1 year.*	3 months
5 years as a Permanent Resident without leaving the United States for trips of 6 months or longer *Note: An absence from the United States for 1 year or more will break your "continuous residence." You may keep your "continuous residence" if you have had at least 1 year of unbroken "continous residence" since becoming a Permanent Resident and you get an approved N-470 at any time before applying for naturalization.*	30 months *Note: Time spent in this type of employment counts as time "physically present" in the United States no matter where you are as long as you get an approved N-470 before you apply for naturalization.*	3 months

(table continues)

283

Immigration

Requirements	Time as Permanent Resident
If you: Are employed by one of the following: • An American institution of research recognized by the Attoney General; • An American-owned firm or corporation engaged in the development of foreign trade and commerce for the United States; or • A public international organization of which the United States is a member by law or treaty (if the employment began after you became a Permanent Resident)	5 years
If you: Have been employed for 5 years or more by a U.S. nonprofit organization that principally promotes the interests of the United States abroad through the communications media	5 years
If you: Are the spouse of a U.S. citizen who is one of the following: • A member of the U.S. Armed Forces; • An employee or an individual under contract to the U.S. Government; • An employee of an American institution of research recognized by the Attorney General; • An employee of an American-owned firm or corporation engaged in the development of foreign trade and commerce for the United States; • An employee of a public international organization of which the United States is a member by a law or treaty; or • A person who perfroms ministerial or priestly functions for a religious denomination or an interdenominational organization with a valid presence in the United States AND Your citizen spouse is working abroad under an employment contract with the qualifying employer for at least 1 year and will continue to be so employed at the time you are naturalized.	You must be a Permanent Resident at the time of your CIS interview

Source: Adapted from *A Guide to Naturalization,* U.S. Citizenship and Immigration Services, pp. 18–21. Also available at URL: http://uscis.gov/graphics/services/natz/English.pdf

Appendix F

Continuous Residence	Physical Presence in the United States	Time in District or State
5 years as a Permanent Resident without leaving the United States for trips of 6 months or longer	30 months	3 months
Note: An absence from the United States for 1 year or more will break your "continuous residence." You may keep your "continuous residence" if you have had at least 1 year of unbroken "continuous residence" since becoming a Permanent Resident and you get an approved N-470 before you have been out of the United States for 1 year.		
Not Required	Not Required	Not Required
Not Required	Not Required	Not Required

INDEX

Index

287

Index

Index

Index

Index

Immigration